Using Data Management Techniques to Modernize Healthcare

Using Data Management Techniques to Modernize Healthcare

Anthony Matthew Hopper, MA, MHA

CRC Press
Taylor & Francis Group
Boca Raton   London   New York

CRC Press is an imprint of the
Taylor & Francis Group, an **informa** business

A PRODUCTIVITY PRESS BOOK

CRC Press
Taylor & Francis Group
6000 Broken Sound Parkway NW, Suite 300
Boca Raton, FL 33487-2742

© 2016 by Anthony Matthew Hopper
CRC Press is an imprint of Taylor & Francis Group, an Informa business

No claim to original U.S. Government works

Printed on acid-free paper
Version Date: 20150626

International Standard Book Number-13: 978-1-4822-2397-2 (Hardback)

Visit the Taylor & Francis Web site at
http://www.taylorandfrancis.com

and the CRC Press Web site at
http://www.crcpress.com

Dedication

I would like to dedicate this book to my family members—the Ferrises, Maloufs, Hoppers, and Picketts—wherever you are.

Contents

Preface

In today's environment, healthcare executives have to ensure that their organizations operate efficiently while, at the same time, keeping customers satisfied. Hospitals and other clinical-based health services firms have the added pressure of meeting certain prescribed patient-safety goals.

Healthcare organizations that possess sound human resources (HR) infrastructures will find it much easier to meet these challenges. Institutions that want to excel in this area will need to accomplish three key objectives. First, they will need to be proficient at identifying and hiring people who match up well with their company-specific needs. These organizations must also do an excellent job of developing and promoting their internal talent. Finally, healthcare firms will need to create corporate cultures that motivate employees to perform at their highest levels as well as entice them to stay on board for long periods of time.

At the meta-level, these workforce-related goals are straightforward and simple. Healthcare companies that want to succeed on the HR front need only to hire the right people, to implement processes that ensure the proper development and promotion of employees, and to create and maintain cultures that motivate these men and women to perform at high levels while also keeping them happy. In reality, many healthcare organizations struggle to achieve these employee-related goals, and some of them fail mightily at these HR tasks.

In this book, I discuss some of the challenges facing healthcare organizations, and especially hospitals, in today's world. I posit some of the reasons why these companies—to succeed in this environment—need to focus on developing excellent HR infrastructures, especially with regard to hiring, developing, and retaining quality employees. At the same time, I discuss some strategies that healthcare executives and managers can use to achieve these HR-related goals. As part of my discourse, I note ways in which healthcare organizations can use information technology (IT) and data management to help them create and maintain superior HR systems.

Specifically, I focus my attention on several key topics. In the first part of the book, I provide readers with a brief historical overview of the growth of the hospital industry and the challenges that it faces in today's world. Readers will note ways in which these historical trends have impacted not only hospitals but also many other types of healthcare organizations. I also briefly explore the changes in technology that have occurred over the past few decades and posit ways in which these developments have and continue to impact healthcare. Next, I discuss HR infrastructures in general terms and posit ways in which HR staff and systems are involved in the hiring process. At that point, I review key elements of this process and denote ways in which healthcare organizations can improve their hiring systems. In the latter part of the book, I move on to other related topics, which include employee development and promotion programs, the proper management (and motivation) of staff, and a review of the unique HR and IT challenges facing rural hospitals. I have also included a section titled "Appendix: Guidelines for Use on the Go" at the end of the text, which contains copies of some key checklists, figures, and tables found throughout the book.

Over the course of the text, I try to view organizational hiring and employee management from both a technical and a sociocultural perspective. This is because I believe that healthcare leaders, when looking to incorporate new technologies or methods into existing corporate schemas, need to focus not just on the merits of specific systems or ideas; these individuals also must determine how their introduction will affect employees, as well as other key stakeholders. At the same time, I feel that healthcare executives, managers, and other key personnel too often focus on micro-department–level issues. I encourage them to take a step back and view their healthcare HR infrastructures in particular and their organizational responsibilities in general at the meta-level.

I think a wide variety of individuals will find this book helpful. As noted by the book's title, I spend time demonstrating for the readers how they can use IT and data management techniques to help them design and implement effective employee hiring and management infrastructures.

However, as important, I try to provide helpful tips to guide managers and other key personnel who work in a range of different organizational environments. I have also included commentary and advice that is geared to resource-challenged institutions, especially rural hospitals. I feel that individuals who work for small healthcare firms will find some of my suggestions to be particularly useful to them.

Acknowledgments

I would like to thank all of the people who helped me to complete this book. I especially want to acknowledge a few individuals who dedicated a significant amount of their time to aiding me in this endeavor. First, I want to thank Carol Jelen, my agent, for helping me to secure the book contract. I would also like to thank Theron Shreve, who is the director of Derryfield Publishing, for spending countless hours reviewing the book's content to ensure its readability and accuracy. Finally, I would like to thank Marje Pollack, my copy editor and typesetter. She devoted a significant amount of attention to the layout of this book as well as to helping me correct errors in grammar and sentence structure.

About the Author

Anthony Hopper has worked in the healthcare industry for over a decade. During the course of his healthcare career, he has spent time with both small healthcare organizations and hospital systems. He has held a number of different positions at these organizations, including analyst and upper-management–level jobs. He also has experience in health policy via an internship with the Center for Studying Health System Change.

Anthony most recently served as a business development officer for Rapid Improvement, Inc. This company utilizes an artificial intelligence algorithm and a unique, one-question survey technique to translate text-based complaints into quantifiable data. He still maintains an affiliation with this company.

Anthony is currently a full-time instructor at ECPI University's Emerywood campus, located in Richmond, Virginia. He recently co-authored an article on sentiment analysis that appeared in the *Journal of Health Organization and Management*. He has an M.A. in English from the University of Virginia and an M.S. in Health Systems Administration from Georgetown University.

Chapter One

Introduction: A Look at the Changing Face of Healthcare

In today's environment, hospital executives have to ensure that their organizations operate efficiently. They have to find ways to cut costs, while at the same time ensuring that their hospitals and ancillary units achieve high marks with regard to patient satisfaction and quality of care. Granted, management can utilize any number of different strategies to achieve these goals. However, in my experience, no organization will succeed in the long term unless it does a good job of utilizing its staff.

It goes without saying that hospitals, and, in fact, all healthcare companies, should strive to hire top-notch employees at all levels. As important, executives and managers have to do an excellent job of matching the skills of their employees to the available positions. Healthcare administrators must also make sure that their organization's workers receive the training required to excel in their jobs. Finally, management needs to foster a work environment and corporate infrastructure that enables their employees to succeed.

On one level, the workforce-related goals appear to be straightforward and simple. If a hospital or other healthcare organization hires the right people and provides them with the proper tools and infrastructure, it will reap the benefits. In reality, most companies have a difficult time achieving these goals. Corporate heads are well aware of the problems that their organizations have in hiring, developing, and promoting the best staff. In one large survey of corporate board directors, the participants "identified talent management as their single greatest strategic challenge" (Groysberg & Bell, 2013). Hospitals and other healthcare organizations do not do a better job in this respect. Per a CareerBuilder survey, almost 80 percent of healthcare companies made at least one bad hire in 2012 (Bouchard, 2012). If a healthcare company wants to buck the trend and excel at hiring and developing its employees, it must utilize proper human resources (HR) strategies and make use of the latest technologies.

In this book, I will discuss some of the HR strategies and information technology (IT)-related practices that hospital systems and other healthcare companies can use to improve their hiring practices and to increase employee efficiency, quality, and productivity. Executives and managers who are interested in this topic can find numerous books that focus on HR. However, they might be surprised (according to a search of Amazon. com) at the dearth of HR texts that focus—at least in part—on topics like data management, and information systems. I hope that this book will help to fill that gap.

Books dealing with these topics might be scarce because, until recently, many healthcare administrators would not have needed to read the texts. They were able to maintain viable organizations without having to worry as much about the bottom line. Hospitals and other health services providers could sometimes get by without focusing on issues such as maximizing efficiency and productivity, reducing waste, and providing the highest level of patient care. This is because they could rely on the federal government or on other insurers to cover the full costs of the procedures—whatever those costs happened to be. However, that is no longer the case because the healthcare environment has changed significantly over the past few decades.

I feel that it is worthwhile for me to take a little time to briefly examine some of these changes. Readers might be able to utilize some of the information to help them better understand the trends that are impacting hospital development, in particular, and the healthcare field, in general. More importantly, I think that it is vital for individuals to possess a general knowledge of the headwinds facing the hospital industry (and the whole healthcare ecosystem), in order for them to make full use of the ideas and suggestions in this book.

1.1 Hospitals—The Golden Years

The first hospitals in the United States got their start in the 1700s. In the beginning, they basically served to quarantine people with infectious diseases and to provide some type of care for the indigent. By the 1920s, modern hospitals, as we know them, had begun to take shape. These institutions provided a range of services and sought both to cure the sick as well as to care for them (Wall, 2013).

Although the hospital industry grew at a brisk pace during the first few decades of the 1900s, it entered a golden age, at least in terms of growth and investment, in the 1940s. This mandala lasted until the 1970s (Evashwick, 2005, 51). During this period, hospitals took center stage, along with physicians' offices, in providing health services for the majority of Americans. Indicative of this trend, the number of hospitals in the United States increased from 6189 in 1937 to 7174 in 1974. At the same time, the number of hospital beds expanded significantly—from 907,133 beds in 1929 to 1,513,000 beds in 1974 (Evashwick, 2005, 53; Shi & Singh, 2004, 287–288). Importantly, the number of community hospital beds per 1000 US residents moved up from 3.2 in 1940 to 4.5 by 1980 (Shi & Singh, 2004, 289).

Though this trend is an important indicator of the hospital industry's growing importance in American life, it does not tell the whole story. That is because, assuming no changes in the hospitals' financial environment, these institutions would have expanded anyway in order to keep pace with the rise in the US population, which increased by approximately 94.8 million people between 1940 and 1980 (Gauthier, 2002, Appendix A). However, as I will demonstrate in the next paragraph, the industry rose to prominence in large part because Americans significantly increased their consumption of hospital services.

After World War II, for the first time, large numbers of Americans began to make use of hospitals when they were sick. Only 74 out of every 1000 Americans visited a hospital in 1940. That figure had increased to 155 out of every 1000 people by 1971 (U.S. Census Bureau, 1973, 78). At the same time, hospitals diversified or increased the numbers of procedures, tests, and other care processes that they offered to each patient (Shi & Singh, 2004, 285). The decline in home births, more than any other statistic, highlights Americans' growing reliance on hospitals during this period. Most Americans consider their children to be their most important asset. In 1940, approximately 44 percent of US women decided to

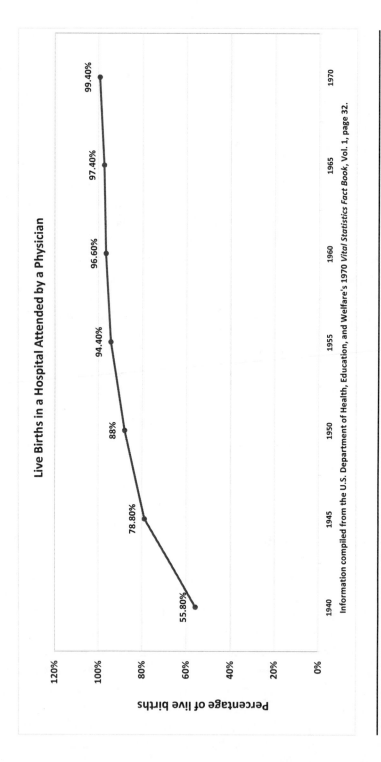

Figure 1.1 The percentage of women who gave birth in hospitals: 1940–1970. Data derived from the U.S. Department of Health, Education, and Welfare. (1970). *Vital Statistics of the United States* (Vol. 1). Centers for Disease Control and Prevention. Retrieved from http://www.cdc.gov/nchs/data/vsus/nat70_1acc.pdf.

give birth to their children in their homes, the remainder of them utilizing hospitals for this service. Within 20 years (in 1969), 99 percent of pregnant women in the United States gave birth in hospitals (MacDorman, Mathews, & Declercq, 2012, 2) (see Figure 1.1).

US hospitals increased their spending significantly in order to meet the needs of their growing clientele (U.S. Census Bureau, 1973, 78; U.S. Census Bureau, 1990, 107). However, in most cases, their costs were offset by increases in revenue. According to economist Thomas Getzen, the amount of money Americans spent on healthcare went up by more than fivefold from 1929 to 1970 (and another 500 percent between 1970 and 2010) (Getzen, 2010, 10). More importantly, the percent of this total going to hospitals increased from 23 percent in 1929 to 37 percent in 1970 (Getzen, 2010, 10). The growth in hospitals' budgets and earnings was significant, even after considering inflation (Getzen, 2010, 10).

1.2 Five Key Drivers of Hospital Growth: 1940s–1970s

Numerous factors contributed to the hospital industry's growth during this period. Some of the more important ones centered on advancements in medical technology, the development of the health insurance industry, the creation of Medicare and Medicaid, the Hill-Burton Act, and the lack of competition. Together, these five issues helped to drive the development of the hospital industry after World War II. Ironically, with the exception perhaps of the Hill-Burton Act, these same factors are also currently responsible for creating some of the headwinds that contemporary hospital executives must navigate.

1.2.1 The Advancements in Medical Technology

Hospitals likely would not have become such prominent features of American life if medical technology had not advanced rapidly in the decades following World War II. During this period, physicians promulgated the use of antibiotics, such as penicillin, to combat bacterial diseases, and researchers developed new drugs and vaccines to combat heretofore deadly germs, such as polio and measles (Atkinson, Hamborsky, Stanton, & Wolfe, 2012, 173–185; Public Broadcasting Service, 1998;

Shi & Singh, 2004, 285). At the same time, scientists and inventors developed new medical devices and made significant improvements to ones, like X-ray machines, which were already in use (Shi & Singh, 2004, 285; The Science Museum, 2013). These changes significantly helped hospitals attract new clientele. Hospitals could use these technologies to improve patient safety, as well as care (Shi & Singh, 2004, 285). As Shi and Singh note in their healthcare text, "Hospitals . . . came to be regarded as a necessity because the superior medical services and surgical procedures could not be obtained at home" (2004, 285).

1.2.2 The Hill-Burton Act

Regardless of any other factors, hospitals would not have added as many beds as they did, and the industry would not have branched out into as many communities, without the passage of the Hill-Burton Act. This legislation, whose official name was The Hospital Survey and Construction Act, "provided federal grants to states for the construction of new hospital beds" (Shi & Singh, 2004, 288). The legislation "assisted in the construction of" approximately four out of every 10 acute care (short-stay) hospital beds in the United States after 1946 (Shi & Singh, 2004, 288) (see Figure 1.2). The Hill-Burton Act, in coordination with other factors, such as the growth in private and government-funded insurance subscriptions, helped millions of Americans access hospital care for the first time.

1.2.3 The Rapid Growth in Private Health Insurance Subscriptions

Even in the 1920s, people found hospital care to be expensive. In an effort to overcome this obstacle, hospitals and hospital associations started to offer non-profit insurance plans to cover hospital expenses, beginning in 1929 (Shi & Singh, 2004, 96). Doctors associations followed suit in the late 1930s and started to offer plans that only covered physicians' expenses (Shi & Singh, 2004, 96). Private insurers jumped onto the proverbial bandwagon a few years later (Shi & Singh, 2004, 97).

At first, the number of Americans who subscribed to these policies was minimal. Only 9 percent of Americans had health insurance of any kind in

SOME KEY PIECES OF LEGISLATION IMPACTING HOSPITALS (1945–2015)

Net Positive Financial Impact

➤ The Hill-Burton Act (1946)

➤ The Creation of Medicare and Medicaid (1965)

➤ The American Recovery and Reinvestment Act (2009)

Net Negative Financial Impact

➤ The Tax Equity and Responsibility Act (1982)

➤ The Health Insurance Portability and Accountability Act (1996)

➤ The Balanced Budget Act (1997)

Unknown Financial Impact

➤ The Patient Protection and Affordable Care Act (2010)

Figure 1.2 This illustration highlights some of the key pieces of government legislation and their net impact on hospitals. It is worth noting that Congress created Medicare and Medicaid by amending the Social Security Act.

1940. However, this rate rose dramatically over the next decade as a result of changes associated with World War II (Shi & Singh, 2004, 96–97). In 1943, in an effort to control prices and wages, the US government instituted a wage freeze but did not apply this proscription to "fringe benefits" (Employee Benefit Research Institute, 2002). Companies and unions negotiated employee benefit packages, which included health insurance, in order to get around the government ban (Shi & Singh, 2004, 97). This trend continued after the war. The number of Americans who possessed hospital insurance jumped to 57 percent by 1950 (Shi & Singh, 2004, 96). The US government's creation of Medicare and Medicaid in 1965 helped to further this trend, and by 1978, almost 90 percent of Americans had some form of health insurance (Cohen, Makuc, Bernstein, Bilheimer, & Powell-Griner, 2009, 5).

1.2.4 The Growth in Private and Government-Funded Insurance and the Subsequent Impact on Hospital Growth

The growth and development of the health insurance industry, including both private and public forms of insurance, in the 1940s through the 1970s helped buoy the hospital system by directing vast numbers of new patients its way. In the past, if people could not afford to go to the hospital, they would either forego care altogether or find someone (e.g,. a physician) to care for them in their homes. When Americans gained health insurance coverage in the decades following World War II, they found that they could use the money paid by their fellow insurance subscribers to help them offset the hospital costs. Millions of Americans could now afford to utilize hospital services for the first time (Bodenheimer & Grumbach, 2009, 10; Shi & Singh, 2004, 288).

Perhaps more importantly, both private and government-funded insurance schemes provided "generous reimbursements" to hospitals (Bodenheimer & Grumbach, 2009, 8). For a number of reasons, which I will not discuss here for brevity's sake, most insurers during this period used a cost-based reimbursement system, or something similar, to remunerate hospitals. In this system, the insurers agreed to pay all of the hospital's costs related to a patient. The hospital had the upper hand in this system, as it could submit a list of its charges for the procedures and expect full payment (Bodenheimer & Grumbach, 2009, 194–195; Ching-To, 1994, 98–99; Office of the Inspector General, 2001).

In general, employers, who paid for a large portion of the private insurance policies, did not worry much about this issue until after 1970 in part because "profits were high and world economic growth was robust" (Bodenheimer & Grumbach, 2009, 194). Additionally, companies' health-care expenditures represented only a "tiny fraction of business expenses" (Bodenheimer & Grumbach, 2009, 194). What is more, the government allowed (and still allows) corporations to deduct these expenses on their taxes, thereby further decreasing the employers' costs (Bodenheimer & Grumbach, 2009, 8). Most of the everyday Americans, who utilized their hospitals' services, also did not worry about the costs because they did not have to pay for their bills out of pocket. Something economists refer to as moral hazard (Getzen, 2010, 92–94).

Although I have discussed the growth of insurance schemes in general during this period, I think it is worthwhile to pay a bit more attention to two specific government programs: Medicare and Medicaid. The US government's sponsorship and creation of these plans in 1965 has had a significant influence on hospital growth and development over the past few decades.

Medicare and Medicaid Provide a Boost

Two important groups, the elderly and the poor, did not significantly benefit from the growth of employer-based insurance plans. For their part, insurers were hesitant to enroll people over 65 because these people generally were in poorer health than their younger counterparts. As a result, "[i]n the late 1950s, less than 15% of the elderly had any health-care insurance" (Bodenheimer & Grumbach, 2009, 10). The poor did not fare much better, as they "tended to work in jobs without the fringe bene-fit of health insurance," when they could find work at all (Bodenheimer & Grumbach, 2009, 10). Congress and the president attempted to ameliorate these deficiencies in 1965 by amending the Social Security Act to include Medicare, Title XVIII, and Medicaid, Title XIX (Klees, Wolfe, & Curtis, 2009, 3). These government programs have been wildly successful, at least when it comes to providing coverage for the elderly and a subsection of the indigent. According to a Census Bureau report, approximately 15.9 percent of Americans had Medicare insurance and

14.5 percent were covered by Medicaid, as of 2010.[1] (DeNavas-Walt, Proctor, & Smith, 2011, 23–24). Importantly, these government-funded plans increased the coffers of acute care and other types of hospitals (see Figure 1.2).

1.2.5 The Lack of Competition among Hospitals

Although the US hospital industry grew significantly between the 1940s and the 1970s, most hospitals did not have to operate in a truly competitive environment (Altman, Shactman, & Eilat 2006, 11–12). Several key factors contributed to this non–market-based environment. For one thing, hospitals located in rural areas oftentimes did not have any direct competitors. These facilities operated in regions that were too sparsely populated to support more than one hospital (Fuchs, 1988, 8). At the same time, they did not have to worry yet about competition from outpatient clinics. Many of the procedures, which are now routinely performed on an outpatient basis, required overnight (or longer) stays in the hospital (Shi & Singh, 2004, 289). Even hospitals that were located close to one another had enough supply (of patients) to negate the need for full-on competition (Fuchs, 1988, 8).

1.3 The Good Times End—Hospitals Forced to Become More Efficient: 1980s–Present

Although individual hospitals might have struggled to survive, as a whole, the industry thrived or at least managed to get by without focusing too much attention on issues such as cost-cutting and economic-waste management. In this environment, hospital executives could sometimes overlook operational deficiencies and occasionally ignore staffing concerns, as long as these issues did not weigh too heavily on the bottom line (Fuchs, 2012, 975; Guterman, Ashby, & Greene, 1996, 134–138; Shi & Singh, 2004, 290–291). Researchers have compared the hospital industry during this time to the airline industry before deregulation (Altman,

---

[1] The number of Americans who have Medicare or Medicaid does not equal 30.4 percent. Some individuals possess both types of insurance.

Shactman, Eilat, 2006, 12). During this period, hospital executives had little to no incentive to maximize productivity and efficiency.

The situation started to change during the latter part of the 1970s and, since that time, the environment has become a progressively more difficult one for hospitals to navigate. In the following section, I will look at some of the key factors that have forced hospital executives and administrators to focus so much attention on the bottom line in recent years. As with the previous section, I will only briefly touch on some issues (and avoid others altogether).

1.4 Five Issues Negatively Impacting Hospital Margins

Over the past few decades, hospitals have faced a number of headwinds. I will focus on five of the factors, which I feel have had the most impact on hospital growth and development in recent decades. The topics center on insurance cuts, an increased focus on the patient, the growth in medical technology, the heightened competitive environment, and the aging of the American populace. These issues differ with regard to their arrival on the historical scene and their importance to the hospital industry's growth and development. However, all five factors share one thing in common: They continue to exert a significant influence on the healthcare ecosystem.

1.4.1 Insurance Payment Cuts

Over the last few decades, federal and state governments have enacted several measures seeking to reduce payments to hospitals and other providers. As a first step, Congress passed The Tax Equity and Fiscal Responsibility Act (TEFRA) in 1982 in an effort to curtail rapidly rising healthcare costs (Guterman, 2000, 4). The law "authorized the conversion of hospital Medicare reimbursement from cost-plus to a prospective system based on DRGs [diagnosis-related groups]" (Shi & Singh, 2004, 290). TEFRA forced hospitals to curtail their charges (to Medicare) and reduce the length of time they kept patients in their facilities (Evashwick, 2005, 57; Fuchs, 1988, 10; Shi & Singh, 2004, 290) (see Figure 1.2).

After the law was enacted, a number of states changed their Medicaid payment schemes to reflect Medicare's model (Shi & Singh, 2004, 290).

TEFRA helped to reduce the federal government's Medicare costs; however, many experts believed that it did not go far enough. In 1997, Congress took another stab at cutting spending when it passed the Balanced Budget Act (BBA). The BBA not only further reduced payments to hospitals for some inpatient procedures; it also limited payments on a variety of other services, including outpatient services, homecare (home health services), and long-term care. Although Congress later reduced some of the BBA's bite, the law nevertheless negatively impacted hospital revenues, as well as the incomes of a host of other healthcare providers (Guterman, 2000, 2–15; see Figure 1.2).

In recent years, the Centers for Medicare & Medicaid Services (CMS) has experimented with using various pay-for-performance programs to reward high-quality care and, more importantly, to penalize hospitals that provide (what Medicare considers to be) substandard care (Centers for Medicare & Medicaid Services, 2014; Johnson, Dawson, & Acquaviva, 2008, 420). State-run Medicaid services have followed Medicare's lead by instituting prospective payment systems and by cutting payments via the use of health maintenance organizations (HMOs) (Duggan, 2002, 2–31; Shi & Singh, 2004, 290).

Private insurance companies have also tightened the purse strings over the last few decades. They have curtailed healthcare costs by "resorting to competitive pricing" and by employing utilization managers who "closely monitored when patients would be in the hospital and for how long" (Shi & Singh, 2004, 290). Many insurance policies, especially HMOs and PPOs, also employ gatekeepers and use other measures to limit or even eliminate their patients' inpatient hospital stays (Bodenheimer & Grumbach, 2009, 61–68; Shi & Singh, 2004, 291). More recently, both public and private insurers, as well as other stakeholders, have been pushing hospitals not only to reduce costs but also to improve patient care.

1.4.2 Increased Focus on Patient Safety and Patient Satisfaction

While insurers have been pushing hospitals and other healthcare providers to cut costs, they have also been asking these facilities to improve patient care. Other stakeholders, including employers, politicians, accrediting agencies, and patients, have allied themselves with insurance companies on this issue (Johnson, Dawson, & Acquaviva, 2008, 407–414). The push for better patient care has manifested itself in a number of different ways. For instance, patient advocates scored a significant victory in 1996 when Congress passed the Health Insurance Portability and Accountability Act (HIPAA), which, among other things, required hospitals and other providers to take significant steps to protect patient privacy (Showalter, 2007, 423–458) (see Figure 1.2). On another front, the CMS has pressured hospitals to improve both patient safety and patient satisfaction at their facilities. The government agency has achieved these results via its reimbursement procedures and by collecting and publicly posting hospital patient quality metrics (CMS, 2015; Johnson, Dawson, & Acquaviva, 2008, 409–411, 420). Many healthcare accrediting agencies, for example, the Joint Commission, have also taken more active roles in assaying the quality of care at the hospitals and other healthcare providers that they accredit (Pawlson & Schyve, 2008, 436–445).

These are only a few of the many ways in which stakeholders are pushing healthcare organizations, especially hospitals, to create a better, safer environment for their patients. Healthcare stakeholders have every right to demand that hospitals and other healthcare providers deliver high-quality patient care. For their part, most hospitals, especially non-profit facilities, should be striving to provide this type of care without any outside pressure. Nonetheless, hospitals have to expend a significant amount of resources (related to direct payments, lost opportunity costs, etc.) to comply with the demands of patient advocates. In many cases, these facilities have had to make significant changes to their technology infrastructures, business processes, and training programs in order to comply with patient safety, satisfaction, and privacy requirements. For instance, hospitals have had to spend billions of dollars over the last few years just to comply with HIPAA regulations (Blackburn, 2004, n.p.; Kilbridge, 2003, 1423–1424).

1.4.3 Medical Technology Becomes More Expensive

As I noted previously, healthcare technological development has progressed rapidly during the last few decades. This phenomenon has had an impact on almost every facet of healthcare—running the gamut from advances in office-based administration and billing systems to the creation of new or improved diagnostic, surgical, and medical devices (Shi & Singh, 2004, 156–159). Americans, as a whole, have benefited from many of the clinically based advances (Shi & Singh, 2004, 168–169). They, therefore, naturally push hospitals to purchase the most up-to-date medical technologies. Hospitals have responded by investing heavily in these new technologies. A CBS Money Watch article suggests that "new technology purchases account for more than half of hospitals' capital spending" (Terry, 2010).

Hospitals have been able to utilize some of these technologies to help them reduce costs (Shi & Singh, 2004, 170–171). However, in many other cases, hospitals feel it necessary to purchase expensive new medical devices or other high-tech systems that are not directly cost-beneficial but which help the facility improve its quality of care or to keep pace with competitors (Strupp, 2008). Many of these new devices are extremely expensive; some of them carry price tags in the tens of millions of dollars (Gold, 2013). A hospital can suffer a major financial set-back if its administrators overestimate the profit potential of an extremely expensive piece of high-tech equipment (Coye & Kell, 2006, 164–168).

Perhaps most important, advances in technology have reduced and sometimes eliminated the need for a hospital's services. Clinicians, using the latest medical devices, can now perform many procedures, which formerly required inpatient stays, on an outpatient basis (Evashwick, 2005, 58; Shi & Singh, 2004, 173, 288–289). Many of these clinicians utilize hospital outpatient facilities; however, they do not necessarily need to do so (refer to the discussion in the next section). Additionally, some patients are now able to obtain home-based care, which could heretofore only be performed in hospitals or in long-term care facilities (Shi & Singh, 2004, 173).

1.4.4 Increased Competition

Over the last few years, hospitals (and hospital chains) have been engaging in an increasingly intense competition with each other "for patients, physicians and insurance dollars" (Toland, 2012). Exacerbating the situation, hospitals have also had to deal with increased competition from other provider types. The competitors run the gamut from freestanding, non-affiliated outpatient centers to home health agencies. Each of these groups has taken away a piece of the hospital industry's market share (Evashwick, 2005, 58; Gustafson, 2009; Shi & Singh, 2004, 289). Finally, as healthcare technology advances, physicians are finding that they can perform an ever-increasing array of patient-related services in their offices (Midey, 2010).

1.4.5 An Aging Population

The American population is aging at a fairly rapid rate. In 1940, approximately nine million Americans, 6.8 percent of the population, were over 65 (U.S. Census Bureau, "Current Population Reports," 1996, 2–3). That figure has skyrocketed over the last few decades; currently, around 43 million Americans—13.7 percent of the population—are over 65 (U.S. Census Bureau, "QuickFacts," 2013). Their numbers are expected to more than double in the coming decades. "In 2050, the number of Americans aged 65 and older is projected to be 88.5 million" (Vincent & Velkoff, 2010, 1).

On the surface, the rapid growth of the nation's 65 and over population would seem like a boon to hospitals. Older patients typically tend to utilize hospital services at a much higher rate than younger and middle-aged individuals (Evashwick, 2005, 60–61). "In 2007, those aged 65 years and over accounted for just 13 percent of the US population, but 37 percent of the hospital discharges, and 43 percent of the days of care" (Hall, DeFrances, Williams, Golosinskiy, & Schwartzman, 2010, 3).

However, CMS has spent a significant amount of time and money over the last few years in an effort to shift some of the elderly care from hospitals and into other, less costly venues, including outpatient clinics and even the patient's home. It is likely that the government agency will ramp up this initiative in the coming years, thereby offsetting the gray tsunami's impact on the hospital industry's inpatient census (York, Kaufman, & Grube, 2013). At the same time, CMS and other insurance carriers are beginning to implement pay-for-performance measures. These initiatives might negatively impact hospitals, and other providers, which treat large numbers of the elderly because, as a group, the elderly are the sickest individuals and so the most prone to contracting staph infections and to suffering unexpected, adverse reactions from surgical procedures and new medications (Anonymous, 2008).

1.5 How Hospitals Have Tried to Cope with the Changing Environment

Hospitals, as a group, have responded to these challenges in a number of different ways. Some facilities have been forced to close their doors; many of the hospitals that remain open have reduced the number of their inpatient beds. A majority of hospitals have either merged into larger conglomerates or in some way aligned themselves with multisystem chains. Most hospitals (and hospital chains) have developed varied, robust outpatient service lines. In recent decades, hospital executives and managers have placed an increasing amount of attention on streamlining their operations by cutting costs and improving worker efficiency.

1.5.1 Some Hospitals Close—Other Facilities Reduce the Number of Inpatient Beds

The total number of hospitals in the United States continued to grow until 1974, when the figure "reached a peak of 7174" (Evashwick, 2005, 53). Almost 20 percent of these hospitals would close their doors over the next few decades until, by 2001, only 5801 hospitals remained (Evashwick, 2005, 53). By 2012, dozens more institutions had closed their doors, reducing the number of registered US hospitals to 5723 (American Hospital Association, 2014).

As a group, hospital executives significantly cut the number of inpatient hospital beds at their facilities in response to the changes discussed earlier in this chapter. In 1975, there were 1.46 million hospital beds in the United States (Evashwick, 2005, 54). By 2012, that number had dropped to less than 921,000 beds (AHA, 2014). Further demonstrating this trend, community hospital beds dropped from 4.5 per every 1000 Americans in 1980 to 2.9 per every 1000 people in 2000 (Shi & Singh, 2004, 289).

1.5.2 Merger Mania

Many hospitals have responded to the headwinds facing the industry by merging into larger conglomerates. The first wave of hospital consolidations began "in the 1980s" and "reached its peak in 1995" (Griffith & White, 2007, 9). The hospital industry's merger mania died down for a while, but started picking back up in 2010 (Anonymous, 2013). In 2004, "two-thirds of all hospitals, with 65 percent of beds [were] part of healthcare systems" (Griffith & White, 2007, 10). That number has likely risen since that time.

Like other industries, the connections between hospitals in a system can be fairly loose, providing individual hospitals with a lot of autonomy, or they can be tightly connected (Griffith & White, 2007, 9–10). In either case, hospital systems possess numerous, potential advantages over their individual facilities, "including increased referral volumes, better access to capital, stronger pricing power, and classic cost economies" (Sutaria, 2013). As such, hospitals, which are part of a larger entity, are naturally better able to overcome some of the headwinds that have faced the industry over the last few decades.

1.5.3 Growth in Outpatient and Other Ancillary Services

Hospitals have responded to the insurance payment changes discussed earlier, in part, by ramping up their outpatient services. The number of hospital outpatient visits has increased substantially in the past few decades—from 254,844,000 in 1975 to 709,960,000 in 2008 (Centers for Disease Control, 2010). Just as important, the "ratio of hospital outpatient visits to inpatient days" more than tripled between 1980 and 2000, going from 0.7 to 2.5 (Shi & Singh, 2004, 290).

Community hospitals have come to rely on the revenues generated from outpatient services to help them remain viable. In fact, the growth in outpatient revenues has been staggering. "Prior to 1985, outpatient care" accounted for "less than 15 [percent] of the total gross patient revenue for all US community hospitals" (Shi & Singh, 2004, 254). By 2009, outpatient procedures had grown to the point where they accounted for, on average, around 40 percent of a community hospital's total gross revenues (AHA and Avalere Health, 2013, 4.3). Many hospitals rely on their ambulatory services to generate more than half of their total gross revenues (Dentler, 2013). Over the course of the next decade, hospitals will come to rely even more on their outpatient services (Dentler, 2013).

1.5.4 Cutting Costs

Many hospitals continue to spend exorbitant amounts of money on new technology in an effort to attract the best physicians and, as a result, maximize the number of patients who visit their facilities (Ferrier, Leleu, Moises, & Valdmanis, 2013, 244–245). However, at the same time, many hospital executives in both for-profit and non-profit facilities have been zealously attempting to cut costs at their facilities. The vast majority of these hospitals have been forced to become more efficient in order to off-set lost revenue from Medicare, Medicaid, and private insurers (Abelson, 2012; Caramenico, 2012). Hospital executives have followed the lead of colleagues in other industries by latching on to strategies like Six Sigma and similar quality-control methods (Arevalo, 2010; Henke, 2009). Words like process control, statistical control charts, and sustainability, which were once foreign to hospital parlance, have become normative terms in managerial meetings (Ferenc, 2013, 9–10; Spath, 2009, 17–20). Some hospital leaders have become so obsessed with cutting costs that they are focusing on even relatively minor expenses, like facility energy costs (Whitson, 2012, 132–138).

1.6 Rosy on the Outside/Bleak on the Inside

On the surface, it appears that hospitals, at least the ones that are still in operation, have done an excellent job in dealing with both external and internal threats to their viability. In 2010, community hospitals earned "$730.9 billion in net revenue . . . [, which] was the highest in decades" (Selvam, 2012). On average, the hospitals secured a 7.2 percent net margin, which is pretty impressive by historical standards (Selvam, 2012). An American Hospital Association (AHA) circular claims that hospitals' current "average operating margin is 5.5 percent" (AHA, 2013). If an individual only looks at these averages, he or she might assume that hospitals, although they might not be cash cows, are nonetheless churning out reasonable profits. This rosy picture darkens somewhat under closer scrutiny.

Averages can be deceiving. A small number of American hospitals generate outsized gains. For instance, A Forbes' survey indicated that "24 hospitals in the country with over 200 beds make an operating margin of 25% or more" (Whelan, 2010). At the other end of the spectrum, the AHA estimates that a quarter of the nation's hospitals "lose money on operations" (AHA, 2013). A sizeable number of hospitals barely make a profit; they are one misstep from disaster (Whelan, 2010). Given the high cost of infrastructure and technology improvements, even high-performing hospitals might lose their way if they make a few poor decisions.

1.7 New Challenges on the Horizon

Unlike in some industries, the healthcare environment is constantly changing. The hospital industry, especially the community hospitals, will have to navigate several major sea changes. This book will touch on one of these seminal events—the move to a more integrated technological environment. However, it is worthwhile for me to focus a bit of time on two other major, external forces that are impacting the industry—the ever-increasing focus on patient safety and the Patient Protection and Affordable Care Act (ACA).

1.7.1 An Ever-Increasing Focus on Improving Patient Care and the Patient Experience

As I have already noted in this chapter, government agencies, private insurers, patient advocates, politicians, and a number of other stakeholders have teamed up to pressure hospitals to improve patient care at their facilities. This chorus is not likely to die down anytime soon. If anything, it will only increase in tempo in the coming years, as a range of stakeholders work to limit the growth in healthcare expenditures (Holahan et al., 2011, 1–26; Lazerow, 2012). At the same time, both private and public agencies are working together to try to improve Americans' overall health. These organizations hope to reduce healthcare costs by keeping people out of hospitals and doctors' offices (Berardo, N.D., 1–11; Scutchfield & Keck, 2009, 37–56).

Some hospitals, along with physicians and other healthcare providers, might thrive in this new environment. However, many other providers will see their bottom lines deteriorate, as the government and other insurance carriers penalize them for failing to meet certain patient safety or satisfaction benchmarks (Lazerow, 2012). And, in a true case of irony, the entire hospital industry might be negatively impacted if Americans become healthier. Healthier people generally spend less time in hospitals, and require fewer services when they do visit these medical facilities (Center for Healthcare Quality & Payment Reform, 2013; Meyer & Smith, 2008; National Council on Aging, 2014).

1.7.2 ACA: Uncharted Waters

Hospitals will also have to deal with the ramifications of the ACA. Some of the ACA's regulations will have a positive impact on hospitals. Millions of Americans, who were previously uninsured, will now be able to obtain coverage through state or federally run healthcare exchanges. Hospitals will benefit from this phenomenon because they usually have an easier time in collecting money from insurance companies than from patients (DuBois, 2013). A large number of poor Americans, who until recently did not have any insurance, will be able to obtain Medicaid. In the past, hospitals would have had to provide many of the services to this patient population for free. Now they will be able to recoup a portion of these expenses (Cowley, 2014; DuBois, 2013).

Although the ACA will benefit hospitals in some ways, it also comes with significant potential costs. For instance, newly enrolled Medicaid recipients might visit hospitals more often and demand a greater array of services than they previously did when they were uninsured (Dubois, 2013). Local, state, and federal authorities currently reimburse hospitals for some of their charity care write-offs. These entities might be less willing to continue this funding, even in cases where the need still exists (Chazin, Friedenzohn, Martinez-Vidal, & Somers, 2010, 7–19). The ACA's push to improve quality of care at hospitals is already having a deleterious impact on many of these institutions' bottom lines (Wolfson & Campbell, 2014) (see Figure 1.2). Some hospitals will likely be further impacted, as the CMS, following ACA directives, implements new policies over the next few years that punish institutions whose quality-of-care metrics do not meet certain standards (Dubois, 2013). It remains to be seen how other portions of the ACA, such as the section establishing accountable care organizations, will impact hospitals in both the near and long term.

Many hospitals will likely see a net benefit from the implementation of the ACA guidelines. However, at least some hospitals will see their bottom lines dwindle, as they struggle to cope with reduced payments and the added costs associated with ACA mandates. At this time, one would be foolhardy to try to pick the winners and losers, or even to estimate what percentage of hospitals will come out on top (see Figure 1.2).

1.8 The 21st-Century Hospital: Maximizing Efficiency without Sacrificing Patient Quality

In the coming decades, some hospitals will be able to weather the aforementioned changes just fine. A percentage of hospitals will find themselves in the exact opposite position; they do not stand a chance of surviving into the future. Even the best, most creative management teams could not save them. However, the majority of hospitals find themselves somewhere between the extremes. They might survive, and even thrive, as long as they achieve certain productivity and efficiency standards without sacrificing patient quality. However, their success is not guaranteed.

Regardless of how their facilities are currently performing, most hospital executives would surely agree that they can do better. Even the best-run hospitals can make improvements. However, management teams often struggle to identify new ways in which to cut costs or to improve efficiency and productivity without sacrificing quality. They have already implemented Six Sigma programs, have cut redundant staff, have reduced waste, and have improved billing systems. However, many hospitals do not yet place enough focus on some of their ancillary (non-clinical) departments, including HR.

1.9 The Mantra for All Healthcare Providers

Hospitals are not the only healthcare organizations that can take these steps to increase their margins and perhaps improve their patient quality metrics as well. Many other healthcare companies give short shrift to their HR departments (as well as to other, non-earning segments within their organizations). Executives' and managers' inattention to HR can impact the whole business in both large and small ways.

In this book, I will identify some of the ways in which executives, managers, and other staff can utilize key methodologies, techniques, and

IT to make better use of their HR resources. They can use my suggestions to help them accomplish goals, improve worker quality, increase employee morale, and achieve higher rates of efficiency.

References

Abelson, R. (2012, May 23). For Hospitals and Insurers, New Fervor to Cut Costs. *The New York Times*. Retrieved from http://www.nytimes.com/2012/05/24/health/hospitals-and-insurers-join-to-cut-health-care-costs.html?_r=0.

Altman, S. H., Shactman, D., & Eilat, E. (2006). Could U.S. Hospitals Go The Way of U.S. Airlines? *Health Affairs* 25(1), 11–21. DOI: 10.1377/hlthaff.25.1.11.

American Hospital Association. (2014, January 2). Fast Facts on U.S. Hospitals. Retrieved from http://www.aha.org/research/rc/stat-studies/fast-facts.shtml.

American Hospital Association. (2013, February 28). Setting the Record Straight on *Time's* article "Bitter Pill." Retrieved from file:///C:/Users/Anthony/Downloads/settingrecordstraight.pdf.

American Hospital Association and Avalere Health. (2013). *Trendwatch Chartbook: Trends in Hospital Management* [PowerPoint, Ch. 4]. Retrieved from http://www.aha.org/research/reports/tw/chartbook/index.shtml.

Anonymous. (2008, October 22). Study: Medicare Pay-for-Performance Penalizes Hospitals that Treat More Elderly Patients. McKnight's Long-Term Care News & Assisted Living. Retrieved from http://www.mcknights.com/study-medicare-pay-for-performance-penalizes-hospitals-that-treat-more-elderly-patients/article/119776/.

Anonymous. (2013, August 12). A Wave of Hospital Mergers. *The New York Times*. Retrieved from http://www.nytimes.com/interactive/2013/08/13/business/A-Wave-of-Hospital-Mergers.html?_r=0.

Arevalo, J. D. (2010, February 12). Hospitals Turning to Lean Six Sigma for Performance Improvement. *AMN Healthcare*. Retrieved from http://www.amnhealthcare.com/latest-healthcare-news/hospitals-turning-lean-six-sigma-performance-improvement/.

Atkinson, W., Hamborsky, J., Stanton, A., & Wolfe, C. (Eds.). (2012, May). *The Pink Book: Epidemiology and Prevention of Vaccine-Preventable Diseases* (12th ed.). The Centers for Disease Control and Prevention. Retrieved from http://www.cdc.gov/vaccines/pubs/pinkbook/downloads/meas.pdf.

Berardo, J., Jr. (N.D.). The New Face of Chronic Care Management. *MagnaCare*. Retrieved from http://www.magnacare.com/newsroom/images/THENEWFACEOFCHRONICCAREMANAGEMENT.pdf.

Blackburn, M. (2004, November). HIPAA, Heal Thyself. *Johns Hopkins Magazine* 56(5), n.p. Retrieved from http://www.jhu.edu/jhumag/1104web/hipaa.html.

Bodenhemer, T. S., & Grumbach, K. (2009). *Understanding Health Policy: A Clinical Approach*. New York: The McGraw-Hill Companies, Inc.

Bouchard, S. (2012, December 20). Survey Finds Eight in 10 Healthcare Businesses Impacted by Bad Hires. *Healthcare Finance News*. Retrieved from http://www.healthcarefinancenews.com/news/survey-finds-eight-10-healthcare-businesses-impacted-bad-hires.

Caramenico, A. (2012, May 24). Hospitals Accelerate Cost-Cutting Efforts. *Fierce Healthcare*. Retrieved from http://www.fiercehealthcare.com/story/hospitals-accelerate-cost-cutting-efforts/2012-05-24.

Center for Healthcare Quality & Payment Reform. (2013). Reducing Hospital Admissions. Retrieved from http://www.chqpr.org/readmissions.html.

Centers for Disease Control and Prevention. (2010). Trend Tables: Table 104. Retrieved from http://www.cdc.gov/nchs/data/hus/2010/104.pdf.

Centers for Medicare & Medicaid Services (2015). Hospital Compare. Retrieved fromhttp://www.medicare.gov/hospitalcompare/search.html?AspxAuto DetectCookieSupport=1.

Centers for Medicare & Medicaid Services. (2014). Readmissions Reduction Program. Retrieved from http://www.cms.gov/Medicare/Medicare-Fee-for-Service-Payment/AcuteInpatientPPS/Readmissions-Reduction-Program.html.

Chazin, S., Friedenzohn, I., Martinez-Vidal, E., & Somers, S. A. (2010, August). The Future of U.S. Charity Care Programs: Implications of Health Reform. Academy Health and the Center for Health Care Strategies, Inc. Retrieved from https://www.academyhealth.org/files/publications/FutureofCharityCarePrograms.pdf.

Ching-To, A. M. (1994). Health Care Payment Systems: Cost and Quality Incentives. *Journal of Economics & Management Strategy* 3(1), 93–112. Retrieved from http://people.bu.edu/ma/Papers_Archive/JEMS_1994.pdf.

Cohen, R. A., Makuc, D. M., Bernstein, A. B., Bilheimer, L. T., & Powell-Griner, E. (2009, July 1). Health Insurance Coverage Trends, 1959–2007: Estimates from the National Health Interview Survey. [issue brief, No. 17]. Centers for Disease Control and Prevention. Retrieved from http://www.cdc.gov/nchs/data/nhsr/nhsr017.pdf.

Cowley, G. (2014, February 19). Obamacare Enrollment Is Up Again. MSNBC. Retrieved from http://www.msnbc.com/msnbc/obamacare-enrollment-up-again.

Coye, M. J., & Kell J. (2006). How Hospitals Confront New Technology. *Health Affairs* 25(1), 163–173. DOI: 10.1377/hlthaff.25.1.163.

DeNavas-Walt, C., Proctor, B. D., & Smith, J. (2011, September). Income, Poverty, and Health Insurance Coverage in the United States: 2010. U.S. Census Bureau. Retrieved from http://www.census.gov/prod/2011pubs/p60-239.pdf.

Dentler, J. (2013, May 23). Winning with Ambulatory Care. *Hospitals & Health Networks*. Retrieved from http://www.hhnmag.com/display/HHN-news-article.dhtml?dcrPath=/templatedata/HF_Common/NewsArticle/data/HHN/Daily/2013/May/dentler052313-6190006017.

DuBois, S. (2013, October 20). Hospitals Face Whole New World under Health Law. *USA Today*. Retrieved from http://www.usatoday.com/story/news/nation/2013/10/20/hospitals-face-whole-new-world-under-health-law/3078353/.

Duggan, M. (2002, August). Does Contracting Out Increase the Efficiency of Government Programs? Evidence from Medicaid HMOs. National Bureau of Economic Research. Retrieved from http://www.nber.org/papers/w9091.

Employee Benefit Research Institute. (2002, March). History of Health Insurance Benefits. Retrieved from http://www.ebri.org/publications/facts/index.cfm?fa=0302fact.

Evashwick, C. J. (2005). *The Continuum of Long-Term Care* (3rd ed.). Clifton Park, NY: Delmar Cengage Learning.

Ferenc, J. (2013, February). Building a Movement: Healthy Hospitals Movement Aims to Boost Sustainability. *Health Facilities Management* 26(2), 9–10. Retrieved from Infotrac Database-GALE|A348310790.

Ferrier, G.D., Leleu, H., Moises, J., & Valdmanis, V. G. (2013). The Focus Efficiency of U.S. Hospitals. *Atlantic Economic Journal* 41(3), 241–263. DOI: 10.1007/s11293-013-9385-z.

Fuchs, V. R. (1988). The "Competition Revolution" in Health Care. *Health Affairs* 7(3), 5–24. DOI: 10.1377/hlthaff.7.3.5.

Fuchs, V. (2012, March 15). Major Trends in the U.S. Health Economy since 1950. *New England Journal of Medicine* 366(11), 973–976. DOI: 10.1056/NEJMp1200478.

Gauthier, J. G. (2002, September). Measuring America: The Decennial Censuses: From 1790 to 2000. U.S. Census Bureau. Retrieved from http://www.census.gov/prod/2002pubs/pol02marv.pdf.

Getzen, T. E. (2010). *Health Economics and Financing* (4th ed.). Hoboken, NJ: John Wiley & Sons, Inc.

Gold, J. (2013, May 31). Proton Beam Therapy Sparks Hospital Arms Race. *National Public Radio*. Retrieved from http://www.npr.org/blogs/health/2013/05/31/187350802/proton-beam-therapy-sparks-hospital-arms-race.

Griffith, J. R., & White, K. R. (2007). *The Well-Managed Healthcare Organization* (6th ed.). Washington, DC: Health Administration Press.

Groysberg, B. & Bell, D. (2013, May 28). Talent Management: Boards Give Their Companies an "F." *Harvard Business Review*. Retrieved from http://blogs.hbr.org/2013/05/talent-management-boards-give/.

Gufstafson, S. (2009, June 1). Medical Imaging: Free-Standing Centers Increase Competition. *MLive*. Retrieved from http://www.mlive.com/businessreview/oakland/index.ssf/2009/06/medical_imaging_freestanding_c.html.

Guterman, S. (2000, July). Putting Medicare in Context: How Does the Balanced Budget Act Affect Hospitals? *Urban Institute*. Retrieved from http://www.urban.org/publications/410247.html.

Guterman, S., Ashby, J., & Greene, T. (1996). Hospital Cost Growth Down. *Health Affairs* 15(3), 134–139. DOI: 10.1377/hlthaff.15.3.134.

Hall, M. J., DeFrances, C. J., Williams, S. N., Golosinskiy, A., & Schwartzman, A. (2010, October 26). National Hospital Discharge Survey: 2007 Summary 29. *Centers for Disease Control and Prevention*. Retrieved from http://www.cdc.gov/nchs/data/nhsr/nhsr029.pdf.

Henke, C. (2009, March 17). Hospitals See Benefits of Lean and Six Sigma. *ASQ*. Retrieved from http://www.asq.org/media-room/press-releases/2009/20090318-hospitals-see-benefits-lss.html.

Holahan, J., Blumberg, L. J., McMorrow, S., Zuckerman, S., Waidmann, T., & Stockley, K. (2011, October). Containing the Growth of Spending in the U.S. Health System. *Urban Institute*. Retrieved from http://www.urban.org/uploadedpdf/412419-Containing-the-Growth-of-Spending-in-the-US-Health-System.pdf.

Johnson, J., Dawson, E., & Acquaviva, K. (2008). The Quality Improvement Landscape. In E. Ransom, M. S. Joshi, D. B. Nash, & S. B. Ranson (Eds.), *The Healthcare Quality Book* (2nd ed.) (pp. 407–432). Washington, DC: Health Administration Press.

Kilbridge, P. (2003, April 10). The Cost of HIPAA Compliance. *New England Journal of Medicine* 348(15), 1423–1424. Retrieved from http://www.mcmaster.ca/ors/ethics/ncehr/2003/apr2003/1423%20NEJM%20HIPAA.pdf.

Klees, B. S., Wolfe, C. J., & Curtis, C. A. (2010, November 1). Brief Summaries of Medicare & Medicaid: Title XVIII and Title XIX of the Social Security Act. Centers for Medicare and Medicaid Services. Retrieved from http://www.cms.gov/Research-Statistics-Data-and-Systems/Statistics-Trends-and-Reports.

Lazerow, R. (2012, May 3). Exploring the Future of Medicare Pay-for-Performance Programs. *The Advisory Board Company*. Retrieved from http://www.advisory.com/research/health-care-advisory-board/blogs/toward-accountable-payment/2012/05/exploring-the-future-of-medicare-pay-for-performance-programs.

MacDorman, M. F., Mathews, T. J., & Declercq, E. (2012, January). Home Births in the United States, 1990–2009. Centers for Disease Control and Prevention. Retrieved from http://www.cdc.gov/nchs/data/databriefs/db84.pdf.

Meyer, J., & Smith, B. M. (2008, November). Chronic Disease Management: Evidence of Predictable Savings. *Health Management Associates*. Retrieved from https://www.idph.state.ia.us/hcr_committees/common/pdf/clinicians/savings_report.pdf.

Midey, C. (2010, November 7). Doctor's Offices Doing More Surgeries. *The Arizona Republic*. Retrieved from http://www.azcentral.com/arizonarepublic/news/articles/2010/11/07/20101107doctors-office-surgery.html.

National Council on Aging. (2014). Chronic Disease Self-Management: Fact Sheet. Retrieved from http://www.ncoa.org/press-room/fact-sheets/chronic-disease.html.

Office of the Inspector General. (2001, August). Medicare Hospital Prospective Payment System: How DRG Rates Are Calculated and Updated. The Department of Health and Human Services. Retrieved from http://oig.hhs.gov/oei/reports/oei-09-00-00200.pdf.

Pawlson, G., & Schyve, P. (2008). Accreditation: Its Role in Driving Accountability in Healthcare. In E. Ransom, M. S. Joshi, D. B. Nash, & S. B. Ranson (Eds.), *The Healthcare Quality Book* (2nd ed.) (pp. 433–455). Washington, DC: Health Administration Press.

Public Broadcasting Service. (1998). People and Discoveries: Salk Produces Polio Vaccine. Retrieved from http://www.pbs.org/wgbh/aso/databank/entries/dm52sa.html.

Scutchfield, F. D., & Keck, C. W. (2009). *Principles of Public Health Practice* (3rd ed.). Clifton Park, NY: Delmar Cengage Learning.

Selvam, A. (2012, January 9). One for the Record Books: Hospital Profit Margins Hit Highest Level in Decades. *Modern Healthcare*. Retrieved from http://www.modernhealthcare.com/article/20120109/MAGAZINE/301099961#.

Shi, L., & Singh, D. A. (2004). *Delivering Health Care in America: A Systems Approach* (3rd ed.). Sudbury, MA: Jones and Bartlett Publishers.

Showalter, J. S. (2007). *The Law of Healthcare Administration* (5th ed.). Chicago: Health Administration Press.

Spath, P. (2009). *Introduction to Healthcare Quality Management*. Chicago: Health Administration Press.

Strupp, D. (2008, June 24). New Technology Fuels Medical Arms Race. *Jacksonville Business Journal*. Retrieved from http://www.bizjournals.com/jacksonville/stories/2008/06/23/focus1.html.

Sutaria, S. (2013, November 18). When M&A Is Not the Best Option for Hospitals. *Harvard Business Review*. Retrieved from: http://blogs.hbr.org/2013/11/when-ma-is-not-the-best-option-for-hospitals/.

Terry, K. (2010, March 17). Hospitals' Dirty Little Secret: Technology Drives Healthcare Costs. *CBS Money Watch*. Retrieved from http://www.cbsnews.com/news/hospitals-dirty-little-secret-technology-drives-healthcare-costs/.

The Science Museum, London (2013). Exploring the History of Medicine: Technology and Medicine. History of Medicine. Retrieved from http://www.sciencemuseum.org.uk/broughttolife.aspx.

Toland, B. (2012, April 12). Hospitals Competing for Patients, Doctors, and Dollars. *Pittsburgh Post-Gazette*. Retrieved from http://www.post-gazette.com/businessnews/2012/04/12/Hospitals-competing-for-patients-doctors-and-dollars/stories/201204120332.

U.S. Census Bureau. (1996). Current Population Reports, Special Studies, 65+ in the United States. Washington, DC. Retrieved from http://www.census.gov/prod/1/pop/p23-190/p23-190.pdf.

U.S. Census Bureau. (2013, December 17). "State and County Quick Facts. Retrieved from http://quickfacts.census.gov/qfd/states/00000.html.

U.S. Census Bureau. (1973). *Statistical Abstract of the United States: 1973* (94th ed.). Washington, DC. Retrieved from http://www.google.com/books.

U.S. Census Bureau. (1990). *Statistical Abstract of the United States: 1990* (110th ed.). Washington, DC. Retrieved from http://books.google.com/books.

Vincent, G. K., & Velkoff, V. A. (2010, May). The Next Four Decades—The Older Population in the United States: 2010–2050. *U.S. Census Bureau*. Retrieved from http://www.census.gov/prod/2010pubs/p25-1138.pdf.

Wall, B. M. (2013). History of Hospitals. University of Pennsylvania. Retrieved from http://www.nursing.upenn.edu/nhhc/Pages/History%20of%20Hospitals.aspx.

Whelan, D. (2010, August 31). America's Most Profitable Hospitals. *Forbes*. Retrieved from http://www.forbes.com/2010/08/30/profitable-hospitals-hca-healthcare-business-mayo-clinic.html.

Whitson, B. A. (2012). The 50 Percent Solution to Reducing Energy Costs: A Systematic Plan for Reducing Hospital Energy Costs, with a Framework that Focuses on Capital Outlay, Performance Tracking, and Cash Inflows and Outflows, Can Result in Big Savings. *Healthcare Financial Management* 66(11), 132–138. Retrieved from Infotrac.

Wolfson, B., & Campbell, R. (2014, February 14). Hospitals Told to Reduce Patient Readmissions or Lose Money. *The Dallas Morning News*. Retrieved from http://www.dallasnews.com/business/health-care/20140214-hospitals-told-to-reduce-patient-readmissions-or-lose-money.ece.

York, R., Kaufman, K., & Grube, M. (2013, March 8). Decline in Utilization Rates Signals a Change in the Inpatient Business Model. *Health Affairs*. Retrieved from http://healthaffairs.org/blog/2013/03/08/decline-in-utilization-rates-signals-a-change-in the-inpatient-business-model/.

Chapter Two

The Digital Revolution and Its Relevance to Healthcare Companies' HR Practices and Infrastructures

I believe that healthcare leaders have to know a little about the history of the technology revolution in order to appreciate the important role that information technology (IT) plays in the current world. The savvy healthcare executive or manager will study technology's past in order to understand the developing interrelationships between IT and human beings. The individual will further use this knowledge to aid him or her in empathizing with workers, especially older ones, who are hesitant to adopt new technologies. The leader could also use history as a guide to aid him or her in identifying ways in which the introduction of new technologies can alter employee behaviors and workflow processes. At the same time, a healthcare administrator who understands technology's historical trends will have a better grasp of where these developments are headed over the next two or three decades, thereby allowing him or her to strategically place the organization in a position to benefit from these changes. Finally—and most importantly—a leader can use what he or she learns about technology's past, as it relates specifically to the health services industry, to help him or her improve human resources (HR) processes, increase overall organizational efficiency and effectiveness, and better manage the office.

2.1 The Early Stages of the Technology Revolution—A Slow Beginning

Anyone who follows computers can attest to the rapid speed at which this industry has progressed over the last few decades. Relative to other innovative technologies, computer development has progressed at breakneck speeds. As recently as the mid-1970s, punch card computers were still in vogue. These machines, which could take up an entire room, were extremely limited by today's standards (Fisk, 2005). The punch cards themselves would typically hold 960 bits or less of data per card (Dyson, N.D.; Lilly, 2009). At the same time, the computer systems were not conducive to supporting vast IT networks. At least not when a company had to "purchase cards by the truckload" in order to ensure that key employees had access to the system (Da Cruz, 2013).

During this period, one could also purchase a computer that utilized magnetic tape storage or even magnetic film, for example, on 8-inch floppy disks (Computer History Museum, 2014; Zetta, 2014). However, these systems were bulky and rather slow by today's standards. One of the workhorses of this era, the IBM System/370 could only hold between 1 million and 3 million bytes in its "core memory." The machine was not cheap either (Ewalt, 2012). "A typical System/370 Model 165 with 1 million bytes of main memory carried a purchase price of $4,674,160" (Ewalt, 2012).

Of course, companies could increase their storage space by linking drives or by purchasing storage facility units. IBM was the leader in this area in the 1970s. IBM introduced the 3340 direct access storage facility (nicknamed the Winchester) to great fanfare in 1973. The state of the art system "provided a storage capacity of up to 280 million bytes" (IBM, N.D.). That equates to the paltry sum of around 267 megabytes (approximately 0.000254 terabytes).

The first home desktop computers, or microcomputers, did not arrive on the scene until the mid-1970s. The first home computers were "of little computing use." Only hobbyists and computer specialists were interested in them. By the end of the 1970s, these computers could perform basic word processing and mathematical tasks, which appealed to both companies and individuals (Fox, 2013, 196–197).

Nonetheless, employees at numerous companies performed many (and, in some cases, all) tasks by hand. Executives would write appointments into calendar books or on sheets of paper. Their staff, including analysts, accountants, and a bevy of other job types, still did things the old-fashioned way; they used pen and paper to perform tasks, ranging from the basic to the complex. Presentations were conducted using large paper sheets or via bulky slide projectors and primitive (by today's standards) overhead projectors (National Museum of American History, N.D.; Rawsthorn, 2013).

2.2 Contemporary IT Systems

Flash forward to today. Companies can purchase desktops and laptops that can process information at astonishing rates of speed when performing linear tasks. Many of these machines can hold more than a terabyte of information in their hard drives, and they can connect to external hard drives, containing additional terabytes of data.* At the same time, each of these computers, while working independently, can communicate with each other, thereby allowing them to divide up tasks between themselves. As a result, companies can create networks of computers. These networks can handle complex, multifaceted tasks, with numerous variables and end products (Rainer & Watson, 2012, 4.1–4.4; Smith, 2011). Companies can also choose to purchase supercomputers. These machines are very

---

* At the time of this writing, one can buy these laptops from most of the major retailers. Here is a page from Amazon.com that contains a list of laptops with at least a terabyte of memory: http://smile.amazon.com/s/ref=nb_sb_noss_1?url=search-alias%3Daps&field-keywords=terabyte%20laptop&sprefix=terabyte+la%2Caps. Another major retailer, Wal-Mart, also sells these machines: http://www.walmart.com/search/?query=laptop%20and%201%20terabyte.

expensive; however, they are much more powerful than even a network of desktops and laptops (Tech News Daily, 2012).

More importantly, computer technology is advancing at a rapid pace. Developments of some computer hardware components and processes are increasing at an exponential pace. As each new generation of computers comes online, their predecessors become less expensive (Kurzweil, 2005, 64–75). Ray Kurzweil, a noted inventor, describes the sheer pace of change and its impact on computer users (both corporate and private):

> I can compare the MIT computer I used as a student in the 1960s to a recent notebook. In 1967, I had access to a multi-million dollar IBM 7094 with 32K (36-bit) words of memory and a quarter of a MIPS processor speed. In 2004 I used a $2000 personal computer with a half-billion bytes of RAM and a processor speed of about 2000 MIPS. (Kurzweil, 2005, 64)

As a result of this phenomenon, many corporations can upgrade parts of their systems (or even whole computer networks) every few years, as opposed to waiting a decade or more between updates. Additionally, companies that are currently priced out of the market for high-end servers, computers, or other devices, might not have to wait too many years before they can purchase comparable models (as newer models come on line, thereby driving down the price of the older varieties).

Companies can also utilize the Internet, something that was in its infancy in the 1970s, to store data, share information, collect data, test market ideas, crowdsource work, and perform any number of other tasks. Just as important, American executives and their workers can utilize an array of other technologies, including tablets and smartphones, to maintain 24-hour connectivity both to their corporation's information system, as well as to publicly available information on the Internet (Forbes & Google, 2010).

In short, contemporary organizations have access to advanced hardware and Wi-Fi connectivity that are light years ahead of the technologies that were available even a few years ago. At the same time, they can purchase or lease advanced software systems. These programs, when used with the correct hardware, can analyze mountains of data in relatively short amounts of time and perform complex calculations. Some of these programs are self-learners. Like human beings, they can adjust their methods or reanalyze data, based on new information.

Although these systems do not approach human level intelligence, they excel at performing a defined set of tasks. For instance, one program might be able to determine whether consumer comments are complaints or praise-based statements. It can then categorize the complaints. Another system might be able to ascertain a person's lifestyle or food choices from his or her web-browsing history. Yet another artificial intelligence (AI) program might be able to review data on hundreds of variables and find patterns within this information (Goertzel, 2008; Rapid Improvement–Minute Surveys).

Corporations in most fields can purchase or lease (or perhaps even develop internally) IT tools that they can use to perform important, complex tasks, for example, matching their products to consumer needs or wants, closely managing complex supply chains, maintaining tight control over product safety and quality, and identifying operational inefficiencies.

2.3 Hospitals Slow to Adopt (and Adapt to) New Technologies

Although American companies have the potential to create integrated IT systems like the ones described above, many of these organizations have not taken this step. This phenomenon is especially pronounced in the healthcare space. Whereas hospitals, and to some extent physicians, have been more than willing to purchase the latest clinical or surgical technologies, they have been averse to upgrading their IT systems. For instance, it is only in the last few years that the majority of hospitals have switched from paper-based charting systems to electronic medical records (EMRs). According to Forbes, "About six percent of U.S. hospitals have yet to convert even the most basic ancillary services of laboratory, pharmacy and radiology to electronic medical record systems despite billions of dollars in funds available to these facilities . . ." (Jaspen, 2014). Many physicians still use flip charts to record their patients' information. Even in some of the facilities, which have upgraded to EMRs, both the clinical and non-clinical staff have difficulty learning how to correctly use the systems (HHS.gov, 2013).

Hospitals and doctors have been almost as reticent to adopt new IT hardware and software for their back-end systems, as they have for their frontline operations (which deal with patients). Their IT systems often contain a patchwork of various programs and hardware designs. Many employees will have to navigate between several different programs in order to complete their assigned tasks. Additionally, they might have to utilize third-party software (for instance a flash drive and either Microsoft Excel or Access) to download information from one system, modify the data, and place it on another system (Judge, 2013; Roney, 2012).

Hospitals and other healthcare providers face another problem that sets them apart from companies in other fields. They are, in some instances, still struggling to develop metrics and procedures to allow them to identify and fix many of the issues that are specific to the healthcare industry. For instance, while the healthcare industry has identified hundreds (if not thousands) of potential metrics for measuring the quality of care in hospitals, it has not yet perfected many of them (Rau, 2012).

At the same time, hospital executives have made strides over the last few years in using Six Sigma and other techniques to improve efficiency, reduce costs, and improve patient care. However, they are still working to perfect many of these systems, which they borrowed from other industries. Even when hospital executives have the ability to streamline their IT systems or possess access to a reliable method for improving performance and patient care, they are sometimes unable to convince their workforces to go along with the changes.

In most industries, one can point to companies that are, for lack of a better term, stuck in the 20th century. However, hospitals (along with physicians and other healthcare providers) have traditionally been more reticent than most other firms about building coordinated IT infrastructures and with regard to adopting modern methods for increasing efficiency, cutting waste, and improving quality of care at their facilities. There are several reasons for this lack of inertia on the part of the hospital industry.

- **Diverse Array of Payers**

  Hospitals have to navigate an extremely diverse and complex regulatory and contractual environment. Hospitals [and other healthcare providers, including durable medical equipment (DME) suppliers, physicians, and ambulatory centers] have to account for hundreds of different insurance payers. A hospital will have negotiated one or more contracts with many of these payers. Each of these contracts will have unique provisions and payment schedules. Hospital staff have to account for all of these differences. One insurance policy might cover a specific procedure, while another one does not. In another instance, one payer might allow a patient to receive inpatient treatment for a surgery, whereas another payer might require the hospital to provide the same surgical procedures on an outpatient basis only (see Figure 2.1). As a result of these complex payment arrangements, hospitals and other healthcare providers sometimes find it difficult to implement holistic, IT infrastructures that can integrate all aspects of the payment process (from contract analysis through payment receipt).

- **Complex Infrastructure**
  Hospitals are extremely complex environments. A community hospital will contain patients of all ages and with an assortment of illnesses. The facility's clinical units will likely consist of an emergency room, a variety of inpatient wards, outpatient units, and even a long-term care wing. The facility will also have to house a plethora of non-clinical departments, including, among others, IT, finance, billing, insurance, and planning. The hospital will also have ancillary units, such as a cafeteria, a gift shop, and a pharmacy. Employees in many of these units, especially the clinical ones, have to deal with a unique set of issues, protocols, and procedures. The hospital might also outsource some functions (such as janitorial work), which adds another layer of complexity to the business model. As a result of this complexity, hospital executives often have a hard time convincing their subordinates to implement holistic, interoperable IT networks.

- **Diverse Employee Community**
  Hospitals contain a diverse array of employee types. The physicians occupy one end of the spectrum. In most cases, hospitals do not directly employ these doctors. Instead, the physicians are independent contractors who utilize the hospital's surgical areas and staff. Doctors have a great deal of autonomy. They will often refuse to take part in hospital cost-cutting or efficiency initiatives. Even when a hospital employs its own physicians, hospital executives and managers can find it difficult to convince this group to adopt new initiatives.

  Non-clinical, entry-level employees, such as insurance verification specialists, occupy the other end of the spectrum. Hospital management can set the protocols, rules, and standards for these workers, and management can correct workers when they do not perform up to these standards. However, I can state from experience that managers will still have a hard time getting these people

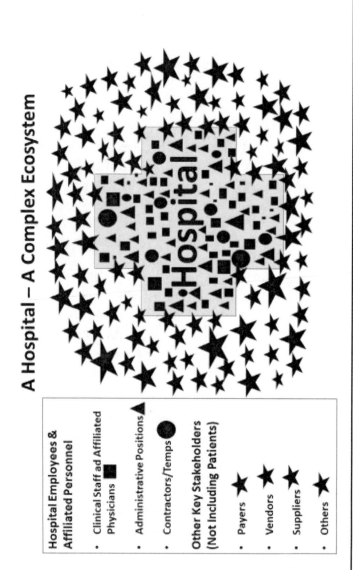

Figure 2.1 Each individual symbol reflects a different employee type (e.g., cardiologists, hemodialysis nurses, medical coders specializing in Medicare claims, etc.) or a different client/stakeholder (Medicare, a particular private insurance company, a supplier, etc.). As this illustration demonstrates, a hospital executive or administrator has to navigate a complex environment, containing a variety of stakeholders. These entities range in size (e.g., the number of employees in a group or the scope of a payer) and possess a wide array of relationships with the facility. Due to space limitations, the image does not list all employee types or accurately denote the number of patients. It also does not include patients. A true representation would contain many more symbols.

to change long-held habits. They also have to deal with issues such as high turnover rates and low morale when they institute a new policy, or install a new technology, which is unpopular with entry-level workers.

A typical hospital can employ thousands of people who run the gamut of points along this spectrum. As such, hospital managers have to contend with a diverse array of employee types when implementing new, global IT systems—for example, EMRs—or when starting new initiatives, which involve a number of departments. They also have to deal with the fact that each group of employees will likely have its own subculture. For instance, oncology physicians might adhere to cultural norms that are quite different from their peers in podiatry (see Figure 2.1).

- **Cost**
  As I noted in the last chapter, many hospitals have problems breaking even. They simply cannot afford to invest the resources necessary to upgrade their IT infrastructure or to adopt innovative employment and HR practices. Many of these hospital executives also tend to be extremely cautious, and who can blame them, when one significant misstep might result in bankruptcy for their facilities and massive layoffs of personnel (Altarum Institute, 2011).

- **History and Tradition**
  One of the key reasons—perhaps the most important factor—why many hospitals utilize outdated technology and methods lies in the industry's history. As I have already noted, hospitals did not have to deal with the same cost pressures facing other industries until relatively recently. Although hospital executives and managers have been working hard to adapt to the changing cost environment, they have had to go through a learning curve. They also have had to overcome antiquated, outdated traditions, which hinder progress.

2.3.1 My Own Firsthand Experiences

I experienced this phenomenon firsthand, while trying to market an innovative technique for identifying patient-care issues at the clinical level. The company had developed an AI system that could identify patient concerns by analyzing text-based comments. Using this method, physicians and hospitals could gain valuable information by simply asking their patients to fill out a one-question, open-ended survey. Patients could voice their complaints, or praises, in their own words. The AI system would then analyze these text-based comments and identify any complaints in real time.

One can easily see the potential advantages with this collection method. Hospitals and physicians could gather valuable information quickly and continuously. Further, these entities could get feedback in real time, which would allow them to quickly identify potential patient-care problems before they got out of hand. Healthcare providers cannot usually achieve these goals with traditional, multi-question surveys.

Regardless of its potential benefits, one would expect healthcare managers and executives to carefully consider a number of factors before they decide to utilize the system. They might, for instance, weigh the costs of leasing the software and purchasing survey forms against the potential benefits. It would be logical for these individuals to ask to see data on patient-completion rates, AI success rates (at correctly identifying patient complaints), and a host of other metrics, which would demonstrate that the company's system would actually do what it was supposed to do.

However, the most difficult issue that I had to surmount was in getting physicians and hospital administrators to overcome what I would term as their "we haven't done this type of thing before" mentality. This result should not be surprising. Both groups are often averse to contemplating using new technologies and new methods, even when the data demonstrates their benefits. Managers and physicians should be cautious when adopting new technologies, business or clinical methods, and protocols. Healthcare companies, which throw caution to the wind and adopt new techniques and technologies, without properly vetting these systems, might end up in bankruptcy court before too long. However, the healthcare organizations, especially hospitals, have often relied too much on tradition and have thus been too slow to change the way they do things.

2.4 Changes Are Afoot

As I noted in the previous chapter, hospital administrators, as well as executives and managers in other sectors of healthcare, are starting to shed old ways of thinking in favor of new and innovative approaches. For instance, they have begun to enthusiastically embrace Six Sigma and other, similar programs. At the same time, hospital administrators, physicians, and others are starting to come around to the idea of using IT for record keeping and as decision support tools—at least to a greater degree than in the past. Many physicians, especially the younger ones, have abandoned their flip charts and other paper tools in favor of tablets and powerful smartphones (Faas, 2012). Some doctors now even use voice recognition software to record their chart notes.

2.5 The Juxtaposition between Old and New Creates Opportunities

If an observer could step back and view the hospital industry—and, in fact, healthcare services in general—he or she would see an industry with one foot firmly planted in the past and one foot tentatively reaching toward the future. Hospitals and other healthcare providers still cling to some outdated methods, and they still sometimes rely on antiquated or under-developed IT infrastructure. However, at the same time, an ever-increasing number of administrators at these facilities are working to modernize their business and clinical processes, as well as to upgrade IT systems.

In other words, the healthcare services field in general—and the hospital industry in particular—finds itself in one of those rare states of flux. The organizations in this arena are in the process of shrugging off many of the low-tech, antiquated traditions that limit growth and hinder the creation of a patient-centered environment. At the same time, these providers still have a long way to go before they can claim victory. Along the way, they will struggle to develop integrated solutions and interoperable IT infrastructures that work in complex environments and meet the needs of their varied stakeholders.

For forward-thinking healthcare leaders, this is an exciting time. They have what might be a once in a lifetime opportunity to introduce new ways of doing things and to purchase or internally develop new IT infrastructures that will literally reshape their facilities and improve the treatment of patients. People who hold positions of power in multi-hospital chains or integrated networks can have an even greater impact.

At the same time, these leaders have to ensure that these systems meet four key criteria if they want to successfully guide their healthcare organizations into the new millennium.

- **Cost Effective**
  First and foremost, healthcare executives and managers have to make sure that the new technologies or ideas work. Beyond that fact, they have to ensure that these systems are cost effective. The corporate world is littered with stories of technologies or ideas that sounded great on paper but did not work in reality. They can achieve this goal by testing the systems in a limited environment before rolling them out in the company at large.

- **Interoperable**
  The best new methodologies and IT systems will be portable. Both managers and, when applicable, frontline employees in all departments and clinical areas should be able to use them. In a best-case scenario, managers in a diverse array of departments will be able to use a particular system without having to make many alterations to it. At the other end of the spectrum, only a few units within the healthcare organization will utilize the system. In either case, the ideal IT system or methodology should fit seamlessly within the organization's overall schema.

- **Buy-in**
  It goes without saying that a majority of employees have to buy-in to any new technologies and methods. At the same time, the people in charge—c-suite leaders, managers, and so forth—have to support these changes. If either of these two constituents—the leadership or frontline staff—do not fully acquiesce to the new changes, then these technologies or methods, regardless of their potential, will likely fail.

- **Adaptability**
  Healthcare leaders must be able and willing to make changes to a new technology or methodology roll-out, when aspects of that roll-out do not work as planned. Most of us have experienced situations at work in which the plans we created on paper did not work as intended when they were implemented at the department or corporate level. Effective leadership teams will be both willing and able to fix any flaws that appear during the roll-out stage (or even at a later point, in response to changes in the corporate culture or in the external environment).

Business experts have identified numerous other issues that relate to this topic. However, in my experience, I have found that new technology or methodology roll-outs, which meet the four aforementioned objectives, usually perform well. On the other hand, a new roll-out, which does not meet these criteria, will often fail to meet its objectives (or perhaps fail altogether).

I think all business leaders would agree that these four criteria are important. However, I have noticed that many seasoned executives and managers fail to follow through on all of them. Most often, corporate leaders (in both healthcare and non–healthcare-related businesses) will do a great job of ensuring that the new roll-out meets initial cost-effectiveness goals (at least on paper) and is interoperable. However, they fail to provide their employees with the right amount of training, coaching, or incentives to convince these people to buy-in to the new system. Just as often, leadership will initially champion something only to abandon it later on. All of us, if we work long enough, will experience this phenomenon for ourselves.

Even when managers or executives fail to correctly implement a new initiative, they can often correct their mistakes. They can adjust the process in situ, by providing additional training for staff, by fixing IT-related issues, or by taking other measures to resolve any problems with a roll-out. However, many otherwise rational and knowledgeable executives will often refuse to make the necessary changes to a new system, even when confronted with the realization that their roll-out, as currently envisioned, is not working. Bolman and Deal discuss this phenomenon in their classic work, *Reframing Organizations* (2008). Suffice it to say, however, that most of us have experienced these circumstances.

Like any other corporate head, hospital executives and other healthcare leaders need to comply with these criteria in order to give their organization's initiatives the best possible chance of success. In fact, they might have to pay more attention to securing stakeholder buy-in than firms in some other industries. In some hierarchically structured firms, management might be able to coerce workers into following new protocols or learning new IT techniques. However, many of the employees and contractors (including doctors) at a hospital or other large healthcare organization are semiautonomous. Healthcare managers have to convince these individuals to adopt new systems. They do not respond well to orders or demands.

I could discuss all of the topics in this chapter in much more depth. However, many other authors have already undertaken this task. Instead, I have sought to provide readers with a brief sketch of the changes in computerization, IT, and AI over the past few decades. The advances in this field have been truly phenomenal. Contemporary healthcare managers can utilize hardware and software to perform complex management, analysis, and oversight tasks, which were unheard of until recently.

Some companies have already leveraged these new technologies to great effect. They have also employed innovated, non-tech methods for analyzing data, streamlining business practices, motivating workers, or finding new talent. However, numerous healthcare corporations, especially hospitals and physicians' practices, have only recently started to adopt these 21st-century technologies and methods. In many cases, they still rely on antiquated IT systems and business practices.

The healthcare services field is transitioning from a low-tech (at least as regards IT infrastructures), tradition-bound industry to one that leverages advanced technologies and methodologies. This is an exciting time for innovative healthcare leaders, as they get the opportunity to help guide fundamental changes in the way that hospitals, doctors' practices, and other healthcare delivery organizations manage their employees, assets, and patients.

Hospital executives and other healthcare leaders will likely be able to identify many areas within their organizations that could benefit from IT upgrades or innovative methodological initiatives. However, these individuals will likely be able to achieve the most significant results by focusing on their HR systems.

References

Alemi, F. (2013, December). Self-Correcting Networks That Maximize Positive Patient Experiences. Rapid Improvement, Inc. Retrieved from https://tellmymd.com/Images/Proposal-to-Optimize-Provider-Network.pdf.

Altarum Institute. (2011). Overcoming Challenges to Health IT Adoption in Small, Rural Hospitals. Retrieved from http://www.healthit.gov/sites/default/files/pdf/OvercomingChallenges_in_SmallRuralHospitals.pdf.

Bolman, L., & Deal, T. (2008). *Reframing Organizations: Artistry, Choice, and Leadership* (4th ed.). San Francisco: Jossey-Bass.

Computer History Museum (2014). Magnetic Hard Disks. Retrieved from http://www.computerhistory.org/revolution/memory-storage/8/259.

Da Cruz, F. (2013). IBM Punch Cards. *Columbia University Computing History.* Retrieved from http://www.columbia.edu/cu/computinghistory/cards.html.

Dyson, G. (N.D.). The Little Secret that Haunts Corporate America . . . A Technology That Won't Go Away. *Wired.* Retrieved from http://www.wired.com/wired/archive/7.03/punchcards_pr.html.

Ewalt, D. M. (2012, March). Mainframe System 370. *Forbes.* Retrieved from http://www.forbes.com/sites/davidewalt/2012/03/19/mainframe-system-370/.

Faas, R. (2012). Majority Of Doctors Will Use iPads on the Job by 2013. *Cult of Mac.* Retrieved from http://www.cultofmac.com/166861/majority-of-doctors-will-use-ipads-on-the-job-by-2013/.

Fisk, D. (2005). Programming with Punched Cards. *Columbia University Computing History.* Retrieved from http://www.columbia.edu/cu/computinghistory/fisk.pdf.

Forbes & Google (2010). The Untethered Executive: Business Information in the Age of Mobility. Retrieved from http://images.forbes.com/forbesinsights/StudyPDFs/The_Untethered_Executive.pdf.

Fox, R. (2013). *Information Technology: An Introduction for Today's Digital World.* Boca Raton, FL: CRC Press.

Goertzel, B. (2008). AI and AGI: Past, Present and Future. *Future Current.* Retrieved from http://www.acceleratingfuture.com/people-blog/2008/ai-and-agi-past-present-and-future/.

International Business Machines. (N.D.). IBM 3340 Direct Access Storage Facility. Retrieved from http://www-03.ibm.com/ibm/history/exhibits/storage/storage_3340.html.

Jaspen, B. (2014, March 29). Despite Stimulus Dollars, Hundreds of Hospitals Still Use Mostly Paper Records. *Forbes.* Retrieved from http://www.forbes.com/sites/brucejapsen/2014/03/29/despite-stimulus-dollars-hundreds-of-hospitals-still-use-mostly-paper-records/.

Judge, M. (2013, November 18). Healthcare IT: A Game-Changer for Coordinated Care. Retrieved from http://www.healthcareitnews.com/blog/healthcare-it-game-changer-coordinated-care.

Kurzweil, R. (2005). *The Singularity Is Near: When Humans Transcend Biology.* New York, NY: Penguin Group.

Lilly, P. (2009, March). Computer Data Storage through the Ages—From Punch Cards to Blu-Ray." *MaximumPC.* Retrieved from http://www.maximumpc.com/article/features/computer_data_storage_through_ages_from_punch_cards_bluray

National Museum of American History. (N.D.). Overhead Projectors. *Smithsonian.* Retrieved from http://americanhistory.si.edu/mobilizing-minds/overhead-projectors.

Rainer, R. K., & Watson, H. J. (2012). *Management Information Systems, Moving Business Forward.* Hoboken, NJ: John Wiley & Sons, Inc.

Rau, J. (2012, February 13). Experts Question Medicare's Effort to Rate Hospitals' Patient Safety Records. *Kaiser Health News*. Retrieved from http://www.kaiserhealthnews.org/Stories/2012/February/13/medicare-hospital-patient-safety-records.aspx.

Roney, K. (2012, December 21). The Rise of Big Data in Hospitals: Opportunities Behind the Phenomenon. *Becker's Hospital CIO*. Retrieved from http://www.beckershospitalreview.com/healthcare-information-technology/the-rise-of-big-data-in-hospitals-opportunities-behind-the-phenomenon.html.

Rawsthorn, A. (2013, January 20). It's a Spaceship! No, It's a Time Machine. *The New York Times*. Retrieved from http://www.nytimes.com/2013/01/21/arts/design/its-a-spaceship-no-its-a-time-machine.html?_r=0.

Smith, D. (2011, April). The 5 Smartest Ways to Connect Multiple Offices. Retrieved from http://www.businessinsider.com/the-5-most-cost-efficient-ways-to-set-up-your-companys-technology-network-across-multiple-offices-2011-4.

Tech News Daily. (2012, November). "World's Fastest Supercomputer" Crowned in US. Retrieved from http://www.technewsdaily.com/15424-world-fastest-supercomputer-crowned.html.

U.S. Department of Health and Human Services. (2013, May 22). Doctors and Hospitals' Use of Health IT More than Doubles Since 2012. Retrieved from http://www.hhs.gov/news/press/2013pres/05/20130522a.html.

Zetta, Inc. (2014). The History of Computer Storage: Innovation from 1928 to Today. Retrieved from http://www.zetta.net/history-of-computer-storage/.

Chapter Three

Healthcare HR at the Crossroads

I think that it is worthwhile to engage in a more general discussion of human resources (HR) before delving into specific healthcare HR structures and processes. As a result, I start out this chapter by defining what I mean by the term "human resources (HR)." I note that, in some ways, every employee of a company—and especially the leadership—is a part of the HR process. I move on from that topic to touch on hiring-related issues and note why it is important for healthcare HR systems to keep bad hires to a minimum. I discuss why healthcare organizations, which have an inherent interest in maintaining well-functioning HR processes (such as those involved in hiring), sometimes perform below par. Finally, I end the chapter by briefly touching on some subjects related to information technology (IT), data management, and culture. In these sections, I lay the groundwork for future chapters, as I will revisit each of these topics in more depth later in the book.

3.1 Understanding HR

Before discussing HR in hospitals and other healthcare organizations, I think it would be worthwhile to define the term. Merriam-Webster provides two definitions for human resources. The first one is "a department within an organization that deals with the people who work for that organization." The second definition refers to the workers themselves (Merriam-Webster, 2014). However, people who have worked in management (and even many frontline workers), would agree that HR encompasses many more aspects than the ones listed in these two definitions.

Myron Fottler, an expert in healthcare HR management, provides a much better definition of these activities. He says that HR (he refers to it as "strategic human resources management") "refers to the comprehensive set of managerial activities and tasks related to developing and maintaining a qualified workforce" (Fottler, 2008, 2). He notes that these tasks include traditional duties, such as recruitment, training and development, appraisal, compensation, and employee relations, "as well as environmental and organizational aspects . . ." (Fottler, 2008, 2). The latter two aspects can encompass more amorphous areas, such as employee morale and corporate culture.

If we use Fottler's definition of HR, then it becomes clear that HR department heads and their staffs are not the only people who are responsible for achieving HR-related goals. Granted, HR managers and their employees play a large part in the process. Most of the organizations that I have been associated with have relied upon HR staff to perform basic employee management tasks, such as processing and distributing (and often vetting) incoming applications, managing the company's healthcare programs, and other traditional HR-related tasks. However, almost everyone in management has some sort of HR-related role to play within their respective organizations.

3.2 HR Focus—Holistic and Progressive

If that is the case, then healthcare organizations need to take a holistic view of HR. They should include all relevant employees—including frontline workers, as appropriate—when they consider changes to their HR infrastructures. After all, a healthcare company's employees are its biggest asset (and its largest expense). As an example, "in many hospitals payments for employees represent around 60% of expenditures" (Cleverley, Song, & Cleverley, 2011).

As important, healthcare organizations, especially labor-intensive ones such as hospitals, should be keen on utilizing the latest HR strategies, HR-related IT infrastructures, and HR-related IT systems. After all, it only makes sense that a hospital or other healthcare entity will gain a competitive advantage if it employs the best methods for managing its human resources—its employees (and all that entails). One researcher affirms this belief by "offering fairly strong evidence that organizations that use more progressive HR approaches achieve significantly better financial results than comparable, although less progressive, organizations do" (Fottler, 2008, 6). Unfortunately, according to available research on this subject, a large proportion of healthcare companies possess inadequate, outdated HR systems.

3.3 HR and Bad Hires

One of the most important—perhaps the most important—jobs of any HR infrastructure is to ensure that its organization hires the right people for open positions. So, it might be surprising to note how often companies (and by association their HR systems) make poor hiring decisions. According to a 2012 Career Builder survey, around 70 percent of companies in a variety of industries, both large and small, admitted to hiring someone who turned out to be a poor fit for the prospective job (Career Builder, 2012). An even larger number of healthcare organizations—79 percent—admitted to making at least one poor hiring decision in 2012 (Bouchard, 2012). It is likely that most of these organizations did not just make one hiring mistake. A survey of hiring managers by The Corporate Executive Board "estimate[s] that 20% of the new hires on their team[s] should never have been brought on" (Tuggle, 2014). One expert predicts that as "many as 70 percent of all hired candidates turn out to be costly 'mis-hires'" (Dickel, 2008).

Companies, in healthcare or in any other industry, will make bad hires from time to time, even if they possess superb HR systems. The larger the organization, the more likely it is to make poor hiring decisions from time to time; however, the available hiring data points to a more systemic problem. Healthcare organizations, and indeed companies in all fields, have issues in hiring the right people due to inadequate HR infrastructures. There are a number of research-related articles and surveys that support this thesis (Career Builder, 2012; Dickel, 2008; Hammonds, 2006).

3.4 Bad Hires and Their Impact on the Bottom Line and on Patient Care

These poor hiring decisions can have a significant, detrimental impact on a healthcare company's bottom line. A business' poor hiring decisions can negatively impact it in a number of ways. These employees can fail to perform their jobs, or they can make mistakes, which can increase expenses and decrease revenues. More worrisome, some of the bad hires could do things that harm department morale or even lead to lawsuits against the corporation. In most of the cases, the organization involved will have to spend hundreds (and more likely) thousands of dollars in training and retraining costs (Career Builder, 2012; Koch, 2006). Healthcare organizations might also have to expend significant sums of money if these employees successfully file for unemployment insurance benefits from their respective states (Anonymous, 2010, 1–2). All of these costs add up.

Forty-one percent of hiring managers interviewed by Career Builder for its survey estimated that each bad hire cost their respective company more than $25,000. "Twenty-four percent said a bad hire cost them more than $50,000" (Career Builder, 2012). Other researchers, while they might disagree about specifics, agree with the premise that a large number of corporations, including a sizeable number of companies in the healthcare field, suffer as a result of poor hires (Koch, 2006, 29–30).

I think that most of the readers of this book can attest to this fact from firsthand experience. Most of us have hired, or at least worked alongside, employees that turned out to be a poor fit for their respective jobs. In some instances, the workers did not possess the skills or abilities necessary to meet the company's production quotas. In other cases, the employees lacked the necessary work ethic. In rarer (but more problematic) cases, these hires engaged in behavior that negatively impacted the productivity of other staff in the department.

We know from experience how much harm these bad hires can do to a company's bottom line. However, healthcare organizations, such as hospitals, which provide hands-on medical care have another issue to worry about in relation to bad hires. These organizations will find it difficult to achieve their mission of providing high-quality patient care if their HR systems are not adept at hiring competent people. When one thinks about it for a moment, it is easy to see how the hiring of even one poor performer on the nursing staff or in another key, frontline position can hinder the healthcare organization's quality-improvement efforts.

Even when a healthcare organization's HR system hires a competent individual, it might not have hired the best person available. I have witnessed numerous occasions when a healthcare organization hired a person who was mediocre at best. That employee might complete his or her tasks, but he or she will not benefit the company as much as a high performer would have.

3.5 HR Infrastructures and Non–Hiring-Related Issues

If healthcare HR infrastructures have problems in performing one of their most important functions—the hiring of new employees—it is likely that they perform suboptimally in other areas as well. As I will demonstrate in subsequent chapters, many healthcare organizations' HR systems do not do as well as possible in other key areas, including the training of employees, analyzing the strengths and weaknesses of current workers, developing and promoting internal candidates, and creating robust internal communications infrastructures, to name a few.

Hospitals and other healthcare entities do not make the best use of their HR infrastructures for a number of reasons, including the following:

- **HR Lacks the Needed Resources**
  Sometimes, healthcare organizations do not devote enough resources to HR processes. For instance, some companies do not possess enough HR staff to properly handle all of their basic human resource functions, let alone to develop a more advanced HR infrastructure. In other cases, healthcare organizations might hire enough HR staff but lack the resources to purchase and maintain the necessary IT systems (including IT personnel). Sometimes these healthcare organizations run very tight budgets and simply do not have the money to devote to HR. In other cases, the corporate leaders might not see a reason to prioritize the needs of HR over those of other areas.

- **IT-Related Issues**
  Many healthcare organizations fall into a different category. They realize the value in a well-constructed HR infrastructure. The

executives of these companies work to ensure that their HR departments are adequately funded. They have also spent money to equip their HR teams with at least some advanced software and updated hardware systems. However, these firms' HR systems do not operate at full potential due to flaws in their placement and usage of IT. In other words, these companies do not make the best use of the computers and software packages that they have on hand.

- **Cultural and Methodological Impediments**
  Even if they were fully funded, some healthcare organizations would still have problems with HR-related tasks, such as hiring, employee promotion and development, and employee management. These corporations perform below expectations in these areas because of issues related to their corporate cultures or to flaws in management strategies. I will delve further into this topic at a later point in the book.

One can view healthcare HR from a number of different angles. An individual will construct a different method for categorizing key HR processes based upon his or her particular vantage point. In this book, I focus my attention on key elements within the HR system.

With that in mind, I discuss ways in which healthcare leaders can use innovative methods and IT-based strategies to improve their respective organizations' HR systems. I focus on several key areas within this domain. They include a number of HR-related strategies.

3.6 HR-Related Strategies

In subsequent sections of this book, I will touch on a number of strategies or techniques that healthcare organizations can and should put in place in order to improve their HR-related infrastructures, including any corporate systems and structures devoted to the hiring, development, and management of employees. Additionally, healthcare executives should not leave it up to their HR departments to accomplish these objectives. Instead, they should include in the process all workers who have a stake in their particular organization's HR processes. I will briefly highlight some of the key HR tactical goals in this section.

3.6.1 Use Objective Data and Processes When Possible

In my experience, HR staff, hiring managers, and others put too much faith in subjective analyses to help them make important HR-related decisions. Sometimes an HR staff member or hiring manager has to use his or her "gut feelings" to aid that person in making a key personnel decision because of the lack of objective, testable information. At other times, a healthcare manager might be justified in "going with his or her gut feeling" if he or she has honed a certain HR skill to the point at which that person can intuitively make excellent decisions. However, anyone involved in a key HR process will usually want to use scientific methods and objective data whenever possible.

Problems with Subjective Data

There are several reasons why a healthcare leader would want to avoid using subjective data and measures when possible. Most basic business statistics books list these reasons in the first couple of chapters. A list of these reasons might note the following:

- **Validity and Reliability Issues**
  Subjective data is prone to errors resulting from human bias. In other words, it is often neither valid nor reliable (Kemp & Kemp, 2004, 2–33). As an example, consider a standard one-on-one interview. I can state from experience that hiring managers will have dramatically different views about a particular candidate's dress, his or her demeanor, and whether or not the interviewee provided good answers to a particular set of questions. Rarely do these subjective views consistently yield the best outcomes, as they are prone to bias and misinterpretation (Grant, 2013). Sometimes the same hiring manager's takeaway from an interview could vary significantly as a result of things like the time of day, the number of other interviews, and so forth.

- **Problems with the Comparability of the Information**
  It is often difficult for management, HR staff, or other key personnel to compare subjective data. To gain a better feel for this issue, the reader might ponder the difficulties that an analyst would have in comparing the reader's assessment on a particular candidate with

those of other HR or management (assuming they interviewed the same candidate)? The person reading this book might correlate the wearing of a bowtie with a strong work ethic. Other individuals might view candidates who wear bowties as socially inept. There is no way (or at least no easy way) for a healthcare HR leader to posit this data into a useful framework.

One can point to the same weaknesses in any process that relies primarily on an individual's subjective or intuitive notions. That is why healthcare experts use empirical approaches, whenever possible, to try to understand and solve health-related issues. Most healthcare executives understand this basic point as well.

Other Healthcare Departments and Areas Utilize Objective Data

Most healthcare executives and managers, at some level, understand the drawbacks of using subjective data and processes. That is why they use a standardized, empirical process for collecting, analyzing, and disseminating financial information (Cleverley, Song, & Cleverley, 2011, 182–187). Healthcare leaders have also sought to bring a scientific, rational focus to many other areas of the organization, running the gamut from inventory control to waste management. Over the past decade or two (as noted in a previous chapter), they have begun to zealously champion the use of statistics and other quantitative methods to improve quality of care. These administrators have even begun to try to force physicians, who heretofore had exclusive control over patient decisions, to follow clinical practice guidelines and other forms of "evidence-based medicine" (American College of Physicians, 2014).

Given the level of attention that healthcare administrators are placing on this topic, some might be surprised to learn that some aspects of healthcare HR remain relatively untouched by the empiricism movement. As I will discuss in the following chapters, hiring managers at many hospitals and other healthcare organizations still rely on subjective measures, such as one-on-one interviews, to vet candidates. HR employees continue to place a lot of faith in cover letters, references, and other pieces of subjective data. In future chapters, I will argue that, whereas HR departments should not totally abandon the use of these documents, they need to place greater emphasis on more objective measures, such as in-house tests, which are less prone to manipulation and bias.

3.6.2 Properly Use IT Software and Hardware

In this book I champion the use of advanced software and hardware— **under the right circumstances**. I think every healthcare leader would agree that his or her company can improve the efficiency of many HR processes if its staff utilizes computer software and hardware, in lieu of more labor-intensive methods. Healthcare workers have lived in the computer age long enough that they can readily discern some of its advantages.

The problem for most healthcare administrators lies in solving three basic problems related to this issue. First, they must determine when it is appropriate to replace human labor with machines. Second, they must identify what automated systems are available and determine which ones are the best fit for their specific organization. Finally, they have to ensure that their employees make the best use of these new technologies.

During the course of this narrative, I will focus attention on all three themes. However, I will eschew some areas. With regard to the first topic, I focus only on issues related to employee hiring, development, and management. For instance, I do not touch on subjects related the automation of pharmacy, clinical, and billing-related tasks. Although I discuss IT-related issues in general, I rarely mention any specific companies or vendors, as I feel that each healthcare organization must decide which particular vendor or supplier is best suited to provide for its specific needs. Finally, my discussions will usually focus on conceptual ideas, as that is the goal of this book. I will leave it to technical manuals to delve into the minutiae of various programming languages, data analytics processes, and so forth.

Instead, I make IT suggestions that healthcare leaders can use to help them improve their HR processes. Importantly, I try to demonstrate, from a cost–benefit perspective, some of the reasons why it makes sense for healthcare executives to purchase, lease, or otherwise obtain these IT tools. At the same time, I focus my attention on general discussions of financial and quality-centered metrics.

Perhaps most importantly, I demonstrate ways in which healthcare organizations can leverage relatively basic IT-related tools, such as Microsoft Excel and Access, to help them collect, manage, and use

HR-related data. Along the same lines, I suggest ways in which healthcare organizations can integrate basic and advanced processes to help them improve the hiring, development, and management of employees. Just as important, I delineate meta-strategies that healthcare executives can use to communicate new or revised HR strategies to pertinent employees and convince these workers to adopt these adjusted goals.

3.6.3 Avoiding Overuse of IT Tools

Sometimes, healthcare administrators will purchase a technology and fail to maximize its use. As I noted in the previous section, I will devote some time to that topic in this book (even if only indirectly). However, at other times, healthcare employees—at all levels—overuse an IT tool or system.

In these scenarios, healthcare administrators use their IT tools to produce information that provides no value to themselves or to their staff. I like to use the old cliché, "like a kid in a candy factory." Managers realize that they can now access data that was heretofore inaccessible due to time constraints involved in manually assaying it. So they busy themselves producing a wide range of new charts, graphs, and tables filled with extraneous information. The data might be eye-catching, but that is the only purpose it serves.

In many cases, the IT system produces information that stymies a healthcare staff's ability to make efficient, productive decisions. For instance, a healthcare company's management team might find itself awash in information. The team members have to spend significant amounts of extra time discerning which information to use in the decision-making process. In other cases, management teams might use the wrong data (for the given task), and thereby make poor decisions.

This issue does not just impact data collecting and project management; it can affect any daily process. The creation of extraneous information streams can take its toll on interdepartmental communications systems (e.g., employees receive so many emails, they don't have time to read them all), worker productivity, hiring processes, and even employee morale (Anonymous, 2011, 59; Chakravorty, 2011, 96; Glen, 2005, 44; Ramsey, 2000, 3–5). HR personnel are especially prone to falling victim to these problems because they deal with so many different types of organizational processes.

I will cover this topic in this book at relevant times. Specifically, I will discuss how healthcare administrators can reduce both the overutilization and the underutilization of HR-related IT systems by creating clear lines of communication between themselves as pertinent employees. I will also denote general methods that healthcare management can use to create a corporate culture that supports the proper use of these technologies.

3.6.4 Clearly Communicate Strategies to Relevant Members of the Workforce

If healthcare leaders want to get the most out of their current HR infrastructures, they need to properly instruct employees with regard to the "ins and outs" of the system. At the same time, these executives and administrators must maintain optimal lines of communication with employees, when these leaders advance initiatives that are designed to improve upon one or more of their HR functions. More specifically, they must clearly delineate to employees the benefits and potential challenges involved in shifting from one system to another. At the same time, they have to provide employees with enough training so that these workers feel comfortable using the new, HR-related IT tools or techniques. I will touch on both issues at later points in the text.

3.6.5 Create the Right Corporate Culture

Earlier in this chapter, I noted that healthcare organizations will often have a hard time implementing successful HR policies unless their corporate cultures—made up of the firm's employees and other key stakeholders—support these initiatives. I think it is worth mentioning again. Even the most progressive and energetic healthcare executive will be unable to change the current HR infrastructure (or any company infrastructure, for that matter), if he or she is unwilling to convince employees to go along with the changes. In recognition of this fact, I will, at relevant points in this book, discuss some of the key workplace and workflow changes that need to go hand in hand with any structural HR adjustments.

In this book, I demonstrate why it is important for healthcare organizations to create corporate cultures that are geared to maintaining high employee-satisfaction rates. Specifically, I will denote correlations between employee contentedness and motivation, productivity, and retention rates. I will also, at various times in the book, suggest methods that employers can use to ease their subordinates' fears with regard to workplace changes, while at the same time encouraging them to adopt new HR-related IT systems and methodologies.

3.6.6 Some Other Suggested Strategies

Over the course of this book, I will also review some other important initiatives, goals, or strategies that healthcare leaders can use to help them improve or maintain HR-related processes. Here are two of the more important ones:

- **Focus on Candidate/Worker Integrity**
  HR departments have to deal with a range of employee-related cheating issues. These problems run the gamut from job applicants lying about their past work experience to employees who find ways to circumvent training-related exercises. Ethical implications aside, healthcare companies can sometimes pay a steep price when potential hires or current workers engage in these behaviors. Even the best HR system is not going to eliminate all of these occurrences—nor should it. However, I would argue that a good HR system can take steps to reduce instances of cheating on hiring documents, training exercises, and in other key areas. I will elaborate on this topic in more detail at relevant points throughout the book.

- **Innovate and Adapt**
  As one would expect from the previous chapters, I am a fan of using innovative methods or IT systems, when appropriate, to help improve HR infrastructures. Throughout the book, I will highlight and explain some of these techniques. At the same time, I will stress the need for healthcare corporations (and indeed all companies) to create and maintain flexible, adaptive HR systems. The well-running HR infrastructure of today could become antiquated in a short time period, given the rapid pace of change in today's society. Healthcare leaders have to be attuned to these changes and adjust their HR strategies accordingly.

3.7 HR Tasks

In this book, I focus most of my attention on HR issues centering on external hiring, internal development and promotion of talent, and employee management. I am especially keen on trying to identify useful strategies and IT tools that my readers can use to improve the hiring, development, and management of potential and current employees at their respective healthcare organizations. I do not devote too much time to delineating other types of HR functions. For example, at no point in this book do I discuss HR's role in labor-management relations, even though HR staff often play prominent roles in these relationships. I also do not delve deeply into any specific type of HR process unless it furthers my meta-hypotheses. Hence, I will eschew a number of HR functions that might be relevant to hiring, development, and management, but which do not relate to the themes in this book. Readers interested in those topics can find numerous HR textbooks, which do a great job of defining and discussing each of these functions in detail.

3.7.1 Hiring

To borrow an old cliché, "a company is only as good as its employees." Hospitals and most other healthcare corporations are labor-intensive entities. Any healthcare company (and, in fact, almost all companies in any industry) needs to possess a workforce that is, at the very least, motivated, capable, and honorable (to a degree anyway). Corporations that, through a series of bad hires, fail to achieve this goal will soon find themselves in bankruptcy court. As I noted earlier in the chapter, a healthcare organization can realize a significant negative impact from even a few bad hires.

Given that information, the most important thing that a good HR system can do is to ensure that its healthcare organization hires the very best candidates for all of its available positions. However, as I noted earlier in this chapter, most healthcare companies (and by extension their HR infrastructures) achieve less than stellar results, when it comes to hiring talent.

Over the course of the next few chapters, I will delve into this issue in more detail. As a first step, I will identify the ways in which healthcare organizations, via their HR networks, try to recruit new hires to fill open positions. I will focus most of my attention on the process of direct hiring (e.g., hiring practices that do not rely on employee referrals or an outside staffing firm). I will describe some of the current practices that HR staff and hiring managers utilize to pick new hires. At the same time, I will look at some of the IT infrastructures that these individuals use to help them in the direct hiring process.

As it stands, the current direct hiring systems at most healthcare organizations do not employ some of the most effective methods for hiring candidates. Just as important, they do not use the latest technologies to help them reduce labor costs and improve the chances of landing the best hires. I will review the weaknesses in these systems, starting with the front-end processes, including things like the collection of candidate data and the sorting of candidate profiles. I will then move on to the second-level vetting processes, such as candidate testing and job interviews.

I do not think that it serves much use to identify the weaknesses in the current direct hiring systems without demonstrating that the costs of maintaining the status quo in this area outweigh the benefits of making substantive (and potentially costly) changes. A healthcare leader would be unwise to change a system—even a flawed one—unless he or she is pretty sure that the new and improved infrastructure would better enable the company to achieve its corporate goals.

With that fact in mind, I will help readers ascertain the costs of maintaining their respective organization's current direct hiring infrastructure. I began that conversation earlier in this chapter when I highlighted the Career Builder survey. I will further develop this thesis to cover other issues related to suboptimal hires.

Finally, I will highlight some of the benefits that might accrue to healthcare organizations that adopt some of the proposed changes to their direct hiring schemes. On an obvious level, companies might realize cost savings, which are related to hiring better candidates. Healthcare executives and managers might also notice more indirect or intangible benefits when they implement some of the suggested changes. For instance, healthcare corporations that hire better candidates might benefit from higher patient-satisfaction scores and improvements in employee morale.

3.7.2 Developing and Promoting Internal Talent

Many healthcare organizations rely on internal transfer and promotion methods that place too much emphasis on subjective selection methods.

These systems also suffer from the fact that they lack a unified, structured process for matching internal talent with the appropriate vacancies. Healthcare organizations that utilize these outdated systems will find it difficult to match employees to their best-fit jobs. These companies will have to deal with a number of issues that stem from this lack of synergy, including extra financial costs, reduced productivity, and employee morale problems. In the greater scheme of things, outdated development and promotion systems can negatively impact a healthcare organization's bottom line, its patient-care standards, and its patient-satisfaction scores.

Following the outline set by the section on direct hiring, I will describe some of the key weaknesses in current internal development and promotion systems. I will then demonstrate how these issues can negatively impact a healthcare organization's mission, vision, and values. Afterwards, I will posit new techniques and IT-based strategies that can help companies avoid employee synchronization issues. Finally, I will show how these suggested improvements can help healthcare organizations increase both the overall efficiency and effectiveness of their operations.

3.8 Looking Ahead

I hope that readers will be able to refer to the remaining chapters as an HR roadmap that they can use to aid them in identifying weaknesses in their hiring, internal development and promotion, and employee-management processes. Like any good roadmap, I have delineated some of the meta-issues and provided general suggestions. Individuals can use this information to aid them in creating improvement initiatives that are geared toward their healthcare organizations' unique, specific needs.

References

American College of Physicians. (2014). ACP Clinical Practice Guidelines. Retrieved from http://www.acponline.org/clinical_information/guidelines/guidelines/.

Anonymous. (2010). HR plays major role in curbing company costs, analysts say. *HR Focus*, 87(9), 1–4. Retrieved from http://search.proquest.com/docview/750368295?accountid=142826.

Anonymous. (2011, July 2). Business: Too Much Information. *The Economist.* Retrieved from http://www.economist.com/node/18895468.

Bouchard, S. (2012, December 20). Survey Finds Eight in 10 Healthcare Businesses Impacted by Bad Hires. *Healthcare Finance* Retrieved from http://www.healthcarefinancenews.com/news/survey-finds-eight-10-healthcare-businesses-impacted-bad-hires.

Career Builder. (2012, December 13). Nearly Seven in Ten Businesses Affected by a Bad Hire in the Past Year. Retrieved from http://www.careerbuilder.com/share/aboutus/pressreleasesdetail.aspx?sd=12%2f13%2f2012&iiiiid=pr730&ed=12%2f31%2f2012.

Chakravorty, S. C. (2011). The Trouble With Too Much Information. *MIT Sloan Management Review* 53(1), 96. Retrieved from ProQuest (Doc. I.D.: 896570327).

Cleverley, W. O., Song, P. H., & Cleverley, J. O. (2011). *Essentials of Health Care Finance* (7th ed.). Sudbury, MA: Jones & Bartlett Learning.

Dickel, T. (2008). Interviewing techniques and pitfalls from the HR perspective. *China Staff* 14(10), 2–6. Retrieved from http://search.proquest.com/docview/191632218?accountid=142826

Fottler, M. D. (2008). Strategic Human Resources Management in *Human Resources in Healthcare: Managing for Success* (3rd ed.). B. J. Fried & M. D. Fottler (Eds.). Chicago: Health Administration Press.

Glen, P. (2005, September 5). Too Much Information. *Computerworld* 39(36), 44. Retrieved from ProQuest (Doc. I.D.: 216091584).

Grant, A. (2013, June 10). What's Wrong with Job Interviews, and How to Fix Them. LinkedIn Pulse. Retrieved from https://www.linkedin.com/pulse/article/20130610025112-69244073-will-smart-companies-interview-your-kids.

Hammonds, K. H. (2006). Why We Hate HR. *Leadership Excellence* 23(2), 20. Retrieved from http://search.proquest.com/docview/204617740?accountid=142826.

Kemp, S. M., & Kemp, S. (2004). *Business Statistics Demystified: A Self-Teaching Guide.* New York: McGraw-Hill.

Koch, W. D. (2006). Better Hires, Less Waste: A Potential Profit Bonanza. *Financial Executive* 22(4), 29–30, 32. Retrieved from http://search.proquest.com/docview/208901262?accountid=142826.

Merriam-Webster. (2014). Human Resources. Retrieved from http://www.merriam-webster.com/dictionary/human%20resources.

Ramsey, R. D. (2000). How Much Technology is Too Much: Strategies for Humanizing a High-Tech Workplace. *SuperVision* 61(1), 3–5. Retrieved from ProQuest (Doc. I.D.: 195590924).

Tuggle, K. (2014, January 17). The Real Cost of a Bad Hire. *The Street.* Retrieved from http://www.thestreet.com/story/12243638/1/the-real-cost-of-a-bad-hire.html.

Chapter Four

A Review of Six Employment Methods

Before I start to discuss what I perceive to be some of the weaknesses in contemporary healthcare human resources (HR) hiring methods, I think it is worthwhile to delineate some of the most popular hiring strategies. Many readers will probably already be familiar with most of the information in the next few pages. However, I feel that it is always a good idea to start with first principles (in this case, a quick delineation of the various methods) before delving into a deeper discussion of these issues.

Healthcare companies, regardless of size, structure, or type, will usually choose from among six different external methods to fill available positions. These include:

- Contracting with employment agencies or staffing firms to identify qualified workers or to deal with short-term needs
- Outsourcing specific tasks, departments, or service lines to third party firms
- Using interns to complete basic or specialized job tasks
- Utilizing a referral method to fill open positions
- Attending job fairs or actively hiring at colleges and universities
- Directly managing the hiring process for external hires

Additionally, healthcare employers can utilize a mix of these techniques during the hiring process. I will touch on some of the potential costs and benefits of using each one of these methods in the following sections (see Figure 4.1 for a brief synopsis).

The Pros and Cons of Five Hiring Methods (Does Not Include Direct Hires)		
Type of Hiring Method	Pros	Cons
Using Employment Agencies or Staffing Firms	* Allows the corporation to utilize additional tools and resources * Provides the company with access to needed personnel * Offers the organization the opportunity to supplement HR functions * Enables the firm to fill temporary and/or permanent positions * Allows the corporation to distribute some of the risks involved in hiring and managing employees	* Temps/Fills might struggle to understand the host company's culture * Temps/Fills may have issues adjusting to the host corporation's protocols (including customs, rules, and regulations) * Problems that derive from the employee-agency-company matrix relationships * The company gives up some control to the staffing or employment agency * The temps/fills might not satisfactorily perform their duties * Liability issues relating to the fact that the temps/fills represent the host company
Outsourcing Work	* Allows the corporation to utilize additional tools and resources * Provides the company with access to needed personnel * Offers the organization the opportunity to supplement HR functions * Enables the firm to fill permanent positions * Allows the corporation to distribute some of the risks involved in hiring and managing employees * Enables the company to focus on what it does best	* The outsourcing agency/workers might struggle to understand and relate to the employer's culture * The outsourcing agency/workers might have difficulty obeying or understanding the host company's protocols (including customs, rules, and regulations) * Problems that derive from the employee-agency-company matrix relationships * The company gives up some control to the staffing agency or outsourcing vendor * The outsourcing firm's employees might not satisfactorily fulfill their duties * Potential liability issues when the outsourced workers represent the host company

(Continued on following page)

The Pros and Cons of Five Hiring Methods (Does Not Include Direct Hires) (Cont'd)		
Type of Hiring Method	Pros	Cons
Utilizing Interns	* The host company procures a source of relatively cheap labor * The host corporation garners some additional labor resources, thereby providing it with increased flexibility *The hosting firm can leverage the internship to help it develop key relationships with universities and other institutions	* Potential liability issues due to the fact that the interns represent the host company * Interns might struggle to succeed because they do not understand the host corporation's culture * Management suffers lost-opportunity costs related to mentoring and training the interns The interns might not perform as expected, or they might engage in improper behaviors, which negatively impact the host company's bottom line
Tapping into Referrals (Direct and Indirect)	* Provides companies with another method for identifying and hiring capable employees (direct and indirect referrals) * Referrals might work harder and perform better than other types of hires (direct and indirect referrals) * Managers can trust referred employees with sensitive information right away (direct referrals) * Companies might not have to spend as much money or time in training referrals vis-à-vis other types of hires (direct and indirect referrals)	* Managers might have more difficulty in firing a bad hire (direct referrals) * Other employees might distrust or dislike the referred employee (direct referrals) * HR might not properly vet these employees (direct and indirect referrals)
Participating in Job Fairs	* Provides companies with another method for identifying and hiring capable employees * Corporations can use these events to help them identify potential hires for positions opening up in the future	* The quality and quantity of potential candidates will vary * Expenses related to attending these fairs and following up with candidates

Figure 4.1   This chart provides the reader with an overview of five of the six hiring methods discussed in this chapter, along with their pros and cons. I do not include the direct hiring method in the chart because I discuss it in detail in the next chapter.

4.1 Staffing Firms

Healthcare companies can outsource many or all of the responsibilities for vetting new candidates to staffing firms. For a fee, staffing firms can perform tasks, which run the gamut from conducting the initial search for qualified individuals—a headhunting process—to providing temporary employees (who receive their pay from the staffing firms). Many healthcare companies utilize staffing agencies to help supplement their internal HR hiring capabilities. For instance, a 2005 Community Tracking Study survey notes that 75 percent of the institutions in its assay utilized temporary nursing staff, including "both per diem nurses and traveling nurses" (May, Bazzoli, & Gerland, 2006, 318). Although the article does not indicate what percentage of these hospitals utilized staffing firms (as opposed to, say, using an Internet job board), the number is probably quite high (May, Bazzoli, & Gerland, 2006, 317–318).

4.2 Outsourcing

Sometimes, a healthcare organization can outsource its whole department to a firm that specializes in this type of work. In these instances, the healthcare company can be said to be hiring (or contracting with) a vendor to perform some of its basic or ancillary tasks. For instance, a smaller healthcare company might find it more cost effective to outsource its payroll processing unit rather than perform those functions in-house. Larger organizations, including hospitals, might contract with another firm to run their support services, such as their in-house cafeterias or laundry and housekeeping duties. A growing number of healthcare companies, perhaps to their eventual chagrin, are outsourcing information technology (IT) as well (Punke, 2013). In some cases, healthcare organizations have even delegated management responsibilities to outside agencies.

4.2.1 Pros and Cons of Using Staffing Services or Outsourcing Work

I do not focus on this type of hiring/outsourcing in this book. However, I think it is worthwhile for me to spend a brief amount of time discussing it. I believe that healthcare organizations can sometimes benefit when they utilize outside firms to make hiring decisions or to supply some of their labor needs. There are several potential advantages to this approach, including:

- **Access to Added HR Resources**
  By working with staffing agencies, healthcare organizations, especially smaller ones, can access resources that would otherwise be unavailable to them due to cost constraints or for other reasons. For instance, healthcare companies, via their relationships with staffing firms, might gain access to additional labor sources, training tools, or employee selection systems (e.g., specialized employee placement tests).

- **Procure Skilled Employment Specialists**
  At many healthcare organizations, especially at small companies, HR staff might wear many hats. They might do everything from managing benefits to vetting résumés. As a result of their diverse work responsibilities, these individuals might not be able to devote the time that is necessary to identify the best candidates for open positions. Even when healthcare HR departments are large enough to employee people who can specialize in external hiring, these individuals often still have to perform a range of tasks or are responsible for a number of disparate departments.

  By contrast, staffing agencies and hiring firms specialize in the business of identifying talent and/or meeting their clients' specific labor needs. The people working for these companies, on the whole, have to be good at what they do, or their firms would not stay in business for long. As such, healthcare companies can use these firms to help them shore up weaknesses or deficiencies in their external hiring systems. One other benefit: By utilizing a staffing agency to procure talent, a healthcare corporation can take this burden off of the department leaders, who might be proficient managers but poor judges of talent.

- **Filling Temporary Needs**
  As I noted earlier in the chapter, healthcare organizations can use staffing agencies to help them fill temporary needs. They can use outsourcing firms to provide services that are outside of the healthcare organizations' areas of expertise. For instance, it makes sense for many hospitals to outsource their cafeteria services. After

all, these institutions are in the business of providing health services to their communities; their employees are often poorly equipped to deal with issues related to food preparation and distribution.

- **Leveraging Risk**
  A healthcare company will sometimes find it useful to contract with staffing companies to reduce the risks that pertain to poor hiring decisions. The organization can essentially borrow workers from staffing agencies. If the employees turn out to be good fits for their respective jobs, the company can keep them on permanently (once the contract with the staffing firm has expired—or via paying a set fee to the employment agency). If not, the healthcare organization can release these individuals and put in a call to the employment firm to send over new temps. The employment agency shoulders much of the costs of vetting these candidates.

  Healthcare firms can transfer even more of the potential risks to an outside staffing firm when they outsource tasks. In many cases, the staffing agency will assume the responsibility for making sure the department meets certain, prearranged goals and for maintaining adequate numbers of personnel. The outsourcing company will likely also shoulder some of the liability risk in case something goes wrong.

The list above is not exhaustive; however, I think the catalogue demonstrates one important point. Namely, it sometimes makes sense for healthcare companies to enlist the aid of a headhunting firm, an employment agency, an outside management company, or some other external staffing entity. However, healthcare administrators should realize that the decision to rely on one of these firms does come with potential downsides. They include:

- **Difficulties in Understanding the Corporate Culture**
  In my experience, it is difficult for HR staff and management at a healthcare organization to determine if potential hires fit in with the corporate culture. It is that much more difficult for an external agency to make that determination. It might be easier in cases where the healthcare organization has outsourced a particular service line; however, there might still be issues if the management firm or staffing provider does not understand its client's mission, vision, values, and traditions.

- **Problems Adjusting to Corporate Protocols**
  Every healthcare company does things a little differently. Employees of two very similar organizations (e.g., two Level 1 trauma centers with approximately the same number of beds and an identical case mix) will often have disparate rules, regulations, and best practices. Even a person who is well-trained in his or her particular field might have difficulty adjusting to a commensurate job with another employer. This might not be a problem in temp-to-hire situations. However, it can pose major challenges for healthcare organizations that need specialized staff for short periods of time (Bae, Mark, & Fried, 2010, 334–336).

- **Problematic Matrix Relationships**
  Whether they are short-term fill-ins, long-term replacements, or temp-to-hire personnel, staffing agency placements often serve two masters. On the one hand, they work for the healthcare organizations that contracted with the employment agency to obtain their services. However, at the same time, they are also beholden to an employment service (their level of reliance on the staffing agency in question depends on contractual obligations between all parties). This matrix type of format can sometimes benefit the healthcare organization, when it helps to reinforce worker accountability. However, the complex relationship can also pose problems for the healthcare provider—running the gamut from increased employee dissatisfaction to confusion over which company does what. The same thing can happen when healthcare organizations outsource tasks.

- **Loss of Control**
  Of course, when a healthcare organization contracts with an outside firm to handle some of its external hiring duties or personnel management functions, it gives up some control. The healthcare company is dependent upon the contractor to deliver quality services—if it is an outsourcing firm—or to perform an admirable job in identifying candidates that match its client's (the healthcare organization's) needs. Oftentimes, the headhunter, the employment agency, or the staffing firm does an excellent job. However, as with any contractual agreement between two parties, sometimes things do not work out as planned.

In my experience, I have noticed that healthcare organizations (and, for that matter, probably all companies) can usually come out ahead when they work with employment agencies to fill many basic, entry-level positions. Workers in these jobs often do not require a lot of training. In many cases, these individuals do not have to worry as much about the corporate culture, especially if they are performing basic or repetitive routines. As a result, these individuals will usually be able to accomplish their assigned tasks (at least in the short term) as long as they are competent and possess at least a minimal work ethic. For example, healthcare organizations that still use paper files could probably utilize temps to do the filing, without worrying too much about the end results (assuming the temps meet the aforementioned, basic criteria). However, as previously noted, corporations that use temps to fill more specialized jobs, such as nursing, might run into problems (Bae, Mark, & Fried, 2010, 334–336). A healthcare administrator should carefully weigh the potential costs and benefits of using an employment agency to fill open positions.

4.3 Interns

Usually, when someone refers to interns, he or she is discussing college students (undergraduate, graduate, or professional) who contract with a company to perform certain tasks for it for a limited amount of time, ranging from a few weeks to several months or longer. Interns often receive college credit for their work. In some cases, companies will remunerate interns for their work; however, many interns do not receive any payment for their services.

Theoretically, all internships, regardless of their type, center on a distinct quid pro quo relationship. Specifically, interns agree to perform certain tasks and/or to work a certain number of hours per week for their host companies. In return, these organizations are supposed to provide the interns with valuable, field-specific training. For instance, a student who is in a graduate healthcare administration program might choose to intern in a hospital's accounts receivable department. He or she would work closely with both frontline staff and managers to get real-world experience in areas including coding, insurance remittance and appeals, and patient collection processes. Oftentimes, both the intern and corporate administrators will have to fill out paperwork demonstrating the completion of certain program-related tasks. The intern might also have to write a paper, create a poster, or complete some other class-related project that summarizes his or her experiences during the internship.

Many internships work exactly as described in the aforementioned paragraph. Both parties in the relationship—the intern and the company—are happy with the results. However, as with any other types of employee–business interactions, there is always the potential for one side or the other to exploit the relationship. For instance, a business can, among other things, force its interns to work more than the stated hours or to perform mundane tasks that do not further their education. For their part, interns might fail to complete all of the requisite tasks (to receive college credit) but succeed in getting their supervisors to sign completion papers anyway.

It is likely that some administrators and students—in both healthcare and in non–health-related internships—violate key parts of their internship agreements. One can probably find a great deal of literature on this subject if he or she has the time to delve into the matter. Suffice it to say that it happens; however, I will assume, for the purposes of this book, that the healthcare companies and the students both comply with the written (and unwritten) rules that govern most internships.

Assuming that everyone follows the rules, healthcare organizations can benefit in a number of ways from internships. For one thing, the organizations can use the interns to help them fill short-term positions without having to pay market wages. Healthcare administrators can also utilize interns to help overworked staff complete vital projects on time. For instance, a manager might choose to allow interns to work on assignments that provide his or her department useful, but not vital, information (e.g., secondary tasks).

In many cases, healthcare organizations use internships to help them vet candidates for salaried or hourly positions. In this type of instance, a manager will bring in an intern with the express intent of hiring that individual if he or she proves to be a solid, capable worker. Viewed from this perspective, internships provide some advantages over direct hiring processes. Some these benefits include:

- **Flexibility**
  A healthcare administrator can move his or her interns around the department and test these individuals' skills by having them perform a variety of tasks. The manager can also vary the risk–reward aspects of these internships. Additionally, a healthcare manager can loan the

interns out to other departments as needed (or as part of the initial intern–company contract). By contrast, healthcare leaders often have less flexibility in dealing with full-time or part-time employees, who are usually hired to perform specific tasks.

- **Lower Labor Costs**
  As I noted earlier, interns usually make much less than comparable wage-earning employees. Many interns do not earn any salary at all.

- **Motivated Workers**
  In many cases, interns might be more motivated than other employees to work hard. This is especially true if the interns believe that they might secure full-time positions with their respective companies at some later date.

- **Create and Maintain Important Candidate Networks**
  Job seekers are not the only ones who can benefit from networking. Healthcare companies can use internships to help them forge valuable relationships with local colleges and technical schools. Healthcare leaders can leverage these relationships to help them identify and hire capable, energetic employees who attend these institutions.

As with anything else, healthcare organizations shoulder some risk when they use interns. The possible downsides will vary by company and position, but can include:

- **Liability Issues**
  When a healthcare organization accepts an intern, it also accepts responsibility for the actions that said intern takes while he or she works for the company. Interns are no different from regular employees in this regard; they can make mistakes or commit crimes that put the company at risk of a lawsuit.

- **Issues Adjusting to Corporate Culture**
  An intern might have difficulty adjusting to a particular company's culture. Similarly, he or she might have problems in complying with the organization's rules and regulations. In these cases, the firm might incur more costs than benefits by onboarding the intern. Depending on the situation, the company might not have any choice but to keep the individual in its employ until the internship period has ended.

- **Management's Lost-Opportunity Costs**
  Many internships require (or at least expect) the mentor—usually a manager or other higher-level administrator—to spend some time training, advising, or otherwise assisting the intern. The time that this individual devotes to the intern represents a lost-opportunity cost. Depending on the mentor's position within the company, these costs can be quite high.

- **Other Issues**
  A healthcare company might experience issues with interns that are similar to its problems with other employee types. For instance, managers might have to deal with interns who are tardy or who have poor work ethics. At the same time, they may have difficulty training some interns or in getting them to perform certain tasks. Compounding the problems—and the resultant costs—administrators might not be able to release these interns (depending on the internship agreement), unless the offenses are egregious.

In short, healthcare organizations should consider entering into agreements with local colleges and universities to bring in a certain number of interns each year. Healthcare companies can reap a number of benefits from these relationships, including the ability to perform additional tasks (over and beyond what they could accomplish with only regular employees) and the establishment of potential new recruitment pipelines. At the same time, healthcare leaders should carefully weigh these and other advantages against the possible risks.

4.4 Referrals

Most healthcare organizations use referrals to help them find capable workers to fill open positions. In my experience, one can break down referrals into two categories. The first type, which I will call a direct referral, involves a higher-level employee, such as a manager, an executive, or an owner, who has the ability to directly influence hiring decisions. This leader uses his or her power to bring in trusted family, friends, or acquaintances. With regard to the other type of instance, which I will call an indirect referral, an employee will recommend a family member, friend, or acquaintance to HR or to a hiring manager. The worker can utilize either a formal or an informal process to remit this type of referral. Either way, the employee, who makes the suggestion, has only a limited say in the final decision.

4.4.1 Direct Referrals

In many cases, especially with smaller companies, healthcare executives or managers will hire close friends, family members, or close acquaintances to work under them. In other instances, they will use their leverage to convince another department head to hire a friend or family member. This type of referral hiring (which many people would call nepotism) can be beneficial to the companies in question. This is because, in most instances, the healthcare administrators are intimately acquainted with the people they are championing. They are cognizant of their new employees' strengths and weaknesses, which allows these leaders, and/or the company in general, to more efficiently direct training resources.

As important to the success of the particular company, the new hires will sometimes work harder than others. After all, they do not want to let close friends or family members down. In addition, healthcare leaders can often place these nepotistic hires in positions of trust, without fear that these people will disobey orders, steal from the company, or commit any other major infringements.

In the right circumstances, it might make sense for healthcare leaders to onboard their friends, family, and close acquaintances. However, when these hiring decisions do not work out, they can cause much greater harm to a company than most other onboarding methods. For one thing, the healthcare administrator will usually find it more difficult than normal to fire a nepotistic hire who turns out to be a bad fit for the job. Too often, the executive or manager will not only refrain from removing the employee, he or she will forego reprimanding the worker. The employee will thus continue to make the same bad choices day in and day out. In these situations, the negative ramifications for a healthcare company can be quite severe. The organizations might have to deal with lost-opportunity costs, employee morale issues, poor productivity, and even lawsuits.

In some cases, the new hire might be a competent worker, but he or she finds it impossible to get along with the family member or friend turned boss. For whatever reason, many relationships, which work well outside of an office, fall apart when moved to a corporate arena. These inter-relational fights can turn nasty and can drag down the morale of everyone in the department.

Even when these nepotistic hires admirably perform their assigned tasks, their very presence might cause problems in the workplace. Staff will tend to assume that the employee in question is receiving preferential treatment from the boss. They will adhere to this belief, even when the exact opposite is true. A healthcare administrator who hires a friend or family member for a position in the company should be aware of this potential risk and should seek to stamp it out immediately. The executive or manager can achieve this result by making it clear to the staff—on day one—that he or she will not treat the new hire any different from the other people under the person's command.

In short, it sometimes makes sense for healthcare administrators to hire friends, family members, or close acquaintances for open positions. These new hires will sometimes work harder than their peers. At the same time, managers can often—within a few days of onboarding—entrust these people with sensitive company information or with important tasks. At the same time, healthcare administrators should be aware that, when these hires do not work out, the results can sometimes be disastrous. For precisely this reason, many healthcare corporations do not allow family members or spouses to work in the same department (or sometimes even in the same company). A manager or executive should carefully weigh the potential costs and benefits before bringing a family member, friend, or close acquaintance on board (or when recommending that another department manager make the hire).

4.4.2 Indirect Referrals

Although many healthcare companies might shun direct referrals (as that term is defined in this book), almost all of them encourage indirect referrals by employees. For the purposes of this book, the term refers to situations in which a worker, at any level in the company, recommends that HR hire a friend or acquaintance. These types of referrals can either be informal or formal.

In some cases, especially in smaller healthcare organizations, this process is informal. Employees might alert HR staff and department managers to potential hires via general email, during a "water cooler conversation," or even after work (at a party, restaurant, or some other locale). In these instances, the employee does not fill out any forms, and often he or she does not expect any remuneration if the company hires the suggested individual.

At the same time, many healthcare companies have formal referral processes in place. In these systems, an employee fills out paperwork, either online or by hand, which connects him or her with the potential hire. HR will keep the information on file and remunerate this individual if the healthcare organization ends up hiring the referred candidate. This process is different for each organization. However, in my experience, two things hold true:

- HR staff and hiring managers often exhibit a preference for these candidates, and they tend to place these applications at the top of the pile. Additionally, companies will sometimes interview these individuals even when their credentials are not as strong (on paper anyway) as those of other, denied candidates. Companies are also more likely to hire referred candidates (Schwartz, 2013).
- The company in question usually pays the referral bonus in installments. The employee will receive a portion of the money upfront. He or she will receive the remainder in stages, which is predicated on whether the referred employee remains with the company for certain prescribed periods of time. A worker will usually receive his or her entire bonus if the recommended employee stays with the organization for six months to a year.

Just like with any other type of hire, referrals come with their share of risks. For instance, the person who referred the candidate might be biased towards his or her recommendation, thereby causing him or her to overestimate the referral's qualifications for the opening. On the other hand, the referring employee might be fully cognizant of the candidate's weaknesses, yet choose to recommend the person anyway, out of a sense of friendship or for some other, personal reason. In either case, it then falls on the company's placement personnel to identify the potential hire's weaknesses during the vetting process. This situation might spell trouble for the company, as its HR personnel and hiring managers might not catch these problems—especially if they put a lot of trust in the employee who posited the referral.

With that being said, healthcare employers can utilize referral programs to help them identify good candidates who would not otherwise apply to their organizations. Companies can also sometimes use these referral systems to help them establish a presence in heretofore unknown informal networking systems (Schwartz, 2013). In these cases, healthcare organizations can benefit from a snowballing process in which one referred candidate brings in another prospect. As a result of this phenomenon, they can, on occasion, procure several good employees from a single, initial referral.

As already noted, healthcare companies do not always hit gold with individual referrals. However, in my experience, these organizations will have success with referred candidates over the long run. The available data supports my anecdotal experiences. Research has shown that referred candidates, on the whole, perform better than job board hires with regards to training time, retention (e.g., how long the employees remain at their jobs), and performance (Schwartz, 2013; Sullivan, 2012). As a testament to the quality of this job-hiring method, "HR executives [in one survey] rated referrals [as] the #1 source of quality candidates, ranking an 8.6 out of 10" (Hollon, 2012).

Over the past few years, many companies have been increasing their use of formal referrals. However, given the potential benefits that come with hiring candidates via this method, it might come as a surprise to many readers to learn that referrals account for only "28%–39% of all hires" (Sullivan, 2012). One can posit any number of reasons for the lack of interest in this method. From anecdotal experience (as I have worked for a number of companies both in healthcare and in non–health services related fields), I can point to three key reasons, including the following:

- In many instances, HR staff and department managers do not provide their workers with enough information about (or sometimes any data on) their respective companies' referral systems, thereby leaving workers to search for the relevant materials on their own. In these instances, a large number of current employees who might know of some good candidates for job openings will refrain from mentioning these people to management because the latter group has not properly communicated information about its referral system—replete with a discussion of the relevant financial incentives—to them.
- Managers and HR staff make the referral process too complicated (e.g., too much paperwork), which discourages employees from referring potential candidates.

- Companies do not provide enough of a financial incentive to spur their employees to submit possible referrals to HR.

Following this logic, I believe that companies will not be able to maximize their referral streams unless they routinely remind employees that they have referral systems in place, ensure that the process (at least in its initial stages) is relatively easy to understand and to complete, and properly incentivize workers with regards to this issue.

In ranking these three things, I would say that it is most important for healthcare HR staff and department managers to remind employees about any existing referral programs on a routine basis. Most healthcare workers, regardless of their positions within their respective companies, have a lot on their plates. They will likely forget about their particular organization's referral program unless management reminds them of it from time to time. Of course, some employees will continuously look for chances to refer friends and acquaintances. These individuals will, on their own impetus, review their organization's guidelines for referring potential hires. However, many—perhaps most—employees are not this proactive; that is why healthcare organizations need to remind them of the existence of these referral systems.

Some might assume that every employee would try to refer friends, family, or acquaintances (especially unemployed friends and acquaintances) if he or she believes that these people are well qualified for an open position at his or her company. Additionally, one might think that current workers—in an effort to maximize their income—would actively seek to learn what they could about their respective company's referral program. However, in my experience, I have not found this scenario to be true. Quite to the contrary, large numbers of people, for a variety of reasons, will not take the initiative to refer well-qualified candidates to their HR departments, unless management gently prods them to do so.

The takeaway from this discussion is straightforward. To put it simply, healthcare leaders who want to increase the number of referrals they receive need to remind employees about their organization's recommendation process. They also need to ensure that the workers can easily understand the system and access the forms.

At the same time, healthcare companies (and, indeed, all corporations) need to properly incentivize employees to refer their friends, their family members, and their acquaintances. In order to achieve this result, any referral bonus has to be commensurate with the particular employee's salary and position. A person who makes $9.00 an hour might be overjoyed at receiving a $500 bonus for providing his or her company with a successful referral. Someone who snags $50.00 an hour, on the other hand, will likely not be motivated by the bonus.

In my experience, healthcare organizations fall short when it comes to matching the incentives to their employees' positions or pay. Many of these companies adhere to "one size fits all" referral bonus structures, or they do not accurately adjust for pay differences when calculating recommendation bonuses. Additionally, it might be common practice for healthcare companies to stagger the referral bonus payments over several months to a year, in order to encourage employees to refer potential hires who are willing and able to stay on for the long term. However, I would suggest that these companies push the payout range even further— perhaps to two years. This action will further encourage employees to refer people who will commit to the company for the long haul. This tactic will prove especially useful if the employee and the referral agree, on their own recognizance, to split any bonuses.

Cash strapped healthcare organizations can include non-monetary awards as part of their referral remuneration packages. For instance, these corporations could offer their employees additional time off, or (if parking is valuable) provide them with choice parking spots. In another example, a healthcare company might provide a raffle ticket to each employee who submits a valid referral within a set period of time. At the end of the time frame, the corporation could raffle off one or two choice prize packages.

An article in *HR World* addresses many of these issues. It showcases 15 businesses (none of them in healthcare) "that deliver fat bonus checks for employee referrals" (Anonymous, 2008). These corporations have a couple things in common. First, most of them are very successful, big name firms. Second, they utilize many of the aforementioned remuneration strategies (Anonymous, 2008).

4.5 Job Fairs

Healthcare companies that are on the lookout for new hires can set up booths at local job fairs. They can also connect with local colleges and universities to arrange on-campus visits (or to attend collegiate job fairs).

At a job fair "[r]ecruiters or hiring managers from each company tend booths throughout the day. Job seekers with resumes in hand can submit on-the-spot applications and for streamlined hiring processes, some job seekers may receive same-day interviews" (Mayhew, N.D.).

I will not go into too much detail about job fairs, as readers who are interested in the subject can find numerous books and articles that deal with almost every aspect of this subject. Suffice it to say that healthcare companies can utilize job fairs or campus visits as one strategy for filling current positions and in procuring potential candidates for future job openings. Healthcare corporations will have varying degrees of success utilizing this strategy, depending on the popularity of the fairs, the type of candidates these events attract, the time of year, the type of positions that healthcare organizations are trying to fill, and so forth. As a result, they should not rely too heavily on job fairs to fill open spots.

4.6 Direct Hiring

Most healthcare organizations need to use internally generated direct hiring methods to fill at least a portion of their open positions. These HR hiring infrastructures will vary significantly from company to company. For instance, small healthcare organizations might only employ one or two HR staff who perform all of that company's HR tasks, including overseeing the candidate identification and selection process. Larger healthcare companies, on the other hand, might employ numerous HR employees who focus exclusively on vetting candidates for a limited number of departments or disciplines (nurses, physicians, CNAs, etc.). In the same way, some healthcare HR infrastructures still utilize labor-intensive, paper-based methods for vetting candidates, whereas HR infrastructures at other organizations are mostly digital (the majority of these systems probably fall somewhere in the middle).

Despite this diversity, I think one can point to some near-universal aspects of the direct hiring process. They include:

- **Onus on the Candidate**
  In some cases, a healthcare company will utilize the services of a headhunting agency. In rarer instances, HR staff at an organization will actively scan databases, such as LinkedIn, looking for potential

candidates. However, most of the time, the potential candidates have to take the initiative and apply directly to the healthcare organization via that company's online site or on a jobsite, such as Indeed.com, which is utilized by the organization.

- **Candidates Apply for Specific Jobs**
  Occasionally, candidates can posit one application, which will make them eligible for all open positions at a healthcare company. The organization's HR staff (or a software program) will consider that person whenever a job opens up that matches his or her capabilities and experience. However, in most instances, candidates apply for specific jobs at the healthcare corporation. The individual must reapply for each job at the organization that he or she is interested in (though the HR software usually retains some or all of the candidate's information, thus making it easier for that person to submit multiple applications).

- **HR Staff–Initial Vetting**
  HR staff, usually (but not always) aided by IT devices and software, will review all of the applications for a specific listing. They will cull this number by weeding out applicants who are not (in the HR staff's opinion) a good fit for the job, due to a lack of experience, credentials, skills, and so forth.

- **Hiring Manager Review**
  After the initial culling process (and assuming that the job opening is not in the c-suite or some other, high-level position), HR staff will send the files of the applicants who are still in contention to the hiring managers.

- **Background Checks**
  At the some point in the process, HR will conduct (or contract with an outside firm to conduct) background checks on the applicants—or sometimes just on the potential hire.

- **Interviews**
  At some point in the process, applicants will need to interview with the company. The potential hires might have to interview once or several times. The interview might consist of a one-on-one with the hiring manager, or a panel interview, or something in between. Nonetheless, almost all hiring procedures include some type of interview.

- **Final Review and Decision**
  The hiring manager, perhaps in conjunction with other company employees, will review the candidate's data and make a final decision. The selection group might use purely objective criteria, or they may go with a gut feeling in deciding who to hire. They will usually use some combination of intuition and rational methods to choose the hire.

- **Informing the Winner**
  In the final step, someone from the company calls the candidate to inform him or her of the selection. The caller might go over the details of the job again, finalize salary and benefits, and discuss other pertinent issues. The employee then gives the candidate a set amount of time to decide whether or not to take the job.

- **Repeat**
  If the chosen candidate does not accept the job offer, the company will have to repeat some or all of the above steps.

I have listed some of the basic steps in the process. An HR textbook might include a number of other bullet points. Its authors would likely go into a significant amount of information (perhaps a chapter) on each of the aforementioned steps in the hiring process. However, I feel that I have covered the topic in sufficient detail for the purposes of this book.

I have provided readers with a brief sketch of six key methods that healthcare corporations use to fill open positions. In some cases, healthcare organizations will rely on outside agencies either to control certain departments (outsourcing) or to help these organizations find candidates to fill temporary or full-time openings. Sometimes, healthcare entities will use internships as a way both to fill temporary jobs and as a method for identifying potential, long-term hires. Healthcare companies can also rely on job fairs to secure this talent. Finally, and sometimes in conjunction with one of the other methods, healthcare HR staff can try to hire candidates directly, via affiliated job boards, through listings on their respective company's website, and sometimes by a paper-based method.

In the next chapter, I will review some of the weaknesses of the direct hiring method. At the same time, I will posit some potential solutions. I hope that companies of varying sizes and technical sophistication can utilize at least some of these suggestions.

References

Anonymous. (2008, March 11). Employee Referral Bonus Jackpots: 15 Companies with Awesome New-Hire Incentives. *HR World*. Retrieved from http://www.hrworld.com/features/referral-bonus-jackpot-031108/.

Bae, S., Mark, B., & Fried, B. (2010). Use of Temporary Nurses and Nurse and Patient Safety Outcomes in Acute Care Hospital Units. *Health Care Management Review* 35(4), 333–344. DOI: 10.1097/HMR.0b013e3181dac01c.

Hollon, J. (2012, May 1). Need Any More Proof? Job Referrals Are REALLY Important. *TLNT*. Retrieved from http://www.tlnt.com/2012/05/01/need-any-more-proof-job-referrals-are-really-important/.

May, J. H., Bazzoli, G. J., & Gerland, A. M. (2006, June). Hospitals' Responses to Nurse Staffing Shortages. *Health Affairs* 25(4), 316–323. DOI: 10.1377/hlthaff.25.w316.

Mayhew, R. (N.D.). Recruiting and Hiring Strategies. *Chron*. Retrieved from http://smallbusiness.chron.com/recruiting-hiring-strategies-21762.html.

Punke, H. (2013, October). Outsourcing is Exploding in Healthcare—Will the Trend Last? *Becker's Hospital Review*. Retrieved from http://www.beckershospitalreview.com/workforce-labor-management/outsourcing-is-exploding-in-healthcare-will-the-trend-last.html.

Schwartz, N. D. (2013, January 27). In Hiring, a Friend in Need Is a Prospect, Indeed. *The New York Times*. Retrieved from http://www.nytimes.com/2013/01/28/business/employers-increasingly-rely-on-internal-referrals-in-hiring.html?pagewanted=all&_r=0.

Sullivan, J. (2012, May). 10 Compelling Numbers That Reveal the Power of Employee Referrals. *ERE*. Retrieved from http://www.ere.net/2012/05/07/10-compelling-numbers-that-reveal-the-power-of-employee-referrals/.

Chapter Five

Suggestions for Improving a Healthcare Organization's Direct Hiring Systems— The Initial Stages

---

Almost all healthcare organizations will use direct hiring techniques to fill at least some of their open positions. Healthcare companies will employ a wide range of strategies with regard to this method. However, almost all of these organizations' hiring protocols will contain some of the same basic processes. I listed many of them at the end of the previous chapter. Here is the list again:

- Onus on the Candidate
- Individuals Apply for Specific Jobs
- Human Resources (HR) Staff Members Perform the Initial Vetting of Applications
- One or More Hiring Managers Review the Finalists' Submissions

- Background Checks
- Interviews
- Final Review and Decision
- The Winner Is Informed and Offered a Contract
- The Company Repeats the Process, if Necessary

In this chapter, I want to focus on hiring strategies and information technology (IT) techniques that healthcare organizations can utilize to help them improve their chances of hiring the right candidates for open positions. As a result, I will focus my discussion around methodologies and software instead of on delineating the individual steps in the direct hiring process. I will forego delineating some of the aforementioned steps, and I will only briefly touch on others.

At the same time, I realize that many healthcare companies never truly separate out direct hiring strategies from the other five hiring methods mentioned in the last chapter. These organizations will almost always utilize a combination of hiring techniques (especially formal and informal referral networks) in order to fill open positions. For the purposes of this narrative, I have chosen to partition the direct hiring method in order to keep the text organized and to focus on key areas for improvement.

5.1 Individual Freedom: Blessing and Bane

In my experience, almost every US company has innate weaknesses in its direct hiring practices that do not derive from any corporate flaws. Instead, many of the business industry's hiring-related issues derive from an external source—the nation's political and philosophical norms. To put it simply, I believe that the American value system, with its focus on individual rights and personal privacy, places key roadblocks in the path of corporations who are seeking to identify and to hire the best candidates.

In making this claim, I do not want the reader to think that I do not value these freedoms. I would rather live in a country that affords me a great deal of personal freedom than I would in one that is autocratic or hierarchical. I also value the corollary rights to personal privacy, which have developed out of America's views on individual rights. I do not want to reside in a nation that is governed by fear and oppression. And while people can differ as to how much freedom they think Americans actually possess, almost everyone will agree that US citizens have significant leeway when it comes to voicing their opinions, keeping their personal information secret (at least from non-federal entities), and making their own decisions. This fact becomes more apparent when one compares the United States to countries like Saudi Arabia, North Korea, and Somalia.

At the same time, American workers, because they live in a country that espouses ideals centered on personal freedom, might be better at doing some things. For instance, it stands to reason that people who live in a country such as the United States may be more willing to go out on a limb and try new things, to espouse creative solutions to problems, and to alert their superiors when they spot weaknesses in their company's strategies, processes, and protocols (Associated Press, 2012; Corbett, 2012; Horth & Buchner, 2009, 19). Almost everyone would agree that there is a strong correlation between free market economies and productivity (though many people might disagree with the way in which those benefits are distributed among the general populace).

Although one can point to a number of benefits that come from living in a free society, it is worth remembering that freedom does have its costs—both for people and for corporations. One downside of our nation's sociopolitical infrastructure is that it puts the onus on the individual to choose his or her path in life. Although this idea is great in theory, it does not always pan out as well in practice because human beings tend to be biased when judging themselves. This aspect of American society places a significant burden on corporate HR departments and hiring managers who have to try to sort through candidate résumés and personal statements in an attempt to determine what parts are true and which aspects are hyperbole.

5.1.1 Human Beings Are Biased

Americans—and probably all human beings—are often not the best judges of themselves. They tend to be biased; they overestimate their strengths and they underestimate their flaws (DeAngelis, 2003, 60; Kruger et al., 2008, 221). As worrisome to HR recruiters and hiring managers, these individuals often seem to have trouble deciding what skills they actually do possess, and they have significant issues in figuring out what job type or position within a company represents an ideal fit for them.

5.1.2 Personal Privacy and Hiring

At the same time, US laws guarantee that most people will be able to keep much of their personal and business affairs private—the recent National Security Agency (NSA) debacle being the exception to the rule. Many state laws are even stricter than the federal standards. This works out well for Americans in general. They can go about their daily lives without having to constantly worry how their private decisions, and personal health issues, will impact their careers, their access to healthcare, and their general public standing in the community (Sharp, 2013).

However, for a healthcare company that is trying to hire people to fill open positions, the US privacy laws can be a challenge; they limit the amount of information that organizations can obtain from (or on) potential hires. For instance, although companies can perform basic background checks, they cannot require candidates to hand over their health records. HR staff and hiring managers often have difficulty in gathering information from previous employers because these entities worry about being sued for defamation or some other breach of employee privacy (Greenblatt, 2012; Lawrence, N.D.; U.S. Department of Health and Human Services, 2014).

Given this situation, it is no wonder that healthcare corporations have, to use an old cliché, difficulty in "sorting the wheat from the chaff." When an organization uses a direct hiring technique to fill a position, it is hoping that the right person finds the job posting. Further, the company has to pray that this individual accurately portrays his or her skills and credentials. Finally HR staff, hiring managers, and other key personnel have to hope that they can root out any potential, candidate-related issues, despite the impediments posed by federal and state privacy regulations. Throw in the fact that many healthcare organizations rely on nonscientific methods to select new employees, and it is not surprising that as many as "20% of [corporations'] new hires . . . should never have been brought on" (Tuggle, 2014).

5.2 Ways to Improve the External Hiring Process for Direct Hires

In my experience, many healthcare companies can improve their direct hiring processes by employing a range of methods and IT strategies at three key points in the candidate vetting process: (a) when candidates first apply for a job—the initial contact; (b) during the initial candidate vetting process; and (c) during the interview/secondary vetting process. In this chapter, I will focus on the first two stages in the hiring process. More specifically, I will focus on certain aspects of the initial contact and vetting process; these are areas that are, in my opinion, most amenable to improvement.

5.3 The Initial Contact

The initial contact phase represents the first time that the candidate interacts with the healthcare corporation. This "meeting" might occur in several different ways. On the one hand, the potential hire might click on the organization's website and research the job openings list. At the same time, he or she might choose instead to contact an HR member or someone else in the company to learn more about open positions—or to try to market himself or herself (e.g., by asking for an informational interview). Alternatively, HR staff or other members of the company might be the ones who make first contact with the candidate, whose information they have found via an Internet-based search.

In some cases, the initial contact phase will conclude without the candidate filing an official application. In other instances, the potential hire will apply to one or more open positons at the healthcare organization. In the latter situation, the initial contact stage will end when the candidate files all relevant materials and/or HR vets the application (as sometimes a candidate, at a later stage in the process, will submit additional information to supplement his or her initial submission).

5.4 The Initial Candidate Vetting Process

Once HR begins to review the application, the second phase begins. During this stage, healthcare companies can utilize artificial intelligence (AI) systems or HR personnel to assay the submission. Regardless of whether a computer or a human being reviews the application, the initial assessment will often be brief. At this point, HR might reject the candidate or hold the application for further review. At this stage, depending on the particular company and position, the HR staff might send the applicant's information to the hiring manager or they might submit it to a second review—in an effort to cull the list before it is submitted to the departmental managers (or in the case of higher-level positions, to company executives or to a committee).

Depending on the corporation, the initial vetting process might be fairly simple or it might be more involved (with HR staff conducting some initial interviews). It is sometimes difficult to tease apart the various steps—the initial contact, the initial vetting, and the interview/secondary vetting process. In the foregoing narrative, I do not attempt to delineate the first two steps. Rather, I will focus my time on reviewing HR techniques that, in some cases, might pertain to either of the first two stages in the candidate selection process.

5.5 HR Should Take the Initiative

In the pre-Internet era, if a healthcare company wanted to fill an open position via direct hire (e.g., without relying on referrals, on staffing agencies, or on job fairs), it would only have a few options open to it. The company could hand out flyers, post "help wanted" ads in newspapers and magazines, and/or let affiliates know it had a job opening available. Those were about the only options that a corporation had available to it had at that time.

Nowadays, healthcare organizations have a range of additional options open to them, as a result of the development of the Internet. One important change is that today's companies can actively search for qualified employees on sites such as LinkedIn, or use search engines, such as Google, to identify the right hires. Healthcare organizations can focus their searches on potential job candidates who are actively looking for work, or on passive job candidates—defined as "someone who isn't deliberately looking for a new position, but could be lured to accept one if the right offer came along" (Halzack, 2013).

Until recently, most companies shunned this practice. They relied almost entirely on passive systems, such as job sites, or on non-direct methods, such as employee referral networks. However, that situation is rapidly changing. According to a Society for Human Resource Management Survey, around 71 percent of the companies it assayed use social networking sites, such as LinkedIn, to actively recruit passive job candidates for some openings (Society for Human Resource Management, 2013, Slide 3). Although that figure is impressive, at least on the surface, its census includes companies that only proactively recruit in a limited number of circumstances (e.g., when searching for directors or c-suite level employees) (Society for Human Resource Management, 2013, Slide 3). Additionally, the survey's member selection, response rate, and margin of error of "+/– 4%" render its conclusions somewhat speculative (Society for Human Resource Management, 2013, Slide 34).

Even if 71 percent of the companies were maximizing this strategy to its fullest potential, it means that around 30 percent of US companies are not using LinkedIn or some other social network to actively search for the right candidates. Whatever the actual number, it is certainly possible that an even smaller percentage of healthcare companies have adopted this proactive strategy, given that organizations in the health services industry are slower to adopt newer methods and technologies than many of their peers (see Chapter 1).

Although I do not have any data (none is available) to support this hypothesis, my experience in the field leads me to believe that many of the healthcare companies who have not yet jumped onto the bandwagon are small to mid-sized organizations, with limited HR resources. When the HR staff (and, to some extent, hiring managers) have to balance a host of job duties, or make do with a limited budget, it might seem like good business sense to forego spending the extra time and money on proactive candidate searches. However, in this instance, I believe that it makes perfect business sense for almost every healthcare company with more than 100 employees to at least try the process out.

Healthcare organizations that primarily rely on passive recruiting systems (even ones that combine referral-based methods with passive recruiting) have to be content with sifting through the candidates that apply to their career portals and job board placements. That figure is necessarily limited. More importantly, the smaller and/or less well known the company, the fewer applicants it is likely to procure via passive methods. Therefore, it makes sense for a healthcare organization, especially if it does not have strong brand awareness, to actively recruit potential candidates to fill its open positions.

Healthcare organizations should focus their efforts on identifying active job seekers who have not yet applied to the company. At the same time, they should also target passive job candidates. According to experts, between 30 and 60 percent of all people, who are currently employed, would be willing to consider switching jobs (Halzack, 2013; Sewell, 2014). Healthcare companies that have the necessary HR budgets might want to utilize specially designed search engines that can help them identify and target employees who are good matches for open positions. For example, healthcare organizations can lease this type of tool from LinkedIn for use on its site. More importantly, they can gain access to the search and target system, along with a limited number of free emails, for a relatively small amount of money (LinkedIn, 2014a, 2014b).

Health services companies that do not have the resources to utilize a search and target system—for example, the one offered by LinkedIn—can still perform searches the old fashioned way, by entering a series of key words and seeing who pops up. They can start their search on LinkedIn or another site and then utilize a variety of search engines to find pertinent information on these applicants. In fact, I have performed searches for potential client/customer phone numbers and emails. One would be surprised how easy it is to obtain some of this information via a simple review on one of the more popular search engines.

Of course, there are times when a healthcare company would be wise not to take the proactive approach to filling positions. For instance, if a healthcare organization is trying to fill a basic, entry-level position, such as a dietary tech post, it might be wiser for the HR team to rely on passive application-collection techniques (or even to just hand this task off to a third-party agency). However, it will often make sense, from a cost–benefit perspective, for a healthcare entity to take a proactive stance in regard to finding the right candidate for a position—and that includes some hourly jobs. HR staff and management should determine in advance which positions require a proactive search, based on a cost–benefit analysis (e.g., costs of the search versus potential losses from a bad hire).

5.6 Get Rid of the Résumé

Along with job interviews, the résumé is a staple of the applicant-selection system. Regardless of the other differences in their hiring processes, almost all companies require (or at least allow) candidates to submit résumés. I admit that these documents can contain useful, unique information about a candidate; however, this fact does not offset its flaws, which include:

- **Too Much Useless Information**
  I think almost everyone would agree that most résumés contain extraneous information, which does not help the vetting process. In fact, if a company's HR staff members, hiring managers, or other hiring personnel are not adept at performing keyword searches, they might devote needless resources to reviewing non-pertinent candidate information.

- **The Data Overlaps the Company Application**
  In many instances, the résumé contains information that is similar to (or the same as) the data requested on corporate applications. Sometimes HR and hiring managers, often with the aid of software, can eliminate these duplicate portions. More often though, the hiring manager or HR staff member will have to comb through the redundant portion in a search for relevant information.

- **Flawed Applicant Screening Processes**
  Many healthcare corporations use applicant screening systems to analyze résumés and identify qualified candidates. They also use these systems to populate candidate databases. However, as one *CIO* article notes, these systems "are flawed. For instance, if a job seeker's resume isn't formatted the right way and doesn't contain the right keywords and phrases, the applicant tracking system will misread it and rank it as a bad match with the job opening, regardless of the candidate's qualifications" (Levinson, 2012).

  Other healthcare companies, especially smaller ones, still rely on HR staff to parse through the résumés in an effort to cull applicants who are a poor match for the respective jobs. Although the human HR personnel will likely do a better job than current AI systems at identifying qualified job seekers, they will also miss good candidates. Human HR staffs are also prone to biases, which might negatively impact their ability to separate the wheat from the chaff.

- **Lack of Standardized Forms**
  One of the key issues with résumés is that there is no set standard governing their creation. Candidates will apply their own unique touches to these documents, and this is a bad thing for companies, as it makes it more difficult for HR staffs and analysts to collect and analyze the candidates' data.

- **Significant Portions of the Data Are Subjective**
  Even if they are telling (what they believe is) the truth, candidates are expressing their views on the résumé. Potential hires are naturally going to be biased with regard to their abilities and their accomplishments. So, for instance, an individual that poured coffee for the president might list one of his or her important job tasks as "helping the president to manage his/her daily affairs." The candidate is not technically lying; however, few outside observers would agree with the potential hire as to the importance of this function.

Healthcare organizations of all sizes and types would be better off if they refused to accept résumés from candidates. Instead, healthcare companies should focus the candidate's full attention on the company application. These organizations, if they have the resources, can include software on the application form itself, which will search the potential hire's résumé for pertinent information and place this data onto the application form (the tools that I have seen for this purpose are far from perfect, but better than nothing). If not, then the candidate will have to enter the information manually. Either way, the application form software should prevent potential hires from submitting their résumés as attachments.

5.7 Move to an Application-Only System

Most healthcare organizations utilize some type of application form. However, they also collect the applicant's résumé. In lieu of this document, the organization's application can ask the candidate to list and describe a certain number ("up to three," "up to five," etc.) of unique instances/traits/abilities that separate him or her from other potential hires.

Healthcare organizations will not fix all of the issues, noted previously, by banning résumé submissions. For one thing, readers will notice that I did not mention lack of truthfulness as a résumé shortcoming. That is because a candidate who is willing to lie about his or her credentials, background, and so forth on a résumé is not suddenly going to tell the truth on a company-sponsored application form. Hence, healthcare organizations probably will not improve this flaw by switching to an all-application process. At the same time, some candidates will still find a way to embellish or misrepresent their experience, credentials, or knowledge. Regardless of any other factors, the information that the potential hire posits in the application will almost certainly contain some subjective data.

Although all that is true, healthcare corporations gain one significant advantage when they move to an application-only system. These organizations can take full control (or nearly complete control) of the initial application process. They can dictate the flow of data they receive and direct it in a way that fits with the particular job type, corporate culture, and so forth. More importantly, healthcare organizations that ban résumé submissions will find it much easier to standardize the process. Finally (and most importantly), healthcare organizations can create application systems that entice applicants to posit any relevant data, including skills, experience, and work history, which is necessary to the vetting process.

Healthcare organizations should be able to realize a number of benefits if they migrate to an application-only system.

- A healthcare company's HR staff can create a format that allows the best candidates to shine, as opposed to what currently happens in many systems that favor candidates who are most adept at adding the right keywords or phrases into their résumés.
- HR staff, hiring managers, and other personnel can more efficiently vet potential hires.
- Theoretically, HR staff can structure the questions on an application in such a way that it reduces bias.
- By reverting to an application-only system, healthcare organizations will be able to standardize the data, which should allow them to quantify and categorize a larger percentage of the candidate information.

Several HR experts have noted the flaws in the current résumé submission process and have suggested at least thinking about doing away with these documents (Adler, 2013; Bharadwaj, 2012). For instance, Lou Adler, who runs a training and consulting firm, wrote an article for *TLNT* in which he critiques current résumés for focusing too much attention on skills and not enough on actual job performance. Although his views differ somewhat from mine, he appears to agree that corporations should set the criteria for selection (Adler, 2013).

Many healthcare organizations utilize third-party, applicant tracking systems (ATS) to help them create and maintain their applicant web pages. They should be able to work with the ATS vendors, when necessary, to adjust their ATS systems to handle application-only formats (though most ATS's should be able to perform this type of thing already). Healthcare companies and vendors can work with job board posting sites, along with other vendors, to ensure that the application-only process is holistic. Of course, not all healthcare organizations use online applications. What should these entities do?

A large number of healthcare companies (mainly small and mid-sized firms) still procure many of their candidate applications via email, fax, or a similar method. They rely primarily on HR staff to collect and analyze the applicant data, cull the list of applications to some manageable number, and then work with the hiring managers to identify the best fit candidate. Sometimes, HR staff will send the list of finalists to the hiring managers, who then take care of further candidate contacts and vetting. Many of these organizations do not have the resources to invest in proprietary ATS's. Yet these companies might benefit most by utilizing an application-only system (or, at the very least, by using some type of automated system).

5.7.1 Creating an Application-Only System on a Budget—Using Open-Source Software

I noted in a previous chapter that a healthcare company can lose thousands (and often tens of thousands) of dollars from just one bad hire. Although painful, mid-sized and large healthcare organizations can usually absorb these losses without too much difficulty. However, smaller corporations can suffer tremendously if they make a few bad hires. Many of these companies are just getting started or they generate very small operating margins; they cannot afford the hit to their brands, the loss of income, the lawsuits, and the other ills that could transpire from even a few poor hiring decisions.

These companies could benefit significantly if they were able to create an online application system that improved their ability to separate solid applicants from weak ones, while at the same time allowing their HR staffs to work more efficiently. Many of these resource-challenged healthcare organizations might still be able to create application-only systems or, at the very least, automate a larger portion of the application process by utilizing an open source ATS, or Microsoft Access and Excel, in combination with a web portal.

Healthcare organizations that cannot afford to pay a third-party vendor to use its ATS system do have another option. They can use an open source ATS program, for example, OpenCATS. Companies that take this route can save significant amounts of money. At the same time, the HR staff and management will still have access to many ATS features, including database management and automatic email creation. These organizations can also add specific modules to the open source ATS to suit their particular needs.

Although healthcare organizations might not have to pay anything to download the open source ATS's, they still have to invest resources in learning how to use the systems and in training others on how to use the systems. More importantly, they have to devote IT hours to modifying the system to fit the needs of their particular companies. Some companies just do not have the IT staff on hand who possess the technical skills to build and maintain these modifications.

5.7.2 Integrating Microsoft Excel and Access into the Application Process

Alternatively, healthcare organizations can take a third route and utilize Microsoft Access and Excel programs to help them build an applicant database. They can use one, or both, of these programs in tandem to do things like sort individuals by category, identify good matches, rank potential hires, and identify good candidates for a position from a previous application job list. HR staff can utilize Access or Excel in coordination with other Microsoft programs, such as Word and Outlook, to send mass emails out to finalists and to non-accepts, to schedule appointments, and to perform other basic HR hiring functions.

Even healthcare organizations that utilize an ATS might choose to use Microsoft Access and/or Excel for some tasks. With that in mind, I have posited a scenario below that demonstrates how a company can work with a web designer to create an application-only portal that utilizes Microsoft Access and Excel. Readers whose corporations use an ATS can substitute their particular system for these programs. The information in the next couple of paragraphs does not provide a precise how-to-guide.

Instead, I describe the process in the most basic terms, to demonstrate how it would work.

To make this work, a healthcare company could work with a website designer to create the application portal interface on the organization's homepage (unless the company has an in-house website designer/developer). The designer would sit down with the organization's IT team to create a portal that contains vital aspects—that is, the job-specific application questions, a response queue, security/data encryption protocols, a collection system, and a method for porting the collected data to Microsoft Access or Excel. The portal should be designed in such a way that it allows the company's HR staff and management to alter the candidate questions, as needed.

The IT staff, working with HR, would have to create an Access-based spreadsheet (or a series of these spreadsheets) that could capture the data from the applications and categorize it. However, once set up, these spreadsheets could separate people based on whatever criteria the HR staff deemed appropriate. At the same time, since the HR staff created the application questions, these individuals should be able to create a matching set of keyword/criteria markers that more accurately capture the qualities of their preferred candidates, vis-à-vis a system that relies on finding keywords in résumés.

Alternatively, the healthcare organization could choose to send the information from the web portal into a series of Microsoft Excel spreadsheets (see Figure 5.1). Excel is not as good as Access in categorizing information, but it does a better job with numerical data. Additionally, HR staff might have to spend more time manually adjusting columns and lines in Excel. Creative and experienced HR/IT teams could even run the two systems, Access and Excel, in tandem, thus leveraging each program's strengths, while minimizing the weaknesses.

Regardless of which method they choose, resource-challenged companies can create application-only processes tailored to their specific needs. These systems would have the advantage of being at least partially automated. Ideally, HR staff would be able to leverage the tools in the web portals, Excel, and/or Access to make better candidate choices in less time. As important, the healthcare organizations should realize cost savings in the long run if they put a lot of forethought and planning into ensuring that the design/process is well constructed and meets their specific needs.

With that being said, a healthcare organization that is interested in taking this route will still have to invest thousands of dollars or more to

Sample Healthcare Organization—Candidate Applications/Dataset for Open Position #31 Applications Received from February 1, 2015–March 2, 2015 (Note: Information Comes from the Online Application Form)

Candidates	Specific Attributes for Task #1 (1 = One Attribute, 5 = Five or More Attributes)	Specific Attributes for Task #2 (1= One Attribute, 5 = Five or More Attributes)	Cultural Fit (Based on Answers to Company Specific Questions, 10–35 and Ranked 1–5)	Job Specific Quantitative Test Results (0%–19.49% = 1, 19.5%–39.49% = 2, 39.5%–59.49% = 3, 59.5%–79.49% = 4, 79.5%–100% = 5)	Job-Related Skills (1 = One Skill, 5 = Five Skills)	Average Overall Score (3.4+ Moves on to Next Round)
1	5	3	2	3	2	3
2	2	2	3	3	3	2.6
3	2	2	4	4	5	3.4
4	1	4	1	2	1	1.8
5	3	1	5	3	3	3
6	4	5	3	4	4	4
7	4	5	2	2	3	3.2
8	1	2	1	1	2	1.4
9	5	3	5	4	5	4.4
10	2	5	5	5	4	4.2
11	3	1	4	4	3	3
12	2	3	2	4	3	2.8
13	5	5	3	3	4	4
14	4	2	4	3	2	3
15	3	1	3	3	4	2.8
16	1	4	2	2	4	2.4
17	3	2	4	3	4	3.2
18	2	3	3	2	1	2.2
19	1	2	3	3	1	2
20	4	3	4	4	3	3.6
Average	2.85	2.9	3.15	3.1	3	3

Figure 5.1 A sample version of an Excel document containing candidate information that has been downloaded from the online application form. Although a real dataset would likely contain many more columns, this figure contains all of the key sections. As important, it demonstrates how an organization can create tailor-made questions and then quantify this data.

get the system up and running, as well as to maintain it. At the same time, if the company does a poor job in planning, development, or launch, it might suffer an even larger financial setback. As with any capital project, the company's management will have to carefully weigh the risks and rewards of undertaking the project—to see if it is right for the organization at that time.

5.8 Maintain a Dynamic Database

As I noted previously, organizations might want to consider moving to an application-only system because it makes it easier for them to standardize more of the applicant data. It is sometimes easier for analysts to quantify data when it is in a standard format. It is certainly easier for HR staff and hiring managers to compare candidates when they are reviewing standardized information. They can, to use an old cliché, "compare apples to apples."

Healthcare companies should input all relevant candidate information into a database, sorted by categories and, when appropriate, ranked. Large or resource-rich corporations can utilize third-party proprietary ATS systems. Smaller organizations can use Microsoft Access and/or Excel. Many companies will use a combination of the two systems. IT staff should ensure that HR personnel, hiring managers, and anyone else who participates in the candidate vetting process have access to these files, when needed.

HR, hiring managers, and other people in management should use these files on a consistent basis to perform a number of tasks, including:

- Collecting and storing applicant information
- Initial candidate vetting
- Tracking applicants through the system
- Communicating with potential hires
- Identifying leads for future job openings and/or mining the database to locate potential hires for jobs that have just become available
- Determining which applicant characteristics and behaviors are most compatible with specific job types at the respective companies
- Identifying applicants who might not fit a particular job profile but who might, nonetheless, be worth bringing onboard with the company

Of course, management can utilize the database for purposes other than the ones listed here. I have chosen to posit examples that are discussed in this book.

In order for healthcare companies to utilize this database to best effect, they should quantify the information, when possible. Management cannot reduce every data point to a number; however, they should try to do so, when possible. By taking this step, healthcare organizations will find it easier to use statistics, especially regressions, to identify patterns in the candidate data and to pick out areas of focus, when mining databases for potential hires. For instance, healthcare HR staff and other personnel can use a numerical system to grade applicants' abilities in key areas, such as verbal skills, quantitative abilities, writing skills, and so forth. They can also translate job experience into a number that takes into account both the time and quality of the candidates' previous work experiences.

Healthcare companies should not translate every piece of a candidate's application into numerical data. At the same time, they should only undertake this task with regard to finalists, the individuals who secure the open positions, and other applicants who seem to be especially promising. It is simply not economically feasible to do it for everyone. Additionally, management might want to forego this process in certain cases, such as when hiring entry-level, non-skilled labor or when they have an overly large pool of potential good hires. Nonetheless, I think it makes sense, from a cost–benefit perspective, for healthcare organizations to quantify as much information as possible for the specific candidate types previously noted.

5.9 Mine Old Candidate Data for Potential Hires

Whether or not healthcare organizations quantify their applicant data, they should store it in this database and render it searchable. HR staff should mine this data for potential hires whenever new positions become available. Often, a previous application process yields several potential good hires for one open position. It therefore makes sense for HR staffs to review their databases to identify these past candidates. They can then search the Internet to see where these people are currently employed and to attempt to reach out to them (Spark, 2012). In many cases, the companies can complete the hiring process in this type of scenario much quicker than they could if they posted the jobs and waited for the new applications to roll in.

Although it may take HR staff some time and effort to review old data, the resources they expend on this process—assuming their search leads to a hire—might pale in comparison to the effort they would need to put forth to start from scratch. Although the costs for conducting this process will vary by company and job type, they will likely be significant. The healthcare organization that is doing the hiring will have to expend resources directly on activities such as creating the hiring notice, disseminating the posting, and vetting the candidates. While the search is going on, the company will suffer from lost-opportunity costs, reduced productivity, and other issues that result from the vacancy (Thompson, 2012). It makes sense that these indirect costs will grow, the longer the position remains unfilled.

5.10 Keep Applicants Informed

Many healthcare organizations do not inform applicants when they are no longer being considered for a particular position. In some cases, these companies might eventually email the failed candidates—sometimes months or even years after their eliminations. Healthcare companies might be able to posit a wide range of legitimate reasons for their failure to notify applicants who are no longer being considered for positions. For one thing, corporations have to expend direct resources to contact these individuals, for instance, by sending out an email blast. At the same time, already harried HR staff or hiring managers would have to set aside precious time to email these people (HR employee, 2012).

While all these things might be true, I would encourage every healthcare company to inform candidates when they are no longer being considered for a particular job opening. That is because the majority of applicants are likely to be locals who live within driving distance of their potential employers (Katzanek, 2012; Wolgemuth, 2009). These are the very same people who make up most healthcare organizations' primary customer bases. This is because most healthcare companies—whether they are hospitals, long-term care facilities, doctors' offices, DME suppliers, or some other type—are regional players. They derive almost all of their business from people who live within a hundred miles or so of their facilities (Anonymous, "Dartmouth Atlas," 2014).

In Chapter 1, I discussed hospitals' renewed focus on creating patient-centered environments. However, healthcare organizations in all markets work hard (or at least should work hard) to keep their customers—whether patients, residents, or some other group—happy. These individuals are the lifeblood of their business. Most companies that I have been associated with would go out of their way to keep their clients happy. And, as anyone with a TV or radio can attest, healthcare organizations spend significant amounts of money on ads depicting them as consumer-friendly places.

So, I am a little bemused by the fact that some healthcare organizations do not dedicate the necessary resources to inform candidates who are no longer in the running for an open position. Most job seekers want to hear back from the companies that they have applied to—even if the response is not positive. That is especially true if they have spent hours researching the particular organization, filling out online application forms, retooling their résumés (an antiquated practice), and doing the other things necessary to apply. The people who receive rejection notices might not be happy about it. However, they will, on average, likely be much more satisfied with the process than their peers who do not hear anything back from their potential places of employment.

If HR staff and management at these organizations took a step back and considered these job seekers as potential customers, they might rethink this practice. The question that they should then ask themselves is, "What is the cost–benefit of sending out rejection notifications to candidates who did not make the cut for one or more open positions at our firm?" I think that in almost every case, management will come to the conclusion that it makes good business sense to send out rejection letters. Further, they should send these notices out to everyone, not just to individuals who are interested in higher-end jobs. The people, who are applying for entry-level jobs are just as likely to be future customers as are the individuals who are applying for mid-level and upper-management positions.

5.11 Survey the Applicants

Over the years, I have held several jobs in healthcare, as well as in other fields. As a result, I have had a chance to view things from the applicant's perspective. What I find amazing is that none of the companies that I applied to asked for my feedback. As almost any business management book will proclaim, corporate leaders need to procure feedback from all stakeholders (Mahajan, 2008, 159). In fact, none of the companies that I have worked with have an applicant feedback process in place.

For some small healthcare organizations, it might not be feasible to survey applicants to get their feedback, due to resource constraints. However, I would recommend that HR staff at all healthcare companies survey the applicants. Large organizations, with thousands of applications per month, would not need to assay everyone. These corporations can send out surveys to a random sample of the applicants, as long they ensure that they include all job types.

Even if a healthcare company uses a predesigned application format, it can benefit from surveying its applicants. Respondents can let the organization know if it needs to adjust any of its questions, alter its format, or perform other measures to ensure that the application process meets the needs of the specific applicant demographic. HR can use these surveys to help it improve various aspects of the vetting process, including the points of interaction (e.g., interviews) between the company's employees and potential hires. Indirectly, the healthcare organization can demonstrate to applicants—even the ones that it rejects early in the process—that it cares about their opinions, which is important because, as previously noted, many of the job seekers will turn into customers at some point.

5.11.1 A Cost-Effective Survey Technique— Open-Ended Surveys

Although I believe that HR departments should survey their applicant population—ideally every candidate—I realize these assays can be expensive (Lee, 2002). Smaller and mid-sized healthcare companies might have an especially difficult time finding the money in the budget to pay for applicant surveys. The organization could incur additional expenses if it uses traditional surveys and wants to ensure a high degree of validity and reliability, as it might have to do things such as send follow-up notices (Trochim, 2006).

Healthcare organizations have another unique issue when it comes to surveying applicants. Namely, unlike other stakeholder groups, a large percentage of the candidates might be upset with the organization. The applicants' frustration comes about from their not getting selected for one or more open positions. This level of discord will differ by company and specific job type, but it might certainly skew the results of a traditional survey. An angry applicant might intentionally misrepresent his or her answers on the assays. A certain percentage of people will do this anyway, but the figures might be higher when dealing with potential hires.

Healthcare organizations could potentially circumvent this problem, as well as keep their survey costs to a minimum, by asking one or two open-ended questions. For instance, healthcare companies, at some point in the application process (perhaps at several places along the way), can include a notice that prompts candidates to provide them with unstructured feedback. For instance, HR might place a survey box at the end of the initial online application that posits this query: "What survey functions work well and which ones do not perform up to your standards" (Rapid Improvement, 2014).

By taking this step, healthcare organizations can keep their costs to a minimum. It will cost companies much less to create one or two open-ended questions than it will for them to conduct an assay that contains a series of closed-ended queries, with accompanying follow-ups (Alemi & Jasper, 2014, 11). More importantly, in a structured assay, the candidates can only provide feedback on particular aspects of the application process, as they are limited to answering the closed-ended queries. By contrast, a survey that utilizes an open-ended method can elicit a wide range of responses, thus pinpointing areas of concern that might have otherwise gone unnoticed (DePoy & Gitlin, 2011, 190–191; Penwarden, 2013). Finally, I would argue that HR can more easily identify and eliminate responses that are biased by the applicant's frustration, when they use an open-ended assay.

Open-ended assays do possess their drawbacks, especially when they are used to analyze a static system, as opposed to one that changes over time. One of these key issues, especially when dealing with static measures such as application portals, relates to their validity and reliability (Penwarden, 2013). However, I do not believe that is an issue here. HR should primarily use applicant assays to identify weaknesses in their hiring processes. I feel that they can better identify the myriad potential problems in this system by utilizing open-ended assays.

If the healthcare organization is small and/or only receives a few hundred or so applications per year, it might make sense for a member of the HR staff to review them. That person can quickly eliminate comments that are inappropriate or not pertinent to the HR hiring process. Additionally, the task will not prove too cumbersome, or result in significant labor expenses, if the HR employee is adept at scanning the candidate comments for key points.

Healthcare HR departments that receive thousands of applications per year might find it too expensive (factoring in full-time equivalents (FTE's) as well as lost-opportunity costs) to manually review all of the open-ended survey responses. In fact, if they take this step, the costs of analyzing and categorizing the data might not be worth the effort. Instead, I would suggest that they utilize AI software to assay the applicant feedback.

Healthcare leaders have a number of different, relatively inexpensive, AI systems to choose from. I am affiliated with one such company, Rapid Improvement, Inc. It employs an adaptive AI system that, for a relatively low price per month, can analyze thousands of comments; determine whether they are complaints or praise statements; isolate the complaint category (e.g., parking, broken website link, etc.); and provide the results of its analysis in real time (Rapid Improvement, 2014). Rapid Improvement is just one of a number of companies out there that can parse the data from HR hiring surveys. Other vendors, including Wise Window and Lymbix, have AI-based systems that can perform similar tasks.

References

Adler, L. (2013, March 7). I'll Say It Again: We Need to Get Rid of Resumes and Job Descriptions. *TLNT*. Retrieved from http://www.tlnt.com/2013/03/07/heres-why-we-finally-need-to-get-rid-of-resumes-and-job-descriptions/#more-103022.

Alemi, F., & Jasper, H. (2014). An Alternative to Satisfaction Surveys: Let the Patients Talk. *Quality Management in Health Care* 23(1), 10–19.

Anonymous. (2014). Data by Region. The Dartmouth Atlas of Healthcare. Retrieved from http://www.dartmouthatlas.org/data/region/.

Associated Press. (2012, Nov. 14). Whistleblower-Protection Bill Sent to the President. First Amendment Center. Retrieved from http://www.firstamendmentcenter.org/whistleblower-protection-bill-sent-to-president.

Bharadwaj, S. (2012, July 28). 4 Reasons Recruiters Should Stop Accepting Traditional Resumes. *Mashable*. Retrieved from http://mashable.com/2012/07/28/traditional-resumes/.

Corbett, A. (2012, July 28). Honor, Freedom, and Entrepreneurship. *Forbes*. Retrieved from http://www.forbes.com/sites/babson/2012/07/28/honor-freedom-and-entrepreneurship/.

DeAngelis, T. (2003). Why We Overestimate Our Competence. *American Psychological Association* 34(2), 60. Retrieved from http://www.apa.org/monitor/feb03/overestimate.aspx.

DePoy, E., & Gitlin, L. N. (2011). *Introduction to Research: Understanding and Applying Multiple Strategies*. St. Louis, MO: Elsevier Mosby.

Greenblatt, A. (2012, May 22). How Much Can Potential Employers Ask about You? *NPR*. Retrieved from http://www.npr.org/2012/05/21/153201730/how-much-can-potential-employers-ask-about-you.

Halzack, S. (2013, August 4). LinkedIn Has Changed the Way Businesses Hunt Talent. *The Washington Post*. Retrieved from http://www.washingtonpost.com/business/capitalbusiness/linkedin-has-changed-the-way-businesses-hunt-talent/2013/08/04/3470860e-e269-11e2-aef3-339619eab080_story.html.

Horth, D., & Buchner, D. (2009). *Innovation Leadership: How to Use Innovation to Lead Effectively, Work Collaboratively and Drive Results*. Center for Creative Leadership. Retrieved from http://www.ccl.org/leadership/pdf/research/InnovationLeadership.pdf.

HR Employee at a Large Hospital. (2012, December 31). Email Correspondence.

Katzanek, J. (2012, January 30). Job Seekers Less Willing to Relocate. *The Press Enterprise*. Retrieved from http://www.pe.com/articles/percent-635742-people-job.html.

Kruger, J., Windschitl, P. D., Burrus, J., Fessel, F., & Chambers, J. R. (2008). The Rational Side of Egocentrism in Social Comparisons. *Journal of Experimental Social Psychology* 44, 220–232. Retrieved from http://www2.psychology.uiowa.edu/Faculty/Windschitl/PDFs/JESP%202008%20%28KWBFC%29.pdf.

Lawrence, G. (N.D.). What Can You Legally Say in Reference to a Fired Employee? *Chron*. Retrieved from http://smallbusiness.chron.com/can-legally-say-reference-fired-employee-21053.html.

Lee, M. (2002, September 30). Conducting Surveys and Focus Groups. *Entrepreneur*. Retrieved from http://www.entrepreneur.com/article/55680.

Levinson, M. (2012, March 1). 5 Insider Secrets for Beating Applicant Tracking Systems. *CIO*. Retrieved from http://www.cio.com/article/2398753/careers-staffing/5-insider-secrets-for-beating-applicant-tracking-systems.html.

LinkedIn (2014a). For Recruiters. Retrieved from https://www.linkedin.com/mnyfe/subscriptionv2?displayProducts=&trk=tlc_buynow_btnt_hero&pid=80002&pids=80011%2C80002&family=talent.

LinkedIn (2014b). Recruiter Tool. Retrieved from http://business.linkedin.com/talent-solutions/products/recruiter.html.

Mahajan, C. P. (2008). *Principles and Techniques of Business.* Jaipur, India: Global Media. Retrieved from Ebrary Reader (online).

Penwarden, R. (2013). Comparing Closed-Ended and Open-Ended Questions. *Fluid Survey University.* Retrieved from http://fluidsurveys.com/university/comparing-closed-ended-and-open-ended-questions/.

Rapid Improvement. (2014). Survey Question. Retrieved from https://tellmymd.com/Surveys.

Sewell, L. (2014). Passive Candidates: Who They Are and How to Find Them. Retrieved from http://www.net-temps.com/recruiters/recart/printer.htm?id=27&pf=1.

Sharp, T. (2013, June 12). Right to Privacy: Constitutional Rights & Privacy Laws. *Live Science.* Retrieved from http://www.livescience.com/37398-right-to-privacy.html.

Society for Human Resource Management. (2013, April 11). Social Networking Websites and Recruiting/Selection. Retrieved from http://www.shrm.org/research/surveyfindings/articles/pages/shrm-social-networking-websites-recruiting-job-candidates.aspx#sthash.KynYaY0c.dpuf

Spark, D. (2012, July 24). 20 Top Tips to Recruit Passive Candidates. *Dice.* Retrieved from http://resources.dice.com/2012/07/24/20-top-tips-to-recruit-passive-candidates/.

Thompson, M. (2012, February). How Much Does It Cost to Hire a New Employee. Dun & Bradstreet Credibility Corp. Retrieved from http://www.dandb.com/smallbusiness/how much-does-it-cost-to-hire-a-new-employee/.

Trochim, M. K. (2006). Selecting the Survey Method. *Research Methods Knowledge Base.* Retrieved from http://www.socialresearchmethods.net/kb/survsel.php.

Tuggle, K. (2014, January 17). The Real Cost of a Bad Hire. *The Street.* Retrieved from http://www.thestreet.com/story/12243638/1/the-real-cost-of-a-bad-hire.html.

U.S. Department of Health and Human Services. (2014). Health Information Privacy. Retrieved from http://www.hhs.gov/ocr/privacy/index.html.

Wolgemuth, L. (2009, July 27). More Job Seekers Are Relocating for Work. *U.S. News.* Retrieved from http://money.usnews.com/money/blogs/the-inside-job/2009/07/27/more-job-seekers-are-relocating-for-work.

Chapter Six

The Initial Stages in the Hiring Process—The Discussion Continues

In the last chapter, I discussed some of the key aspects of the passive candidate selection process, and I made some suggestions for improving the early stages of that system. In this section, I will continue that conversation; however, I will—for the most part—focus on more abstract, generalizable topics. Readers can utilize some of the ideas in this section not only to help them in fixing specific issues with their hiring schemas but also to aid them in making systemic improvements to their hiring and promotion methodologies.

6.1 It Is Hard to Find Good Workers— Even in a Recession

Although many healthcare corporations struggled during the Great Recession, they also benefited from high unemployment. During this period, a much larger percentage of the US population than usual was out of work. At the recession's peak in 2009, unemployment reached as high as 10% (Bureau of Labor Statistics, "The Recession," 2012, 2). If one includes people who have quit searching for work, along with people who are underemployed, then almost one out of every four Americans was either unemployed or underemployed at the Great Recession's peak (Slack, 2014). Several years after the phenomenon ended, both the unemployment and underemployment rates are still well above norms (BLS, 2014).

As a result, corporations in many fields, including healthcare, have been able to choose individuals from among a much larger applicant pool. Healthcare human resources (HR) staff have focused their attention on candidates with the most experience and credentials. In recent years, they have tended to eschew candidates who have lots of potential but are lacking either the experience or the credentials (or sometimes both) (Cappelli, 2011; Holland, 2014). At the same time, many of these companies have cut back on training programs for new entries (Holland, 2014).

Ironically, many of these organizations still complain that they are often not able to find the right people to fill open positions (Cappelli, 2011; Holland, 2014). And as I noted in a previous chapter, most healthcare organizations have made at least one bad hire (and many of them make lots of bad hires) in the previous year. How can these companies fill their open positions with the best applicants (or at least capable individuals)? In this chapter and in the following one, I will posit several techniques and tools that healthcare HR staff and hiring managers can utilize to help them identify the best candidates for specific positions. However, before I begin that process, I would like to offer a general solution to this dilemma, which does not require companies to purchase new technologies or come up with innovative techniques.

6.2 Focus Less on Credentials and More on Potential

As I noted previously, healthcare companies, and indeed corporations in most fields, have become extremely picky. They want people who already have the experience and credentials—the more of these, the merrier (Holland, 2014). In some cases, they are completely justified in taking this route. Healthcare providers should ensure that some personnel, such as physicians and nurses, have the requisite credentials. In other cases, healthcare organizations will want to fill many key positions with experienced workers. For instance, few executives would want to trust a neophyte to craft a strategic plan for a new service line.

At the same time, healthcare organizations can save on training costs if they hire people whose technical expertise and experience closely match the job-posting requirements. Hiring managers can forego technical training and instead focus on introducing the individual to the particular department's culture and protocols. It might be especially tempting for hiring managers to take this route if their budgets are tight.

It makes sense for healthcare organizations to focus much of their attention on experienced, credentialed candidates. At the same time, I would argue that they should not overlook applicants with little experience but a lot of potential. Healthcare corporations will likely expend more resources in training these people; however, they might reap the benefits over the long term.

6.2.1 Look for High-I.Q. Individuals

Before proceeding with this discussion, I think it is worthwhile to define these (what I will call) "high-potential candidates." Most managers would probably agree that ideal employees, at least the ones in specialist and mid-level positions, will possess three key attributes: high-I.Q.'s, excellent technical knowledge, and strong emotional intelligence (EI) skills (otherwise known as "people skills") (Goleman, 1998, 93–94; Kemper, 1999, 15–16). In this book, I refer to I.Q. as "verbal/linguistic and logical/mathematical" skills (Ehrlich, 2003, 51). The other two skills are self-explanatory.

I put much more emphasis on verbal and logical/mathematical abilities than I do on the other two categories when assessing potential candidates, for one important reason. Namely, although human beings can learn new things and improve their EI skills, they find it difficult, if not impossible, to raise their I.Q. scores. Provided that their minds are healthy, adults of any age can increase their technical knowledge and skills. Most experts would agree that they can also develop their EI skills (Mayer et al., 2012). However, researchers, by and large, do not believe that men and women can improve their cognitive potentials (Cox, 2012). Even if adults can increase their raw I.Q. scores (as opposed to the weighted scores, with the average at 100), the process for doing so is still shrouded in mystery (Cox, 2012; Nisbett et al., 2012, 130–152).

This fact is important because the higher one's I.Q., the better he or she is at solving some types of problems and at pattern recognition.

In my experience, people who have above average I.Q.'s are, more often than not, excellent at identifying macro-level, systemic problems. They are also more adept at learning new skills, at multitasking, and in solving the everyday conundrums that employees—at least the ones whose jobs are not based on rote routines—have to overcome.

In short, high-I.Q. individuals have the potential to perform admirably at a wide range of tasks. More importantly, their numbers are limited. Healthcare corporations cannot—at this time—onboard individuals with average I.Q.'s and, via training, transform these men and women into geniuses.

So, it makes sense for healthcare corporations, at least on occasion, to hire high-I.Q. individuals who might not yet have the requisite experience for a particular job and/or finely honed EI skills. The healthcare companies can aid these people in imbibing new techniques or in developing their EI skills over time. Although these individuals might not perform as well as their peers at the outset, the high-I.Q. performers hold the potential to far outpace their colleagues over the long run.

I should mention one key caveat here. Namely, the healthcare leader should ensure that these high-I.Q. individuals have good work ethics. He or she should also try to discern whether these men and women are amenable to change. Someone who is lazy or who is stubborn is unlikely to succeed, irrespective of his or her I.Q.

I also believe that it is easier for HR staff and management to identify individuals who possess excellent cognitive skills than it is to identify people who rank high in categories related to EI. That is because I believe that cognitive tests are more objective measures of the skills they assay (e.g., verbal and analytical skills) than are personality surveys. An individual can manipulate his or her score on many personality tests. Assuming that the company takes proper measures to prevent cheating, that person will find it much more difficult to perform this task on quantitative and verbal reasoning assessments.

Of course, if a healthcare company's HR staff and management can devise methods for accurately identifying raw recruits who possess high-EI potential, they can actively seek those individuals as well. Healthcare organizations should also be on the lookout for overachievers who fit into this category (e.g., little experience or lacking some key credentials) as well. Much of what I have to say in the next couple of paragraphs also applies to these individuals.

To sum this section up, I would equate high-potential candidates, as I have defined them, as equivalent to rookies in baseball. These individuals possess significant intellectual potential. They can quickly master new technologies and business processes while, at the same time, proving adept at solving complex problems. These men and women are also often excellent autodidacts, who are able to pick up on things without formal training. Assuming they are hard workers, these individuals, regardless of any initial deficiencies, will grow to become star performers who are capable of moving rapidly up the ranks.

6.2.2 Take a Risk—Hire Individuals with No Background in Business or in Healthcare

Additionally, healthcare organizations should take on high-potential candidates whose training is neither in business nor in healthcare (e.g., they might have history, sociology, or other humanities degrees). Some of these people might not even have a degree at all. I have had the pleasure of working with a number of highly capable individuals who, for one reason or another, opted not to attend college. These individuals process information differently from people with business degrees, and that is a good thing. Healthcare companies can utilize these diverse viewpoints to help give them an edge in complex, fast-changing environments (Llopis, 2011).

Of course, as I noted before, companies will have to expend additional resources in training these people. Many healthcare executives (and indeed executives in many different types of corporations) are hesitant to spend significant amounts of money on training because they are worried that the employees will not stay with the company for the long run. This is a significant concern, as the company will not reap any benefits from hiring these people if they head to greener pastures the first chance they get.

6.2.3 These Workers Are Often More Loyal to Their Employers

Employers' fears might be prompted by data showing that the average American readily switches from job to job—partaking in, on average, as many as "seven careers in a lifetime" (Bialik, 2010). According to the

Bureau of Labor Statistics, the median number of years that employees remain with the same company is less than five (BLS, "Tenure," 2012). However, I believe their fears are misplaced.

For one thing, the data is likely skewed by teenagers and people attending college, who might switch employers several times in a short period of time (Bialik, 2010). Regardless, in my experience, high-potential candidates are usually less willing to hire on with a new employer, even when they obtain the desired training. There are several reasons for this hesitancy, which include:

- Their feelings of gratitude to their current employers for "giving them a chance," when no one else would . . .
- They might have the skills but still not possess the credentials. As a result, other companies might not be willing to hire them.
- For other reasons, they tend to be more loyal to the companies that brought them onboard and provided the requisite training.

In fact, I would argue that, for these reasons, high-potential candidates might be the least likely to bail on a company, as long as they are somewhat satisfied with the corporate culture and their level of remuneration. By contrast, it makes sense that employees, who come in with the perfect credentials and experience would be the most likely switch companies if the opportunity arises. After all, these individuals have both the incentives and the requisite backgrounds to "play the field."

6.2.4 Personal Case Studies—My Interactions with High-Potential Employees Who Lacked Field Experience or Training

My first job out of college, I worked for a small healthcare company in which management routinely took a chance on high-potential candidates. In some cases, these hires did not work out; however, in many more instances, the individuals would perform exceptionally well (or at least at an above-average level). Some of these people would go on to become managers or even directors with the organization. On the whole, they also proved exceedingly loyal to the corporation; they stayed for many years—and, in some cases, well over a decade. The company relied on this talent to grow its business. Over the years, it increased both the number of its employees and its revenues many times over. The owners eventually sold the company to a much larger firm for a significant sum of money.

I have heard of many more such success stories, where healthcare organizations utilized raw, untapped talent to great effect. Of course, not all healthcare organizations will reap the same level of benefits from these hires. However, my experience leads me to believe that, in many cases, it behooves healthcare executives and managers to at least consider bringing some of these high-potential candidates aboard—even ones with only high school diplomas.

6.3 Record Everything in a Database

As I noted in the last chapter, healthcare HR staff and management should try to record all candidate information in one database. My previous suggestions hold true for both the initial and final vetting processes. At the same time, they should seek to quantify the data, whenever possible (previous chapter).

Healthcare companies will want to keep this data on file for a number of important reasons. For one thing, HR staff and management can assay the data to help them identify excellent candidates and, later in the process, to more objectively analyze the strengths and weaknesses of finalists. They can also utilize the data to help them expedite their search for potential hires when the position opens up again in the future. Perhaps most importantly, healthcare organizations can use the information that they collect during all three stages of the hiring process to help them determine what types of candidates are best suited to particular roles in the company.

Perhaps some healthcare organizations, working with their applicant tracking systems (ATS) providers, already perform these assays. However, none of the organizations that I have been affiliated with have utilized candidate tracking information to help them in identifying ideal employee characteristics for certain job types. In fact, many companies do not perform any type of objective, empirical analysis on this subject. Instead, they rely on the knowledge that their human HR staff and management personnel have procured over their work lives.

Before continuing with the discussion about candidate databases, I think it might be worthwhile to take a second to focus on why healthcare organizations should expend resources in creating and maintaining these databases, when they possess competent, long-time employees who are adept at locating talent.

Healthcare organizations, and indeed all companies, build up a knowledge and experience base over time, often through trial and error. In many cases, this accumulated wisdom is almost entirely ensconced within the minds of its individual employees (Mort, 2001, 222). To put this in HR terms, a healthcare organization might be very good at identifying talent for particular positions because its HR employees and hiring managers are long-time employees; they have been in their positions long enough to develop an intimate understanding of their particular corporate culture, as well as the specific demands of each job type.

Healthcare organizations that rely too much on individuals to keep and maintain the corporate knowledge base can pay a heavy price when these people retire or transfer to another corporation. At the same time, it might be difficult for all pertinent staff within a company to share in the benefits of this knowledge (Clarke & Rollo, 2001, 208–209). From an HR perspective, one hiring manager might be great at identifying talent, but he or she does not pass this knowledge onto managers in other departments.

Of course, management at most healthcare companies are cognizant of these shortfalls. It is why they often codify this knowledge (Contractor, 2000, 246–247). In the HR realm, healthcare organizations will rely on their HR staff and managers to create detailed job descriptions. These documents will include assessments of the skills required to perform the job and the tasks related to the position. Managers and HR staff might even include some basic personality notations, such as "employees should be willing to engage customers."

From my experience in the healthcare world, I believe that it might be possible for companies to derive even more specific inferences. Further, I believe that they can use the data they collect during the hiring process to help them better refine their assessments for each position. I believe that this is possible because not only are certain types of people better suited for some jobs than for others (a known fact that everyone would agree on), but individuals also exhibit certain tendencies that reflect their personalities, experiences, and skills. Many psychologists would agree with my assessment (McCrae, 2010, 57–64).

To bring the topic back to the subject at hand, healthcare organizations that maintain a detailed, searchable, quantifiable, and comparable database on candidates can use statistical assays, such as regressions, to see if they can ascertain any correlations between successful (or unsuccessful) hires and application patterns. Perhaps successful employees have things in common that would not appear anywhere except on the initial application forms. On the other hand, maybe all of the unsuccessful hires had a tendency to exhibit certain traits during the interview process. Unless HR staff undertake these analyses, they will not be able to empirically confirm any of their hunches. At the same time, they can use statistics to help them transfer some of their personal knowledge (hunches/intuition) into written records that are readily accessible by other, pertinent employees.

Of course, healthcare organizations that choose to assay the data in this way will incur costs. They also run the risk that their analyses will not turn up any meaningful correlations. At the same time, if these companies can identify just a few statistically significant correlations, they might be able to use them to greatly enhance their hiring processes. Given the cost of just one bad hire, it would behoove healthcare organizations, if nothing else, to run pilot assays for a few, select positions. If the pilots generate successful data, then the companies can expand the data analysis further.

6.4 Testing

Potential hires can manipulate, embellish, or otherwise misrepresent almost any aspect of their applications. They can falsely claim to possess certain skills, experience, or credentials. Underwhelming candidates can often posit references who speak in glowing terms about these individuals' abilities and potential. Employers cannot trust high school and college grades, as institutions vary widely in how they assess students (though HR staff and management should put value in an applicant's class rank) (Pollio, N.D.). However, as long as companies utilize proper protocols, they will find that applicants' test scores provide an objective, clear picture of their abilities—at least in certain areas.

I think that it is important for healthcare organizations either to test applicants or to have those individuals submit tests from non-affiliated third parties (SAT, GRE, etc.). Organizations can use testing information to help them develop an objective overview of a candidate's current intellectual strengths and weaknesses, as well as his or her potential (I will discuss this issue in more detail in the next chapter). They can also test for key skills that are relevant to the particular job.

Healthcare organizations do not have to take this step during the initial round. They can wait until later in the process. However, if the healthcare organizations can utilize test information at this stage, it might prove useful to them in helping to eliminate candidates. At the same time, depending on how the companies handle testing during this phase, they might need to test the individuals again at the final stage. Namely, if companies utilize non-proctored exams, even ones with strict time limits, they cannot guarantee against cheating. In this case, they will want to test the mid-round candidates, or at the very least the finalists, again, in a proctored setting.

Some companies contract with third-party vendors to create specialized tests that all applicants must take. Examples can include typing tests, as well as tests that are designed to determine a person's familiarity with key software, such as Microsoft Word and Excel. Other firms utilize non-specialized math, verbal, logic/I.Q. tests. In my experience, companies that use these tests to filter out candidates during the initial vetting process often allow the individuals to take the tests from their home computers, where they are not proctored. All of these tests are (or should) be timed.

Many healthcare organizations cannot afford to pay vendors to test all of their applicants. If they still want to ensure that they utilize testing data in their initial candidate assays, they can create their own tests. A healthcare organization can rely on a key employee, with expertise or knowledge in a certain area, to create its tests. The company can, all things considered, often save a significant amount of money if it is able to develop tests in-house. Healthcare management will find some tests easier than others to create. For instance, if a company is testing a candidate's basic math skills, it might not be hard for that organization's staff to create tests of addition, multiplication, square roots, fractions, and so forth. (see Figure 6.1) It might be much more difficult for them to assay an individual's knowledge of healthcare laws (due to the difficulty in creating questions that carry equal weight/difficulty).

If a healthcare organization wants to take this step, it should first identify staff who possess a keen knowledge of the areas it wants to test. The company might preferably seek out ex-educators or individuals who serve as adjunct professors at local universities and community colleges. These people would have an intimate knowledge of testing processes. Next, it would have these staff members create a large number of questions—perhaps as many as 100. They should rank each question as to difficulty,

Sample Healthcare Organization
Open Position #31
Company/Job-Specific Exam
Quantitative Section

Instructions: You have 25 minutes to complete 30 multiple choice questions. Please choose the best answer to each question. Do not spend too much time on any one answer. These queries pertain to actual work-related tasks that you will be required to perform if you are chosen for this job.

Question #1: Your department has, on behalf of a client, billed Insurance A for 300 test strips. The insurance company has allowed 3/5 of your total charges. It has paid 100% of its allowed amount. Assuming your price (billed to Insurance A), per 100 strips, is $37.95, how much do you receive from Insurance A?

A. $68.31
B. $56.93
C. $70.00
D. None of the above

Question #2: . . . .

Figure 6.1   An example of a type of test that can be created in-house by even the smallest healthcare organizations.

using a number system, for example, "3 = hard, 2 = medium, 1 = easy." Finally, they have to determine how many of these each candidate will receive, as well as the time that they will give the applicants to complete the queries.

Healthcare HR staff should make sure that, at a minimum:

- The testing packet contains a fairly sizeable number of questions. Each candidate will only see a small number of these queries. By taking this step, companies make it more difficult for individuals to cheat, via sharing answers to questions online.
- The questions are weighted by difficulty level. As I noted previously, it will be easier for staff to accurately weight some tests than others. One can readily create equal weight addition questions, for example, there is little difference in difficulty levels between "8 + 7 = 15" and "9 + 3 = 12." In other cases, this task will be difficult. However, staff must try to do the best job that they can in this area. If they weight

the questions incorrectly, they will not be able to accurately compare individual candidate's scores.

- The tests are timed. This is a must-do step, as it deters cheating.

Once a healthcare organization has created a test, the organization will need to add it to the applicant module. If it utilizes a third-party ATS service, it can work with this service to create the testing program module and integrate it into the application site. If the company has created its own site, or it is working with a web developer/designer, it will need to create a module that (a) integrates with the application system; (b) will randomly choose a set number of questions from each of the weighted classes; (c) will accurately time the tests; and (d) will collect the data, grade the tests, and remit the grades to the candidate's profile, as well as to the general database.

Some healthcare organizations might not want to create their own tests or pay a third-party vendor for a test set. At the same time, they might still want to use test information to help them eliminate candidates during the initial vetting stage. These organizations could try to make use of shareware or free, online tests, such as tests of typing speed. At the same time, they can require that candidates submit scores from a test such as the SAT, GRE, LSAT, or GMAT.

The aforementioned tests have their weaknesses, and some would argue that they are also biased against certain groups (Anonymous, 2007). At the same time, these tests do provide a fairly objective, comparable measure of individual aptitude in certain key areas. The one drawback is that each of these tests, with the exception of the SAT and GRE (which basically measure the same things), focuses either on different cognitive abilities or on different aspects of these skills. However, that should not stop HR staffs from using these measures. They just have to keep the differences in these tests in mind when using them to assay a candidate's strengths and weaknesses.

6.5 Objectively Assess a Candidate's Verbal Reasoning Abilities

I believe that all healthcare organizations, regardless of their size or resource base, should test the applicants who make it past the initial assays.

However, it would be cost prohibitive for many of these companies to test all of the initial applicants. With that said, there is a way that HR staff at these organizations can assess verbal skills.

Once HR staff have eliminated the applications that do not meet their basic criteria, they can often, via a quick scan, assess a candidate's writing skills (which usually directly relate to his or her verbal reasoning skills). Obviously, an individual whose application contains numerous grammatical errors, especially ones that involve issues with sentence structure, has demonstrated either an inattention to detail or an inability to write well. However, even a person who has had someone else edit the document will sometimes still display tendencies that should raise red flags for the reader.

For one thing, the HR staff member should notate an application that does not utilize a diverse array of words. If the applicant constantly uses the same words over and over again, it might indicate that his or her vocabulary is limited. In my experience, individuals who have difficulty diversifying their text also often (but not always) exhibit other writing-related issues.

Other things that HR staff could look out for:

- The candidate might use words that do not make sense within the context of the application.
- He or she might have difficulty in creating coherent narratives. For instance, the individual might posit ideas out of order, or she or he might place information in illogical places.
- The application may contain more than one writing style, which might mean that the candidate had other people fill out the application.

In some cases, HR might not need to assess a candidate's writing abilities because the job does not require individuals to possess highly developed verbal reasoning skills. At the same time, HR should not necessarily dismiss an application just because it contains any of the above issues. However, if the job requires good communication, writing, or verbal reasoning skills, an HR staff member will want to note these issues (for reference in the next round of vetting). If the application contains the aforementioned errors and has any other issues, then HR staff might consider eliminating the applicant from consideration at the initial vetting stage.

6.6 A Managed Approach

As I noted in the last chapter, if HR staff utilize an application-only process, they can manage the information they collect. HR personnel can control the process to a greater extent. They can structure the questions in such a way that these queries will allow them to better discern good candidates from bad ones.

During the early stages in the candidate-selection process, HR staff should not worry overly much as to the authenticity of the candidate information. They can verify—or attempt to verify—the data in the next phase of the hiring process. However, they should know what key aspects they are looking for in candidates. As noted before, organizations should have structured the queries to guide applicant answers in such a way as to allow HR staff to identify a larger number of good candidates (vis-à-vis other methods that rely on keyword searches on résumés). At this point, they can leverage information technology (IT) strategies to help them pinpoint the best candidates for an open position.

Many organizations' HR staff members will create hiring checklists or utilize a mental series of checklists. During this process, they deny candidates who do not possess certain requisite skills or job experience. They might also, depending on the time available to them, review an applicant's statements to search for issues with veracity, verbal skills, and so forth. (Anonymous, 2012). This vetting process is rather crude in that it does not always cull enough people. HR staffs will then dedicate significant amounts of time to winnow the field further; however, they will not necessarily utilize any statistical methods in this process (Overman, 2012).

HR staff can reduce the secondary workload by leveraging IT to help them conduct a more rigorous, yet celeritous, applicant assay. Healthcare organizations that utilize ATS providers can work with these third-party vendors to set up the system discussed in the next few paragraphs. Some healthcare companies already likely have these systems in place. However, many healthcare companies do not utilize an initial, rigorous assay method and/or they cannot afford to utilize a third party to help them create one. I will use the next few paragraphs to demonstrate how these healthcare entities can create detailed assays using relatively common and inexpensive IT tools, such as Microsoft Excel and Access.

First, the HR staff, in coordination with management, should perform web-based and internal research to determine what characteristics are most important for success for any given job. They should then rank these characteristics by their predicative value—the correlation between the trait and an employee's work results. HR can then create a panel of key traits that they believe every employee will need in order to succeed. They should then use weighted means to come up with a relative value for each trait. HR staff might also want to create a formula that further combines the trait with a measure of time. For instance, HR might note that, over the last 15 years, employees who have succeeded at job A* have all had X experience. At the same time, workers with five years of X experience perform __ % better than individuals who possess less than five years' experience (see Figure 6.2).

A healthcare organization can work with a web developer to create a program that searches for these traits and a corresponding number (e.g., years), within the text, and posits the information into an Access or Excel database that has been pre-programmed to translate this information into a worker score. HR staff can then sort the candidates by overall score. At the same time, they can view all of the candidates' sub-scores.

At first, management and HR might have difficulty in quantifying these characteristics. They might also have problems in obtaining all of the necessary information. Additionally, a healthcare company will have to expend at least some resources—lost opportunity costs for managers, web design and program-related costs, labor costs, and so forth—to undertake this project. Finally, whenever a corporation quantifies a process, it loses some of its ability to identify beneficial outliers and to act holistically.

Although all of the foregoing are true, I think that healthcare companies will benefit when they ensure that the initial hiring process—and for that matter, the entire process—is as empirical as possible. By taking this step, HR and management can eliminate some of the viewer bias, determine which variables are most important to employee success, and, over time, create a system that is more efficient and effective than a more holistic one.

Some people might argue that companies cannot utilize a quantitative system to judge candidates. Human beings are too complex and diverse. One has, therefore, to utilize a holistic approach—to capture all of a candidate's unique attributes and skills, in order to find the right employee. I do not agree with that viewpoint. I believe that one can use statistics to identify key variables that will lead to success in certain positions and to determine their relative strength. Most managers and executives, if they stop to think about it, would agree with this point. After all, they use

Sample Healthcare Organization
Specific Position in the Accounts Receivable Department
Data Derived from Hires — October 10, 2001–January 18, 2013
Note: Information Comes from Candidate/Employee Tracking Information

New Hires 10/10/2001-01/18/2013	Quantitative Score on the Entrance Exam (0%-19.49% = 1, 19.5%-39.49% = 2, 39.5%-59.49% = 3, 59.5%-79.49% = 4, 79.5%-100% = 5)	Medicare Billing Experience Noted on the Employment Application Section (No = 0, Yes = 1)	Used the Term "Organized" to Describe Himself/Herself on the Employment Application (No = 0, Yes = 1)	Performance Reviews (1 = Poor, 5 = Excellent) Averaged over Number of Years with Company and Rounded	Promoted During Tenure with Company (5 = Three Promotions, 3 = Two Promotions, 2 = One Promotion, 0 = No Promotions)	Fired or Laid Off? (5 = No, 0 = Yes)
1	5	0	1	4	5	5
2	3	1	1	3	2	5
3	1	1	0	1	0	0
4	4	0	1	3	2	5
5	2	0	0	1	0	0
6	3	1	1	3	0	5
7	4	1	1	4	3	5
8	4	0	1	3	0	5
9	3	1	1	2	0	0
10	2	0	0	2	0	0
11	3	1	1	3	0	5
12	3	1	1	3	0	5
13	5	0	1	4	3	5
14	4	1	1	4	3	5

Figure 6.2   This dataset is simplistic. A real data sheet would likely contain many more columns and lines. Nonetheless, it does a good job of denoting some of the ways in which healthcare companies can utilize candidate hiring data, in combination with employee statistics, to identify key traits that denote successful workers in certain job positions. Note how a healthcare analyst can, with the help of statistics, identify interrelationships between categories or determine the cohort's medians and means in certain key areas.

empirical systems to monitor and control human activities—think productivity, patient safety, patient satisfaction, and marketing.

In Chapters 5 and 6, I have argued that healthcare organizations need to move away from passive recruitment systems that allow applicants to dictate the style, type, and quantity of information that they remit to HR. Healthcare companies need to replace them with systems that they control—from beginning to end. The HR staff and other pertinent personnel at these facilities also have to place a greater reliance on quantitative methods to assay applicants.

If one stops to think about the issue, it makes sense for healthcare companies to closely manage the initial candidate data collection and vetting processes. After all, these organizations have had success in other areas, such as supply chain management, when they decided to closely oversee the processes instead of letting external factors (or individual employees' desires) dictate their purchases. And even the most talented HR staff are compromised by their need to review a large number of applications quickly—sometimes in a matter of seconds (Giang, 2012). In that environment, I would argue that a healthcare HR staff, which manages the incoming data and utilizes objective, quantitative measures to assay applications, will have better success, over the long run, than its non-organized peers.

References

Anonymous. (2007, August). The SAT: Questions and Answers. *Fair Test*. Retrieved from http://fairtest.org/facts/satfact.htm.

Anonymous. (2012). How to Review a Résumé. Staffing and Recruiting Essentials. Retrieved from http://www.staffing-and-recruiting-essentials. com/How-To-Review-A-Resume.html#axzz38HnTgWZY.

Bialik, C. (2010, September). Seven Careers in Our Lifetime? Think Twice, Researchers Say. *The Wall Street Journal*. Retrieved from http://online.wsj. com/news/articles/SB10001424052748704206804575468162805877990.

Bureau of Labor Statistics. (2012, September). Employee Tenure Summary. U.S. Department of Labor. Retrieved from http://www.bls.gov/news.release/ tenure.nr0.htm.

Bureau of Labor Statistics. (2012, February). The Recession of 2007–2009. U.S. Department of Labor. Retrieved from http://www.bls.gov/spotlight/2012/ recession/pdf/recession_bls_spotlight.pdf.

Bureau of Labor Statistics. (2014, July). Economy at a Glance. U.S. Department of Labor. Retrieved from http://www.bls.gov/eag/eag.us.htm.

Cappelli, P. (2011, October). Why Companies Aren't Getting the Employees They Need. *The Wall Street Journal.* Retrieved from http://online.wsj.com/news/articles/SB10001424052970204422404576596630897409182.

Clarke, T., & Rollo, C. (2001). Corporate Initiatives in Knowledge Management. *Education and Training* 43 (4/5), 206–214. Retrieved from ProQuest.

Contractor, F. (2000). Valuing Corporate Knowledge and Intangible Assets: Some General Principles. *Knowledge and Process Management* 7(4), 242. Retrieved from ProQuest.

Cox, L. (2012, February 9). 5 Experts Answer: Can Your IQ Change? *Live Science.* Retrieved from http://www.livescience.com/36143-iq-change-time.html.

Ehrlich, R. (2003). Are People Getting Smarter or Dumber? Skeptic 10(2), 50–53, 55–61. Retrieved from ProQuest.

Giang, V. (2012). What Recruiters Look At During The 6 Seconds They Spend On Your Resume. *Business Insider.* Retrieved from http://www.businessinsider.com/heres-what-recruiters-look-at-during-the-6-seconds-they-spend-on-your-resume-2012-4.

Goleman, D. (1998). What Makes a Leader. *Harvard Business Review* 76(6), 93–94. Retrieved from ProQuest.

Holland, K. (2014, May). Another Rude Awakening for Millennials. *CNBC.* Retrieved from http://www.cnbc.com/id/101660087.

Kemper, C. (1999). EQ vs. IQ. *Communication World* 16(9), 15–19. Retrieved from ProQuest.

Llopis, G. (2011, August). America's Most Wanted: What Diversity Can Do for Business. *Forbes.* Retrieved from http://www.forbes.com/sites/glennllopis/2011/08/29/americas-most-wanted-what-diversity-can-do-for-business/.

Mayer J. D., et al. (2012). Improving Emotional Knowledge and Social Effectiveness. University of New Hampshire. Retrieved from http://www.unh.edu/emotional_intelligence/ei%20Improve/ei%20Rasing%20EI.htm.

McCrae, R. R. (2010). The Place of the FFM in Personality Psychology. *Psychological Inquiry* 21, 57–64. Retrieved from http://www.psychometric-assessment.com/wp   content/uploads/2013/01/Five-Factor-Model-in-Personality-Psychology-Psychological-Inquiry-2010.pdf.

Mort, J. (2001). Nature, Value and Pursuit of Reliable Corporate Knowledge. *Journal of Knowledge Management* 5(3), 222–230. Retrieved from ProQuest.

Nisbett, R. E. et al. (2012). Intelligence: New Findings and Theoretical Developments. *American Psychological Association* 67(2), 130–159. Retrieved from http://www.apa.org/pubs/journals/releases/amp-67-2-130.pdf.

Overman, S. (2012, May). Use the Right Data to Make Hiring Decisions. *Society for Human Resource Management*. Retrieved from http://www.shrm.org/hrdisciplines/staffingmanagement/articles/pages/userightdatatomakehires.aspx.

Pollio, H. R. (N.D.). Grading Systems. *Education Encyclopedia*. Retrieved from http://education.stateuniversity.com/pages/2017/Grading-Systems.html.

Slack, T. (2014, March). The Great Recession and America's Underemployment Crisis. *Scholars Strategy Network*. Retrieved from http://www.scholarsstrategynetwork.org/sites/default/files/ssn_key_findings_slack_and_jenseiiiin_on_underemployment_and_the_great_recession1.pdf.

Chapter Seven

Suggestions for Improving HR's Direct Hiring Systems— The Intermediate/ Final Stages

In Chapter 5, I broke the candidate selection process down into three key stages, including the first contact between the potential hire and the corporation, the initial candidate vetting process, and the interview/ secondary vetting process. In Chapters 5 and 6, I focused my attention on the initial two steps in this cycle. In this chapter, I will devote my attention to the interview/vetting process.

At this point, I think it is worth remembering that one can break this final stage in the process into a number of steps. If I were creating a human resources (HR) textbook, I would likely take that action. I would then carefully delineate and organize each of these steps. However, that is not the goal of the book. At the same time, most (if not all) of the readers of this text will be familiar enough with the hiring process to allow me to forego such an analysis. Suffice it to say that the final step in the three-part process— the candidate interview/vetting process—can itself be broken down into a number of phases. At the same time, learned individuals might disagree as to which specific components belong to this stage and which ones are part of the two earlier steps.

I acknowledge these issues; however, they are not important here. What does matter is that the interview/vetting step, regardless of any other considerations, represents the intermediate and end stages in the hiring process. And just like with a chess player, a healthcare organization needs to adjust its overall methodologies and goals. It needs to create a game plan that is designed to find the best person not only for the specific job but for the company. That is an important distinction, as it requires sometimes myopic HR staff and department managers to think holistically—to take into account not only the needs of their own particular departments but also the interests of the corporation as a whole.

In this chapter, I will devote some time to this issue. I posit some strategies that healthcare leaders can use to help them, as well as other key personnel at their respective companies, to think from a big picture standpoint when vetting potential hires. I also look at some of the key, corporate-wide needs that can be satisfied by hiring the right type of people in certain situations. Finally, I touch on some of the questions that executives, HR staff, hiring managers, and other personnel can utilize in helping them to identify the best candidate from among a short list of applicants.

Although healthcare corporations have to adjust their strategies to meet the new demands imposed upon them by the later phases in the hiring process, they still need to adhere to some overall norms. With this in mind, I will reiterate some of the themes that I introduced in the previous two chapters. I will further develop them in this section and—in some cases—demonstrate how a healthcare leader can alter them to better fit with the requirements of the various phases in the candidate interview/secondary vetting process.

I think that executives, managers, and other personnel from healthcare companies at all stages in their growth process will benefit from reading this chapter. However, I think employees of smaller healthcare companies will be especially pleased with the information in the proceeding paragraphs. That is because I discuss some of the unique challenges that smaller healthcare organizations face as they struggle to grow their businesses while, at the same time, keeping costs down. I have posited a number of the suggestions in this chapter with an eye to these types of healthcare firms.

Perhaps most importantly, I have tried to include information in this chapter that is innovative—or at least that departs from the hackneyed information that one can find in numerous texts. I have drawn on my years of experience in the healthcare field—and especially my familiarity with small healthcare firms—to aid me in positing viable, sometimes cutting edge, ideas that healthcare leaders can use to help their companies succeed. When appropriate, I have supplemented my own knowledge with key research or commentary from other healthcare experts.

7.1 What Are You Hiring the Person to Do?

When a healthcare company's management decides to hire individuals for new positions they almost always ask, "Why are we hiring an individual at this time?" The organization's leaders (or whoever is in charge of authorizing the hire) might not consciously think about this topic; instead, they automatically seek to hire a new employee to replace one that has vacated a position via promotion, termination, or resignation. Even in those cases, management has still asked the question—at least implicitly—and answered it.

In many cases, hiring managers and HR staff, if pressed on the question, would respond by stating that they want to hire the right person for the position. That is the reason that many of them create (or ask their employees to create) detailed descriptions of each job, which include elements such as the job's tasks and the requisite employee skills and experience. These men and women will then spend hours reviewing applications, interviewing candidates, and taking other steps to identify the right hire for that position.

7.1.1 Two Questions to Keep in Mind When Looking for New Hires

Obviously, healthcare leaders who are involved in the hiring process want to find the right people to fill open positions. At the same time, I think that they should also ask two other important questions: "How far can this applicant advance in the company?" and "Can this candidate fill any other job roles, if necessary?" I began this discussion in the last chapter, when I focused on the initial vetting process. I will continue it here and focus on aspects that accord with the intermediate and final stages of the candidate selection process.

Hiring managers, at least, often ponder these two questions when they are considering candidates. However, they too often approach the topic from the wrong perspective. Instead of favoring candidates with a diverse range of skills and a high degree of potential, they often prefer individuals with narrow skill sets and limited potential. This makes sense from the hiring managers' perspectives. They want to bring in people who, while competent and capable at their positions, will remain in the department for a long period of time. These individuals naturally would rather refrain from having to deal with the all of the issues that derive from employee turnover.

Of course, not all hiring managers think this way. Some of them are more than happy to hire a candidate with the potential to move up rapidly in the organization or who is likely to switch jobs (within the company) within six months to a year. At other times, when a healthcare organization contains plenty of high-performing or high-potential talent, a hiring manager is right in focusing on candidates who are best suited for his or her department.

In short, a hiring manager, when left to his or her own devices, will often make self-interested hiring decisions, which place the needs of his or her individual departments above those of the company as a whole. Sometimes, this motivation is valid, such as when the company has a large number of high-performing or high-potential candidates. However, in many cases, the manager's decision negatively impacts the company as a whole because it deprives the organization of needed talent or flexibility.

7.2 Create Proactive Action Plans

For this reason, I believe that upper-level management at all healthcare companies should have a plan of action in place that ensures that their organizations hire a certain percentage of high-performing, high-potential, and highly flexible workers. C-suite personnel can create these plans to fit the needs of their particular corporations. As an example, a large healthcare entity with a strong brand and plenty of in-house and redundant talent can focus its attention on identifying extremely gifted individuals. On the other hand, executives at a smaller company that does not have a lot of built-in redundancy might choose to more closely oversee a larger portion of the process.

Many healthcare organizations have already created action plans to help them identify and fast track superb talent. Other corporations sponsor dedicated hiring and training programs for high-potential or high-performing individuals. For instance, Hospital Corporation of America (HCA) sponsors COO, CNO (chief networking officers), and CFO training programs, which seek to identify and groom high-potential individuals for these c-suite posts [Hospital Corporation of America (HCA), 2014]. As another example, Medical Facilities of America (MFA), a long-term care organization based in Roanoke, Virginia, has a program in place to train "future leaders" for administrator positions at its network of long-term care facilities (MFA, 2014).

7.3 Small Healthcare Organizations Should Think Like Baseball Teams—Focus on Flexibility

At the same time, many healthcare organizations, especially mid-sized and small ones, do not possess either external (e.g., dedicated programs that seek out high-potential/flexible candidates and train them) or internal programs to identify and onboard high-potential or highly flexible employees. In the next few paragraphs, I will demonstrate why it is especially necessary for small companies to create action plans for hiring a certain percentage of these types of workers. I will then posit a sample plan. Many of the elements in this discussion also apply to mid-sized and large healthcare entities.

In my experience, small healthcare organizations often do not have a lot of redundancy at key positions. At the same time, these corporations place a significant amount of responsibilities on the shoulders of even lower-level employees. Many of these companies run on tight margins and have to get things done with less personnel. As a result, a small healthcare organization can suffer a severe setback when an employee either leaves the company unexpectedly or has to take an extended sabbatical. This issue becomes a much bigger problem if management is not able to temporarily place another of its employees in this job position.

One can gain an understanding for the scope of this problem by using a baseball analogy. In order for it to win, the baseball team needs all of its key personnel—the pitcher, the infield, the outfield—to play well. Occasionally, a key team member will get injured. Assume in this case that the team's first baseman gets hurt. If the team cannot replace him (or her) with someone who can at least do an adequate job covering first base, then the team will struggle to win games. That is why baseball teams ensure that at least a few of the players on the bench—the utility players—can play multiple positions, if and when needed (Anonymous, 2014).

Small companies, like baseball teams, have to ensure that their organizations contain at least a few utility players. They should, as a further step, make sure that they have at least one utility personnel for each key corporate position. To borrow an old baseball cliché, "They need to make sure that they have all of their bases covered."

Of course, management in small healthcare companies can cross-train individuals to ensure that their workers possess a diverse range of talents. In fact, I would argue that businesses should conduct this type of training. However, it takes both time and resources [in full-time equivalents (FTEs), lost-opportunity costs, etc.] to implement and maintain these types of programs. Small companies will find it much more efficient to cross-train employees who already possess many of the requisite skills and experience or who are quick, adaptive learners. These individuals are the very same types that I recommend hiring.

I should note one other reason as to why small healthcare companies want to ensure that at least a percentage of their hires meet my standards for flexibility and high potential. To wit, many (but not all) small organizations rely on their workers to perform a wider array of tasks than their peers at larger corporations. For instance, a large hospital chain might allocate revenue cycle management tasks, such as insurance billing, insurance appeals, patient records management, and patient collections, to separate teams. A smaller healthcare organization, on the other hand, might require that its accounts receivable team members be able to perform all of those tasks on a daily basis. In these scenarios, small healthcare companies need employees who are intelligent and adaptive, and who ideally possess a breadth of experiences (see Figure 7.1).

The Ideal Flex Employee

The Ultimate Utility Person

* Can perform a number of different roles at the department level
* Is capable – in a pinch – of helping out in other departments
* Can take on multiple roles in two or more departments when the company is short-staffed

A Flex Player

* Is willing to adjust his or her work schedule when necessary
* Can work nights and weekends
* Can be trusted to work by himself/herself at the site or at home

*High Intelligence Quotient (I.Q.)
*Excellent 'People Skills'
*A Diverse Array of Interests
*A Wide Range of Experiences

A People Person

* Gets along well with most personality types
* Can easily switch roles – from leader to team member to follower
* Is a person that others trust

A Cosmopolitan Outlook

* Can see the big picture – how the various job roles and/or departments interconnect
* Is also adept at completing detailed, narrowly focused tasks and is successful in handling mundane, everyday occurrences
* Can easily switch from thinking about the big picture to analyzing the minutiae

Figure 7.1 Some of the key traits and abilities of flexible employees.

7.4 Small Healthcare Companies— Key in on a Candidate's Potential

In my opinion, small healthcare companies also need to focus on ensuring that at least a certain percentage of their hires have the potential to move up the corporate ladder. In other words, these organizations should make sure that they hire people—at all levels except c-suite positions—who possess the skills to advance out of their current jobs, once they obtain the necessary experience.

There are a number of reasons why small companies should actively seek to hire high-potential people. I have listed them below; however, keep in mind that all of these factors are interrelated.

- Small healthcare organizations often have distinctive corporate cultures. As a result, they operate more efficiently when they can promote from within the ranks. Simply put, current employees are already cognizant of their respective company's values and ways of doing things. Unlike outside hires, they can quickly take over the reins of a new job, as long as they can master the new position's tasks (Adams, 2012).
- Small healthcare companies are often running on tight budgets. Therefore, it makes sense for them, whenever possible, to promote internally rather than try to hire someone to fill a mid-level or specialist role. By taking this step, companies can often save thousands of dollars. This is money that they would have otherwise thrown into the external hiring process—factoring in all of the costs of hiring someone from outside the organization for a mid-level or specialist position (Aerotek, 2014; Thompson, 2012).
- According to a Forbes article, research demonstrates that "external hires made 18% more than the internal promotes in the same jobs" (Adams, 2012). This is a huge boon to smaller companies, who are often running on shoestring budgets.
- At the same time, small healthcare organizations do not have the luxury of hiring thousands of employees in the hopes that a few of these individuals blossom into middle/upper management or specialist-level material. They have, at most, a thousand people, and often less than a hundred individuals, on their payrolls. As a result, smaller healthcare companies have to take a more proactive stance when it comes to identifying and hiring high-potential individuals.

- All of these issues are compounded by the fact that many small healthcare companies are in the initial stages of their growth trajectories. They are constantly growing (or at least that is what one shoots for at this stage). However, these companies do not exhibit consistent growth. They sometimes have to ramp up very quickly when, for instance, they secure a new, large contract or client. In these instances, the companies that can quickly fill any important, new openings with internal staff will perform better.

7.5 A Hiring Game Plan for Small Companies

C-suite and upper management at small healthcare companies, working in conjunction with HR, should create a blueprint for managing the hiring of flexible, high-potential, and high-performance employees. Healthcare leaders at each company will need to create a plan that matches their specific organization's unique corporate structure, culture, and needs. Companies with flatter organizational structures will often require a larger percentage of adaptive, high-potential employees. By contrast, organizations that are structured along hierarchical lines, and who exhibit a small ratio of managers/specialists to entry-level employees, might not need nearly as many of these types of employees. Despite these differences, there are some techniques that executives and other key personnel at all healthcare organizations can use to help guide their hiring strategies.

- **The leadership team, working with HR, should create a meta-plan of action**
  This statement might seem like an obvious one, given the discussion. However, I think that too often leaders of small (and large) healthcare organizations do not devote the time to creating a conscious, careful plan of action. Instead, they express their desires to subordinates (e.g., middle managers and specialists) and rely on these people to get the job done.

  That type of management style works in some cases; however, in this instance, self-interest, inertia, and similar issues might foil such a strategy. Therefore, leaders want to ensure that they create a meta-plan of action. They will want to ensure that this guide contains specific goals and methods for measuring success or failure.

- **The c-suite and upper management need to champion the initiative**

  If one searches online libraries and the Internet, he or she will find numerous articles, books, and guides that demonstrate a strong correlation between a project's success and the amount of backing it receives from management (Czarnowski, 2008, 44–45; Kehoe, 2014, 69–70). I can personally attest to the validity of this one.

  One would think that healthcare leaders would have learned this lesson a long time ago and that management in most companies would provide continued support to projects that they green light, as long as these programs prove useful. However, in my experience, leaders too often latch onto an idea, push to turn it into reality, and then lose interest in it after a short span of time.

  One could posit a number of reasons as to why healthcare leaders sometimes initially support projects, only to lose interest in them a few weeks or months later. However, regardless of the factors behind the phenomenon, it does happen. Healthcare leaders who want to implement my suggested, holistic changes to their hiring schemes should make sure that it does not happen in this instance.

- **Create a culture that supports hiring flexible, high-potential individuals**

  Healthcare leaders need to create a culture that supports this hiring strategy. In small companies, they can achieve this goal by talking with directors and managers to make sure they understand the plan. Additionally, the leaders might want to ensure that both mid- and upper-level management have access to written guidelines regarding hiring. The leadership should also, on occasion, remind everyone about the hiring strategies that their respective companies have adopted. Finally, and perhaps most importantly, they need to ensure that their healthcare corporations properly incentivize directors and managers.

  Almost everyone who ·is reading this chapter can point to at least one occasion (and probably numerous instances) where upper management implemented a new policy or set of procedures but did not properly incentivize workers to adhere to them. In most of these cases, the company's leaders probably did not see the results that they anticipated. This issue is no different. Healthcare executives have to ensure that hiring managers are not penalized for putting the needs of their companies over those of their individual departments.

7.6 Place Everything into a Database

As I noted in the last chapter, all healthcare organizations, regardless of size, should utilize a candidate database. It should be designed to allow pertinent staff to access individual candidate profiles/information and, at the same time, to be able to aggregate, collate, and compare the data vis-à-vis other candidates (or even the entire database of all applicants). HR and other staff involved in the hiring process might not be able to posit all applicant information into this system. However, they should try to place as large a percentage of it as possible in the database. Additionally, the personnel involved in the hiring process should try to quantify as much of the material as possible.

7.7 Adopt a Paperless Hiring System

Regardless of whether a healthcare corporation chooses to utilize a candidate database, it should ensure that the hiring process is as paper free as possible. To this end, HR staff should require that candidates submit all materials electronically. In the event that this is not possible, HR staff members should scan and digitize any paper documents that they receive. Everyone who is involved in the hiring process should have the ability to access pertinent candidate information from any location. These individuals also need to possess the ability to edit key documents.

Numerous experts have expounded on the benefits of moving to a paperless environment. Hospitals, doctors offices, and other health services companies have recognized (or been forced to see) the benefits both to patients and themselves in utilizing a digitized system to maintain clinical records and other related documents (see Chapter 1). Healthcare organizations can achieve several notable advantages by digitizing the entire hiring process:

- **More Accurate Candidate Records**
  If HR staff, hiring managers, and other pertinent employees utilize a computer system for the creation and maintenance of all candidate

records, they do not have to worry about things like misplaced files and miscopied information (Frazee, 1996, 70).

- **More Powerful Statistical Assays**
  Healthcare employees will find it much easier to parse, analyze, and compare like data between different candidates—and even among the entire pool of candidates—when everything is computerized. Think about it this way: It is much easier to run regressions and other statistical assays when the requisite information is already in an electronic database.

- **More Efficient Processes**
  Healthcare organizations can potentially achieve significant efficiency gains if they utilize a hiring process that is fully digitized, as opposed to one that relies on a combination of paper files and computers. With a paperless system, HR staff and hiring managers do not need to spend time rifling through papers or scanning documents to find a phrase or topic. Instead, they can quickly locate the material online and (hopefully) use shortcuts and hotkeys, such as CTRL F, to jump right to the portion of the candidate file that interests them (Hilgen, 2000, 124–125).

- **A Number of Other Reasons**
  Healthcare companies can also leverage a number of other advantages by transitioning from a mixed electronic–paper candidate selection process to one that is entirely paperless. These benefits can run the gamut from improved security—it is much more difficult for someone to steal encrypted files than it is to snatch paper documents—to "enhanced team communication" (Frazee, 1996, 70).

- **Cost Savings Specific to HR**
  A number of business experts have assayed the potential cost savings that derive from the shift to a paperless HR system. One researcher estimates that organizations that migrate to fully electronic HR infrastructures can realize significant cost savings across the board. When viewing it just in terms of the hiring process, the researcher notes that paperless systems can cut as much as 30 percent off of "[t]he cost per hire" (Anonymous, 2003, 8).

In short, healthcare organizations can benefit from implementing and maintaining a paperless hiring process. However, few if any of the companies that I have come into contact with over the last few years have transitioned to a fully paper-free system. These corporations have ranged in size from small, 100- to 300-person organizations to companies with more than 10,000 employees. Regardless of their size, almost all of them still utilize paper documents at some point in the process. Most notably, hiring managers and other personnel involved in interviews will tend to print out the candidate files. They will make notes on the files during the interviews and then either transfer these remarks into a computer file/ email or send the paper sheets to the HR department for processing.

7.8 Corporate Culture: One Key Barrier to a Paperless Hiring System

HR staff and other key personnel at these organizations might have a variety of reasons for sticking with a mixed (paper and electronic) system, despite the fact that numerous studies have demonstrated the efficacy of going paperless. Personally, I believe that they are hesitant to go all in on electronic systems for the same reasons that doctors, nurses, and other clinical staff balked, for the longest time, at adopting full electronic medical records (EMRs). Chiefly, these individuals have a hard time letting go of traditional practices, and at the same time, they worry about the costs of such a transition (Garcia, 2010; Miller & Sim, 2004, 119–122).

There is a lot of talk in the business world about the need for corporations to be adaptive to changing environments. However, it is common knowledge in the business world that employees (including upper management) are resistant to change. That is especially true when it comes to using computers and other technology. Large numbers of healthcare workers, including many c-suite personnel, started in the business world before the technology revolution really started to get going in the 1990s and 2000s. They learned how to read and write using pen, paper, and hardbound (or softbound) textbooks (Anonymous, 2009; Stratton, 2013, 44–45).

Many of these individuals have not yet fully integrated into a technology-based society, and who can blame them? It is difficult for anyone to learn an entirely new system. And for most people, switching from a paper-based system to a paperless one is tantamount to doing just that. They not only have to learn new technologies, but they also have to change some of their old behaviors and ways of doing things (Stratton, 2013, 44–45).

7.9 Overcoming These Cultural Barriers

This issue would pose a significant hurdle if a healthcare corporation were implementing an EMR or some other, global, system that involved numerous stakeholders. In this case, healthcare leaders will most likely only have to worry about a relatively small percentage of individuals within the company—the HR staff, hiring managers, and anyone else who is directly involved in the candidate selection process.

Healthcare organizations that still utilize a number of paper-based processes in the candidate selection process will want to first switch to a paperless system. They can sign on with an ATS, or utilize the strategies I noted in the last chapter. Even when using an ATS, the healthcare organizations might still need to create some modules (mods) to account for areas the ATS does not cover. Once that is done, they would train HR staff and other key personnel to utilize the new system(s). Healthcare leaders who oversee the training can use whatever protocols are already in place to train these employees.

Most healthcare organizations can create adequate training programs to prepare relevant staff to utilize a paperless HR system. Many companies have already taken this step. The difficult part for many organizations is in keeping employees from cheating and creating shadow documents. In these instances, a worker will circumvent the paperless system by printing out documents. He or she will then handwrite notes on these paper forms and retype these notes in the system. Employees will often utilize shadow documents when they have not fully acclimated themselves to a new, electronic format. HR staff and hiring managers have several opportunities during the candidate selection process when they might be tempted to revert to old habits—to print out the documents to review and/or notate.

Healthcare leaders can implement a number of different measures to encourage HR staff and hiring managers to eschew these old habits. They could, for instance, remove the printers from HR offices and from mangers' desks. This draconian measure might solve the problem but would create a host of other, obvious concerns. Healthcare executives could also try to break their staff of the bad habits by penalizing them. I would suggest that upper management forego this practice as well. In my experience, an office that works on a penalty system tends to suffer from employee morale problems. At the same time, staff will often find a way to continue printing the forms while avoiding the prying eyes of their superiors.

In contrast to these punitive measures, healthcare executives could choose to reward hiring managers, HR staff, or other pertinent employees for cutting the cord—so to speak—with the old paper system. In my experience, people respond much more positively to this type of incentive. However, I believe that healthcare leaders can wean key staff off of their old habits without having to provide cash incentives. They can achieve these results by identifying with the needs of these employees. Here is how it might work:

- **Step 1**

  Healthcare leaders should pinpoint the areas in the hiring process where staff members tend to fall back on old paper-based habits.

- **Step 2**

  They should try to put themselves in those employees' shoes (so to speak) and identify the key factors that motivate these people to forego the electronic process in favor of the old paper system.

- **Step 3**

  Healthcare executives will want to attempt to meet the staff halfway. In other words, they should see if they can work with the information technology (IT) department and other key stakeholders to get the new technology-based systems to conform, as closely as possible, to their employees' old workflow habits and/or needs.

- **Step 4**

  Healthcare leaders should pilot these projects to see if they are effective in convincing key personnel to migrate fully to the new electronic systems. If the ideas do not work as planned, the leaders might need to come up with another solution, or they might want to tweak the current idea. Their decision in this regard will depend on factors such as project cost outlays.

Later in this chapter I will posit an example that readers of this book can use to help guide them in undertaking projects that incorporate the aforementioned steps.

7.10 Benefits Outweigh the Costs

Healthcare companies that create a paperless candidate selection process might incur significant upfront costs. This might be especially true for companies that transition a large portion of their HR processses from mixed paper–computer systems to electronic ones (a move that I will recommend in a later chapter). However, research has demonstrated that, in the long run, most companies will benefit from taking this step (Anonymous, 2003, 6–8; Sage HRMS, 2012). What is more, resource-challenged healthcare corporations can spread the e-initiative over several years in order to reduce costs (Anonymous, 2003, 6–8), or they can work out payment arrangements with third-party vendors. And healthcare organizations that do not/cannot utilize a third-party vendor might still be able to create a fully electronic hiring process by utilizing a variety of in-house programs in combination with Microsoft Access and Excel (please see the last chapter for more details on how to construct such a system).

At the same time, many healthcare organizations have already implemented hiring systems that are, technically speaking, as fully electronic as possible (excepting the fact that they might need to keep paper forms of some documents to satisfy certain legal requirements). These companies' HR systems only need to deter employees from creating shadow documents in order to become fully electronic. In those instances, the healthcare entities might not have to expend significant resources in order to complete the transition to an electronic candidate selection system. I will posit one such hypothetical example in the following section.

7.11 A Case in Point: How to Convince Hiring Managers to Go Digital

Jerry Green is the CEO of a 500+ employee, durable medical equipment (DME) supply company. His business is small enough that he can actively participate in all meetings with his directors and managers. The healthcare corporation has transitioned to a paperless system for its candidate selection process; however, Green has noticed that the hiring managers have a tendency to print out applicant materials before each interview. They will take notes on these documents during these meetings and upload the information into the computer system at a later time.

Green discusses the issue with his hiring managers at the next corporate meeting. He encourages their honest input on the issue. The managers state that they often utilize the meeting room for interviews. The meeting area does not have a computer terminal. At the same time, even if it did, the hiring managers would be loath to use it. They prefer to read the material in a horizontal to near horizontal position; they claim that they can review material faster this way. The hiring managers cannot perform this action on their desktops. Finally, the managers note that they are more comfortable, during an interview, writing out their notes than they are in typing them into a computer system. After all, many of them grew up in an age before computers became ubiquitous.

Green, though a tech nerd himself, tries to empathize with the needs of his employees. When viewing it from the hiring managers' perspectives, he can see where they might have difficulty in adhering to the company's e-hiring process. To remedy the matter, the CEO decides to buy five used tablets, at a cost of less than $350 apiece. Each of these devices comes equipped with a handwriting recognition program and stylus. He sets up a lending system, where a hiring manager and other pertinent staff can check out the tablets for use in interviews and other relevant events, such as company meetings. In creating the lending/checkout system, Green saves money, as he does not need to buy tablets for all of his managers. As a further remedy, Green authorizes the IT staff to work with a local provider to ensure that the meeting room has Wi-Fi.

Green believes that his solution will meet the needs of his hiring managers while, at the same time, closing the electronic loop. He announces his plan at the next managers' meeting and sets aside time for each manager to train on the new device. The CEO carefully monitors his staff's use of the tablets for candidate interviews and is pleased to note that, after two months, almost all of the hiring managers and the other pertinent staff members (who sit in on the panel interviews) are using the devices during the interviews. As an added bonus, some of the managers also utilize the tablets at other times, such as during conversations with vendors and at office meetings.

In this chapter, I have tailored my discussion to small healthcare companies. However, I believe that healthcare organizations of all sizes can utilize the suggestions in this chapter to help them improve their mid- and late-stage hiring procedures. Too many of these corporations, at least since the Great Recession, have taken an ultra-conservative approach to new hires. As a result, they lose out on procuring top quality talent— people who can move up the ranks to lead the corporation in the future.

Just as important, many healthcare companies—both big and small— do not fully leverage the capabilities of modern IT systems. Some healthcare leaders might feel that the necessary hardware and software are too expensive for their companies. However, by eschewing these technologies, they limit the ability of their HR infrastructures to manage the hiring process and to identify beneficial or detrimental patterns in hiring practices. Healthcare organizations are also losing out on the opportunity to store a larger portion of their HR knowledge in a digital database. As such, they are often not able to cushion the blow when a key HR staff member or other pertinent employee resigns or is fired.

References

Adams, S. (2012, April). Why Promoting From Within Usually Beats Hiring From Outside. *Forbes*. Retrieved from http://www.forbes.com/sites/susanadams/2012/04/05/why-promoting-from-within-usually-beats-hiring-from-outside/.

Aerotek. (2014). Cost per Hire Calculator. Retrieved from http://www.aerotek.com/staffing-services/staffing-resources/cost-per-hire-calculator.aspx.

Anonymous. (2003). Lose the Paper, Gain HR Efficiency—and Cut Costs. *HR Focus* 80(8), 6–8. Retrieved from ProQuest.

Anonymous. (2009). Lessons learned from a journey to EMR. *Health Management Technology* 30(11), 24–27. Retrieved from ProQuest.

Anonymous. (2014). Utility Player. Sporting Charts. Retrieved from http://www.sportingcharts.com/dictionary/mlb/utility-player.aspx.

Czarnowsky, M. (2008). Executive Development. *T + D*, 62(9), 44–45. Retrieved from ProQuest.

Frazee, V. (1996). Six Reasons for Going Paperless. *Personnel Journal* 75(11), 70. Retrieved from ProQuest.

Garcia, K. (2010, June 14). How to Switch to a Paperless Office. *Inc.* Retrieved from http://www.inc.com/guides/2010/06/switch-to-paperless-office.html.

Hilgen, D. (2000). Going Paperless. *Best's Review* 101(3), 124–127. Retrieved from ProQuest.

Hospital Corporation of America. (2014). HCA Executive Development. Retrieved from http://www.hcaexecutivedevelopment.com/.

Kehoe, B. (2014). Supply Chain: Optimization through Collaboration. *Hospitals & Health Networks* 88(7), 62–71. Retrieved from ProQuest.

Miller, R. H., & Sim, I. (2004). Physicians' Use of Electronic Medical Records: Barriers and Solutions. *Health Affairs* 23(2), 116–126. DOI: 10.1377/hlthaff.23.2.116.

Medical Facilities of America. (2014). Healthcare Administration— Future Leaders. Retrieved from http://www.mfa.net/main/careers/ job-details?id=1839.

Sage HRMS. (2012, August). The Benefits of Paperless HR: Sustainable, Cost-Effective, and Within Your Reach. Retrieved from http://www.slideshare.net/ SageHRMS/the-benefits-of-paperless-hr.

Stratton, A. (2013). Pursuing the Possibility of a Paperless Office. *Information Management* 47(5), 44–47. Retrieved from ProQuest.

Thompson, M. (2012, February). How Much Does It Cost to Hire a New Employee. Dun & Bradstreet Credibility Corp. Retrieved from http://www. dandb.com/smallbusiness/how much-does-it-cost-to-hire-a-new-employee/.

Chapter Eight

Additional Suggestions for Improving the Hiring Process

In today's world, social media has garnered a significant place in many Americans' daily lives. Over the past few years, a growing number of healthcare human resources (HR) staff and hiring managers have sought to take advantage of this fact by reviewing the posts, pictures, and other material that candidates (and their friends and acquaintances) leave on social media sites. At the same time, many healthcare organizations have not yet jumped on the social media search bandwagon. In this chapter, I provide information that both of these camps can use.

In this chapter, I posit some background on the growth of social media. More importantly, I discuss how healthcare organizations could potentially benefit when their HR staff and hiring managers check their candidates' social media footprints. On the other hand, healthcare companies run risks when they add social media searches to their hiring regimens; I discuss some of these potential problems. I end the section on social media by positing some suggestions for healthcare leaders who want to add social media mining to their hiring process toolkits. As a part of this discussion, I encourage these administrators to create action plans that account for the risks involved in social media assays while trying to maximize the benefits of these searches.

In the second part of the chapter, I focus on interviews. Specifically, I pinpoint some of the problems that are associated with traditional interviews. I propose that healthcare HR staff and hiring managers eliminate (or sharply reduce) their use of one-on-one interviews in favor of panel assays. I go on to delineate some of the advantages that the latter technique possesses vis-à-vis traditional interviews. I end the chapter by going one step further and suggesting that hiring managers invite the finalists in for an extended demonstration event.

8.1 A Review—Focusing on Electronic Processes and High-Potential Hires

In the previous chapter, I noted that healthcare leaders should consider transitioning to a paperless hiring process. I believe that almost all healthcare companies can realize beneficial results if they completely digitize their candidate selection systems. By utilizing an electronic system, these corporations should be able (after an initial learning stage) to make their hiring systems more efficient and effective. At the same time, they can store a range of candidate datasets. They can use a variety of information technology (IT) tools to analyze this information to identify general skills, personalities, or behaviors that best conform to certain job types.

Building on this point, healthcare organizations can use their IT tools to create corporate memory banks. Healthcare leaders can encourage their HR staff and hiring managers to input successful hiring techniques and strategies into a computer database. In this way, their companies can record at least some of the knowledge and accumulated wisdom that HR staff members and hiring managers have obtained from their experiences in dealing with candidate selections. By taking this step, healthcare executives will be able to reduce the HR "brain drain" that usually results when a key employee resigns or is fired.

In short, healthcare companies can and should use their IT systems to build up databases containing hiring best practices; these memory systems should conform to these organizations' specific external environments, corporate cultures, and needs. Healthcare companies can leverage their IT networks to help them collect and analyze pertinent information and employee experiences. Just as important, healthcare organizations can disseminate this knowledge to relevant staff who are involved in the hiring processes. By taking these steps, healthcare corporations can more successfully create and maintain hiring systems that are robust, adaptive, and, to some extent, interoperable (key personnel in any department can access and understand the information).

In the previous chapter, I also suggested that healthcare companies take a proactive approach to the hiring process. They should focus not just on hiring people for the jobs at hand. Rather, these corporations need to look for employees who have the potential both to move up the corporate ladder and to perform non-related job tasks in a pinch. I believe that healthcare companies that employ this approach will be find it much easier to identify capable, future leaders and to insulate themselves from the negative impacts of employee turnover.

8.2 Other Suggestions

In the previous chapter, I focused on more holistic, globally focused strategies. Although it is important for healthcare leaders to devote attention to the macro-issues, they will usually need to spend more time dealing with issues at the department and employee levels. In my experience, healthcare companies will not succeed unless management successfully handles these micro-issues. Most readers will agree that an organization can have a great game plan, but it will all be for naught if its members cannot execute the plays.

As important, I think that almost everyone can glean something from this chapter. Even if readers do not feel that the time is right to implement the suggestions in the previous section, they can still utilize the ones I bring up in the next few pages. This is in part because each of the topics in this chapter can serve as standalone pieces, although the individual narratives still fit within the overall themes iterated throughout the book. I feel that people who work in a range of different business environments can utilize this information to help them improve their organizations' hiring processes.

8.3 Social Media—The New Way to Connect

Social media sites such as Facebook and Instagram (and MySpace before them) are relative newcomers. One source traces their origins back to the mid-1990s; however, the phenomenon did not really "hit its stride" until around 10 to 15 years ago (Anonymous, 2014). Suffice it to say that I did not grow up with social networking sites, nor, when I first entered the business world, did I have to worry about the benefits and potential risks of utilizing them (either as a frontline employee or while in management).

However, like millions of other Americans, I have become accustomed to using social media to communicate with friends, relatives, and acquaintances. I also utilize social media sites to market ideas, to gather information on a range of topics, and to learn more about business acquaintances or companies. I have begun to use them to help me organize my daily routine and to keep track of birthdays and important events. A number of my friends and acquaintances have gone a step further; they have integrated social media into almost all aspects of their daily lives. For these people, the sites have become almost an extension of themselves.

These individuals are not alone. Today it seems that almost all Americans are using social networking sites to post videos and pictures of themselves. Most of these entries are mundane, G-rated images that would not draw any attention—images of them at the beach, in a shopping mall, playing sports, and so forth. However, sometimes people post images of themselves in, from a business's point of view, inappropriate places, or they posit pictures of themselves performing (again from a corporation's standpoint) inappropriate acts. These photographs and videos can run the gamut from illicit activities to the more mundane—an image of the individual with a beer in his or her hand.

A large number of people also use social media to publish their views on certain issues. As with videos, most of these posts are innocuous or at least engender few negative emotional responses. However, sometimes individuals say things online that are racist, sexist, or homophobic. In other cases, people discuss taboo or X-rated subject matter. In each of these instances, a section of the public will take offense to these comments. Sometimes, even seemingly mundane posts, such as on a well-trod political topic, will engender an array of passionate responses—both positive and negative.

8.4 Companies Now Using Social Media in the Hiring Process

Over the last few years, HR staff and hiring managers at many companies have started to mine this information to gain additional insights on applicants. In fact, according to a CareerBuilder survey, "[N]early two in five companies (39 percent) use social networking sites to research job candidates" (2013). According to the survey, employers look for negative candidate traits, including the types of inappropriate behavior discussed above, as well as "information that contradicted . . . listed qualifications" (CareerBuilder, 2013). At the same time, companies are reviewing applicants' social media data in search of what I will call positive information—key skills, professionalism, positive recommendations, and so forth. (CareerBuilder, 2013).

The CareerBuilder survey does not provide more detailed information, such as whether these organizations use social media screenings in all cases or only in certain instances. Nonetheless, it does show that a large number of hiring managers and HR staff are using these networks to help them assess applicants. With that said, I would urge relevant personnel to use caution, when searching candidates' social media records, for two key reasons. For one thing, there is currently a lack of information demonstrating the effectiveness of these searches. At the same time, if staff are not careful, they can run afoul of ethical norms or legal codes when performing these searches.

8.5 Social Media Mining and the Hiring Process—The Potential

As I have noted previously in this book, I would, whenever possible, eschew subjective processes in favor of more objective ones. I am not a fan of many personality tests because I feel that they are easy to game—at least to some extent. On the surface, it would appear that a hiring manager could use social media to supplement, validate, or perhaps even replace personality assays. This might be especially true for applicants who spend significant amounts of time on Facebook, Instagram, or similar sites.

Hiring managers and HR staff could also potentially utilize social media assays to supplement, verify, or replace other popular but flawed application materials (Slovensky & Ross, 2012, 56–57). They include:

- **Cover Letters**
  These documents are subject to a number of flaws. For one thing, the writer's views are subjective, and his or her statements have to be taken with a grain of salt. Worse, an applicant could intentionally include incorrect or fraudulent information without HR catching on to this fact. Sometimes, the candidate might even get someone

else to write the letters for him or her (or the ghost writers might edit the letter so thoroughly that the document is essentially the surrogate's work).

- **Résumés**
  I have discussed the potential issues with these documents in a previous portion of this book. They can contain a number of problematic issues, which run the gamut from embellishments to outright fraudulent statements.

- **One-on-One Interviews**
  Hiring managers should use the information obtained from these types of interviews with caution. I will discuss this issue in more depth at a later point in this chapter.

- **References and/or Reference Letters**
  It might surprise some readers to note that the individuals who compose the reference letters are often biased. Even when this is not the case, the individuals who draft these letters (in my experience anyway) tend to focus almost solely on the positive aspects of the respective candidates. This myopic focus limits these documents' usefulness to hiring managers and HR staff.

In addition to these items, one might think that hiring managers and HR staff could reliably use social media to identify potentially undesirable employee behaviors, such as the tendency to party excessively or to use illicit drugs. At the same time, it seems reasonable to assume that company personnel could peruse a candidate's online record to identify (seemingly) unsolicited referrals and positive comments about these people, which come from other individuals. The hiring managers and HR staff could then use this information to help them identify applicants, who will work hard, meet deadlines, arrive to work on time, and perform laudably in other key areas. In a perfect world, those assumptions might hold true; however, the real word is far from perfect.

8.6 Social Media Mining and the Hiring Process—The Problems

Although all of those assumptions might eventually turn out to be correct—at least to some extent, it is worth noting that currently there is very little peer-reviewed data supporting the efficacy of using social media in the hiring process. Victoria Brown and E. Daly Vaughn remark on the dearth of research on this subject in a 2011 article in the Journal of Business Psychology (2011, 221–222). What is more, they and other researchers have noted the potential liability issues, which include, among other things, potential discriminatory behaviors, privacy concerns, and breach of contract issues with the social media websites (Brown & Vaughn, 2011, 222–223; Slovensky & Ross, 2012, 62–65).

Experts also worry that hiring managers and other key personnel, due to their personal biases, will not be able to successfully utilize the information they obtain from social media mining (Sovensky & Ross, 2012, 61). In short, a hiring manager might place too much emphasis on the information he or she finds on a candidate's social media profile. As an example, assume the manager looks at the applicant's profile and is impressed with what he or she finds on these sites. The individual's initial optimism might lead him or her to overlook some potentially important, negative issues centering on the candidate's background, skills, and so forth.

The issue regarding biases is important. However, with regard to social media searches, I am more concerned with what Brown and Vaughn call "the fundamental attribution error" (2011, 221). To put it simply, human beings have a tendency to act differently depending on the situation, and this fact might significantly limit the usefulness of social media assays. Having worked in healthcare, as well as in other fields, for a number of years, I can attest to the veracity of the phenomenon.

During my career, I have had the pleasure of working with a large number of individuals who possessed a diverse array of personalities, skills, and work backgrounds. I have also had the opportunity to interact with many of these people outside of work. One thing that I learned from these experiences is that many people are able to compartmentalize and separate their work selves from their personal lives.

I have known men and women who would party hard on weekdays as well as weekends, yet they still managed to arrive at work on time. More importantly, they worked as hard as anyone else in the building. It is not just the hard partiers who were able to maintain this bifurcated lifestyle. I have known many people who were introverts when they were not at work. However, they turned into marketing mavens when placed in certain environments. Along the same lines, I have met individuals who were paragons of virtue (at least regarding adherence to company rules), during their 9–5 shifts, but they exhibited less than saintly behavior outside of the office. Ditto for employees with odd behaviors, radical views, and so forth. They did not let their personal beliefs intrude upon their work lives.

I worked with many of these people in the era before the growth of social media. However, hiring managers and HR staff who perform social media assays likely find similar types of behavior online. If these employers immediately jump to the conclusion that workers' personal lifestyles correlate with on-the-job behaviors, they might end up tossing many excellent candidates into the reject piles. They might instead hire lesser candidates who are either more adept at hiding their peccadillos from the public eye or who do not have an online presence.

I think it is important to mention one other important issue with social media mining data by HR and hiring managers. It deals with the candidates themselves. A large percentage of applicants are aware of the potential dangers in publicly posting risqué photos to or making inappropriate comments on a social media site. As such, they hide all of this material by limiting its viewing to friends only, or by refraining from putting it on the Web; however, they do not eschew these behaviors.

Many HR staff and hiring managers might not consider this issue to be problematic. However, these individuals might have a more difficult time comparing candidates, as they will have more data on some than on others. This leaves the hiring staff trying to compare "apples to oranges."

Savvy candidates can also create false virtual personas. For instance, immediately before beginning the hiring search, they can have their friends and colleagues post positive comments to their social media sites. People who do not know each other that well in real life can sometimes also trade positive recommendations (when this option is available on a social media site).

As an example, assume that George is applying for healthcare jobs. He has numerous connections on his social media sites. George does not know most of these people. He simply asked them to join his network, and they accepted his invitations. George is also in the habit of posting positive recommendations or notes on his connections' sites. They return the favor in a quid pro quo manner, even though they do not personally know George. They make these blanket recommendations because there is no penalty for doing so (and significant potential benefits).

A hiring manager who reviews George's social media profiles might come away impressed by these recommendations. The employer might wrongly think that they are honest assessments of George's abilities—written by his colleagues and close associates. The hiring manager decides to offer George the job and is surprised when he does not perform well.

With those caveats in mind, I do believe that employers can use social media searches to help them flesh out candidate profiles, or to weed out bad actors—in certain circumstances. In the next few paragraphs, I will posit my suggestions for correctly utilizing this medium as a part of the hiring process.

8.7 A Guide to Using Social Media Mining as a Part of the Hiring Process

In this section, I lay out a step-by-step guide that an organization's HR staff and hiring managers can utilize to help them create effective social media mining systems. The goal of this plan is twofold. On the one hand, I map out a process that healthcare leaders can use to help them sort the wheat from the chaff when it comes to candidate information on the Internet. At the same time, I point out risks that might be involved in these searches; some of my suggestions are designed to protect companies against these potential pitfalls.

- **Step 1—Identify Specific Ways in which Social Media Mining Can Improve the Hiring Process**
  Before a healthcare company adds social media data mining to its candidate selection procedures, it makes sense for a dedicated individual (or group) within the organization to analyze the costs and benefits of taking this action. As part of this review, the employee or employees should define both the scope and the focus of its proposed social media mining system. As part of the review, the individual or individuals should ascertain any potential legal risks that might result from HR's social media assays.

- **Step 2—Create and Enforce Guidelines to Govern Social Media Searches**
  Sometimes it makes sense for a healthcare corporation to allow its staff some autonomy in how they go about completing a project or a series of tasks. However, this is not one of those instances. A healthcare company's implementation team, working with management and HR, should create a series of guidelines for using social media

data mining as part of the hiring process. The healthcare corporation should take these steps for several reasons, including:

○ **By standardizing the process, the company can help to ensure that the data is both valid and comparable.**
The organization can strengthen the validity of any hiring data obtained from social media searches by creating best practice guidelines. These rules, if designed correctly, can focus on the collection of more objective information. At the same time, the healthcare company can reduce a hiring manager's or HR employee's tendencies toward biasing the results. The latter correlation will be readily apparent to readers and needs no further exegesis.

○ **Healthcare organizations might limit or eliminate any potential liability issues by creating a plan and sticking to it.**
Readers probably are fully aware of this fact; however, it is worth listing here, nonetheless.

○ **Management maintains control over the process.**
As in the last bullet point, the more control the c-suite/upper management has over this process, the better the corporation will be at eliminating rogue behaviors, which, if left unchecked, might lead to lawsuits or other problems.

- **Step 3—Routinely Review the Social Media Search Process**
The healthcare organization should routinely collect data related to HR's social media mining activities. As with any other business-related process, the company needs to make sure that it procures data that will yield useful information when organized and analyzed. At certain points throughout the year, healthcare analysts and leaders will want to review this information to identify the strengths and weaknesses in their social media mining processes.

- **Step 4—Periodically Review the Literature to Make Sure that HR's Use of Social Media Searches Adheres to Current Best Practices and Legal Codes**
The healthcare organization should designate an employee whose job is to ensure that the firm's social media mining processes are following best practices. In order to achieve this goal, the worker should occasionally scan the Internet for new information on the efficacy of and legal issues surrounding social media data mining.

He or she should alert management if the search yields any pertinent results.

A healthcare company that follows these steps will incur expenses related to the research, discussion, analysis, and review phases of this action plan. However, the benefits of going through this process will outweigh the costs if it helps the corporation avoid legal issues related to improper social media assays, or if it allows the firm to construct searches that are more efficient and effective than would otherwise be the case.

8.8 A Different Type of Interview

As I have previously noted in this book, traditional HR staff and hiring managers often do not derive many benefits from conducting one-on-one interviews with prospective hires. In fact, they might sometimes be negatively impacting the hiring process by relying on this method to interview candidates. This is especially true when these interviews result in bad hires. Although traditional interviews might still have a place in the hiring process, they should be used with caution. In fact, hiring managers and HR staff should rely on other group or panel interviews, when possible.

In this section, I will note the occasions when healthcare leaders are justified in utilizing a traditional interview technique. However, I will spend the majority of my time discussing panel or group interviews. I will also denote question types that interviewers can use to reduce bias and elicit responses from a candidate, which can then be compared with answers from other interviewees (see Figure 8.1).

8.8.1 The Traditional One-on-One Interview

Many hiring managers, in healthcare as well as in other industries, seem to favor one-on-one interviews. They still tend to use these interviews to assess candidates, despite the fact that researchers have posited numerous flaws in this type of candidate assay (Grant, 2013). If one asked a hundred healthcare managers why they utilize personal interviews, that person is likely to receive a wide variety of answers. In my experience, hiring managers tend to stick with this type of interview for one of a few reasons.

Sample Healthcare Organization
Open Position #31
Panel Interview Results: Candidate 12 (14 potential hires interviewed)
Ranking System: 5 = Excellent/Highly Qualified and 1 = Poor/Not Qualified
Note: Does Not Include (open-ended) Questions 4, 7, 9, and 15;
        "I" = Interviewer

Questions	I #1	I #2	I #3	I #4	Total	Avg.	Weight	Category Score	Avg. of All Candidates
1	4	3	3	4	14	3.5	0.05	0.175	0.1759
2	2	1	4	2	9	2.25	0.1	0.225	0.3679
3	5	4	3	4	16	4	0.1	0.4	0.3893
5	4	3	4	3	14	3.5	0.1	0.35	0.4196
6	2	2	1	2	7	1.75	0.05	0.0875	0.158
8	3	3	3	3	12	3	0.1	0.3	0.3929
10	4	5	4	4	17	4.25	0.1	0.425	0.4036
11	4	5	5	4	18	4.5	0.1	0.45	0.3107
12	1	2	5	2	10	2.5	0.1	0.25	0.3429
13	3	2	3	3	11	2.75	0.1	0.275	0.3196
14	5	4	4	5	18	4.5	0.1	0.45	0.425
Total Score								3.3875	3.7054

Figure 8.1   Healthcare corporations can use a system similar to the one above to quantify company-specific interview questions. In this graphic, the interviewers ranked the candidate's responses to certain queries on a scale from 1 to 5. The HR staff transferred this data to Excel and came up with a composite score for the applicant. The hiring manager and/or HR staff can use this sheet to compare this individual's interview responses to those of his or her peers. Note that some open-ended questions could not be quantified.

- **One-on-One Interviews Are Cheaper**
  If healthcare leaders want to conduct panel interviews, they have to pull several key personnel away from their daily jobs or routine tasks, which results in lost-opportunity costs (Dixon et al., 2002, 397). These expenses can add up over the course of several interview sessions. Healthcare organizations will also have to expend resources in training their employees on how to conduct panel interviews (Wheeler, 2011). As a result, healthcare organizations (or sometimes the hiring manager acting on his or her own behalf)

choose to stick with the one-on-one interview process because it is cheaper than the alternative. This is probably true even when the organization uses multiple one-on-one interviews—for example, one interview with an HR staff member and one with the hiring manager—for each finalist.

- **Managers and Candidates Prefer Personal Interviews**
  Both candidates and interviewees alike are usually more comfortable engaging in one-on-one interviews, than in group settings. In a group setting, applicants might feel like they are in front of a panel of judges (which, in a way, is true). These individuals are less relaxed in these settings, as opposed to a one-on-one discussion, because they believe that they have to please not just the hiring manager, but several other participants as well (Traci K. & BrightMove, Inc., 2010).

  Hiring managers sometimes also become more anxious than otherwise during panel interviews; their anxiety might result from their feelings of being watched by peers or superiors. In this situation, a hiring manager might not feel comfortable asking the candidate certain questions, or that person may posit more demanding queries, just to please his or her bosses. Given this scenario, many hiring managers—and candidates—prefer more intimate, personal interviews to panel or group interviews.

- **The Personal Interview Is a Tradition**
  I think it is common knowledge that people, in general, are averse to changing habits and customs, especially ones that have existed for decades or longer. By extension, healthcare HR staff and managers might opt to conduct one-on-one interviews with candidates, even when they could potentially choose another option, because these individuals have always done it this way. They will not adopt a new interview method, unless they are forced to take this step by their superiors, or unless their departments suffer through a number of bad hires.

- **Hiring Managers Think They Are Great at Identifying Talent**
  In at least some cases, hiring managers, or other key personnel, utilize one-on-one interviews because they think they are great at identifying candidates who are excellent fits for their respective departments.

- **Multiple Interviews**

  In some cases, healthcare corporations will ask candidates to take part in several interviews. In some cases, all of these interviews will consist of one-on-ones; however, in other instances, the applicant might have a personal interview with the hiring manager or a member of the HR team. He or she might then have to participate in a panel interview.

8.8.2 Traditional Interview Questions and Techniques

Going hand in hand with the personal interview, HR staff and hiring managers often rely on a ubiquitous series of questions. Some of the more popular ones are very general in nature. One HR expert lists a few of the more popular ones, including such stock queries as "Where do you see yourself in the next 5 years?" and "What would you do if someone asked you to overlook a problem with your project?" (Bliga, 2011). Another one, which I have heard a lot is, "Tell me about a time that you had to deal with a difficult client . . . How did you handle the situation?"

Traditionally, interviewers do not ask all candidates the same series of questions. For instance, a hiring manager will ask one candidate about his or her greatest accomplishment in the last job. However, the manager will not pose that query to the next applicant (Grant, 2013). In my experience, even when the interviewer has a sheet with a structured series of interview questions, he or she rarely sticks to that script. After about five or six queries, the person will inevitably start to ask ad hoc questions. These questions and techniques are flawed for any number of obvious reasons, including issues related to bias, candidate preparation, and the comparability of candidate data.

8.8.3 When to Use Traditional Interview Techniques

Sometimes, it is okay for hiring managers or HR staff to utilize one-on-one interviews that focus on an ad hoc, laid-back question-and-answer session. I would recommend this type of interview session when management has already identified its likely hire, even before the interview process begins. In these instances, the hiring manager or the HR staff member might want to use the interview session to hammer out the final details of the employment contract, or to better acquaint himself or herself with the "new hire" and vice versa.

This type of interview session is appropriate in a couple of scenarios. In some instances, the organization's HR staff has a difficult time finding qualified candidates. After a thorough search, HR only attracts one really good applicant. At other times, one applicant, due to his or her experience and skills, is heads and shoulders above the competition. Both situations result in the same outcome. Namely, the hiring manager has already penciled the candidate's name into the open position.

When this situation occurs, the employer might be justified in using the interview primarily as an informal meet-and-greet session, instead of as an assessment tool. After all, the manager will change his or her mind about the potential hire only if something dramatic and unexpected comes up in the interview, or the applicant refuses the job (assuming that the healthcare organization allows its hiring managers to make the final decision on things like wage/salary levels).

I was a part of one such interview session. I had recently been promoted to team leader. In this position, I would sit in on all of the new hire interviews for my department. At the time, the economy was humming, and my manager was having difficulty finding employees to fill open positions. Due to these staffing issues, the department was having difficulties meeting its production goals. After what seemed like forever, HR identified a qualified candidate who was willing to accept the proffered wage level. My manager decided, in advance, to hire the individual, barring any interview bombshells. As a result, we focused more on getting to know the applicant—and helping the candidate to familiarize herself with us, as well as her co-workers—than we did on assessing the individual's relevant skills and experiences.

8.8.4 Traditional Interviews Are Not Good Assessment Tools

When a healthcare corporation has already decided on a candidate before the interview process begins, then its management should utilize the traditional interview process. However, when the organization must choose between several good candidates, it needs to use the interview as an assessment tool. Researchers have demonstrated that the aforementioned interview techniques are not good at accurately assaying a candidate's job potential (Grant, 2013; Wheeler, 2011; Prencipe, 1997, 65). In fact, according to Adam Grant, a professor with the University of Pennsylvania's Wharton School of Business, "Interviews are terrible predictors of job performance" (Grant, 2013). One might be better off choosing from among the finalists by throwing darts at their profiles then by using a traditional interview as a means of selecting the winner.

Experts in the field have pointed to a number of reasons as to why traditional interviews (as defined in the previous section) are not effective in identifying the best candidates. However, the three factors that I consider, from personal experience, to be most important are:

- HR staff and hiring managers view the candidates' responses through their own, biased worldviews. These assessments, due to their lack of objectivity, are necessarily flawed (Grant, 2013).
- Interviewers ask each candidate a different set of questions, which inhibits their ability to compare one applicant's answers against the responses from other potential hires (Wheeler, 2011).
- "Studies have demonstrated that most people are poor judges of when they are being told the truth and when they are being deceived" (Rosen, 2009). Ergo, interviewers will usually have little success in determining when candidates are not being truthful.

I can attest to the validity of these three principles. I have sat in on more than one interview in which the applicants portrayed themselves as excellent fits for the job. Just as important, they appeared to be sincere when describing themselves, their skills, and their experiences. However, once hired, they turned out to be mediocre to poor employees. In other words, to use an old cliché, "They talked a good game, but they did not deliver." Using the traditional interview approach, as described in the previous section, neither I nor anyone else in these meetings were able to predict these results. Otherwise, management would not have hired these individuals in the first place.

8.8.5 A Better Way to Interview

In accord with my views throughout this book, I feel that management should try to ensure that the interview process yields as much objective, comparable data on the candidates as possible. Research has indicated that the aforementioned interview techniques do not work. As such, I suggest that healthcare corporations jettison the one-on-one interviews in favor of panel interviews. Additionally, I feel that they should replace unstructured sessions with a scripted list of questions. However, in my opinion, neither of these changes will help all that much unless healthcare companies also replace the overused (traditional) questions with innovative ones that draw attention to a candidate's cognitive and behavioral abilities.

I would suggest that healthcare organizations ensure that most interviews—especially the ones that involve mid-level or specialist positions—be conducted by a group or panel. The group should consist of the hiring manager and at least two other employees. Some researchers recommend that these groups contain "three to six" members (Dixon et al., 2002, 420). Ideally, at least one of the other members of the panel should hold a position in the company that is on a par or higher than that of the hiring manager—to ensure that he or she will not take control of the meeting. Finally, the group should receive thorough training with regard to conducting structured, panel interviews (Wheeler, 2011).

A panel interview provides several potential advantages over a one-on-one session, including:

- **The Reduced Potential for Interviewer Bias**
  In a one-on-one interview, the hiring manager or HR person might allow his or her subjective views to bias the results. By conducting panel interviews instead of traditional ones, healthcare organizations should be able to reduce the level of interviewer bias, as the interviewers in the group can analyze each other's notes. Viewing the results from a number of perspectives will help the group identify and eliminate individual biases (Dixon et al., 2002, 420). One potential caveat: Organizations that do not ensure that their panel contains a diverse group of individuals might not realize the aforementioned benefits.

- **Everyone Stays on Script**
  The individuals involved in the panel interview are more likely to adhere to the assigned questions and not go off script. As a result, they are more likely to generate candidate data that is comparable (more on scripted questions in the next section) (Doan, 2009).

- **Better Analysis of the Response Data**
  I think most of the readers will agree that teams are often better adept at analyzing data than any one individual. This is because, among other things, they can view the data from a wider array of angles or perspectives.

I believe that it often makes sense to conduct panel interviews instead of one-on-one sessions. However, I do not feel that group interviews will be of much benefit to a healthcare corporation unless it also ensures that its interviewers pose the same questions to each candidate. Kevin Wheeler, an HR expert, sums it up nicely when he says that the questions "to be most effective, have to be delivered in a similar way (ideally exactly the same way) to each candidate for the job" (2011). By using a structured series of questions, management and HR can ensure that the candidate responses are, to some extent anyway, comparable. One study demonstrated that structured interviews were three times more likely to account for "variance in job performance" than an unstructured one (Grant, 2013).

Finally, the individuals involved in these interviews should create questions that center on the skills and experience needed for the position itself, as opposed to queries that are more general in nature. The employers should also try to create questions that test the candidate's cognitive abilities, as well as any traits or skills that are related specifically to the job tasks he or she will be responsible for completing if hired (Bliga, 2011; Wheeler, 2011). If nothing else, the interviewers should create a series of questions that an applicant has not heard, verbatim at other interviews, thereby reducing his or her ability to game the system.

Many experts insist that organizations utilizing these techniques have a greater likelihood of choosing the right candidate for any open positions. Having sat through a number of interviews from both sides of the aisle (as an employer and as a candidate), I agree with these assessments. I feel that, by correctly using these methods, HR staff and hiring managers can increase the reliability and validity of the candidate data that they collect from their interviews. I am aware of many healthcare organizations that now use structured panel interviews.

Although I would encourage healthcare organizations to utilize these interview techniques, they are not foolproof. Additionally, companies that utilize structured panel interviews will realize a larger upfront cost. I feel that healthcare companies can increase their odds of finding the right candidate by taking an additional step.

8.9 Utilize Candidate Show Days

Many companies will go beyond the basics, such as application review and interviews, in an effort to make the right hire. For instance, an organization might require all applicants for a call center job to demonstrate their proficiency in answering phones and solving customer complaints (in these cases, the hiring managers take on the customer's role). In other instances, a hiring manager or HR staff member might give the applicant a specific task to perform and observe that person as he or she works to complete the project. In both cases, management requires candidates to demonstrate their job-specific skills in real time.

Almost all healthcare organizations that I have been affiliated with place most new hires on probation, lasting anywhere from 30 days to 6 months. During this period, the neophyte employees will not receive key benefits, such as healthcare or vacation days. In this way, management hopes to limit any negative impact that comes from making poor hiring decisions. If a new employee does not "pan out," management can release that individual, at a reduced cost.

Both of these methods have their merits. However, they also possess some important drawbacks. In the former case, candidates usually do not spend a significant amount of time performing these real-world tests. As a result, the organization in question can obtain only a limited amount of feedback. At the same time, the company's management is not able to learn whether these applicants are a good cultural fit. At the same time, a company that cuts an employee during the probation period is, at best, putting a band-aid on a bad hire. Management might save some money; however, they will still likely have to expend significant resources to hire another person for the job and to train that individual. This is assuming that the bad hire did not create additional expenses for the corporation by, for instance, negatively impacting employee morale.

I would suggest that healthcare leaders, as part of their hiring processes, think about bringing the final few candidates into the office for a full day. During this period, the hiring managers can ask the applicants to shadow other employees and/or to complete basic, job-related tasks. The department heads and their staffs can gain valuable information about potential hires' job-related skills. Just as important, they should be able to get some sense of how each candidate will respond to the respective department's regulations and culture.

Readers who wish to try this strategy out at their organizations should keep in mind that their companies will have to shoulder some costs related to bringing these candidates in for a day. First off, organizations will want review any state laws that might limit or otherwise proscribe such activities. They might, for instance, have to remunerate potential hires who agree to this type of arrangement. If nothing else, organizations will incur expenses related to lost-opportunity costs involving the time that managers and their staffs spend in observing and overseeing the candidates. At the same time, healthcare firms might not find it feasible to create shadow programs for all job types. I can foresee situations where it is not practicable, especially for positions in clinical areas.

With that said, I believe that healthcare organizations should employ this strategy, when feasible. I think hiring managers can learn a lot more about a potential hire via this one-day event than they can intuit from interviews. At the same time, the applicants have a chance to learn about the respective department's rules, expectations, and culture. In some cases, a new hire is the one who cuts the cord after a few months with a company due to issues related to the workplace culture. Candidate visits, like the ones that I suggest, should decrease these cases of employee buyer remorse.

References

Anonymous. (2014, August 5). The History of Social Networking. *Digital Trends*. Retrieved from http://www.digitaltrends.com/features/the-history-of-social-networking/#!bNMRY8.

Bliga, F. (2011, May 23). Behavioral Interviewing vs. Traditional Interviewing. ApplicationStack. Retrieved from http://blog.applicantstack.com/2011/behavioral-interviewing-vs-traditional-interviewing.

Brown, V. R., & Vaughn, E. D. (2011). The Writing on the (Facebook) Wall: The Use of Social Networking Sites in Hiring Decisions. *Journal of Business and Psychology* 26(2), 219–225. DOI: http://dx.doi.org/10.1007/s10869-011-9221-x.

CareerBuilder. (2013, June 27). More Employers Finding Reasons Not to Hire Candidates on Social Media. Retrieved from http://www.careerbuilder.com/

share/aboutus/pressreleasesdetail.aspx?sd=6%2f26%2f2013&=pr766&ed=1 2%2f31%2f2013.

Dixon, M., Wang, S., Calvin, J., Dineen, B., & Tomlinson, E. (2002). The Panel Interview: A Review of Empirical Research and Guidelines for Practice. *Public Personnel Management* 31(3), 397–428. Retrieved from ProQuest.

Doan, T. (2009, February 4). Panel Interview. Retrieved from http://www. humanresources.hrvinet.com/panel-interview/.

Grant, A. (2013, June 10). What's Wrong with Job Interviews, and How to Fix Them. LinkedIn Pulse. Retrieved from https://www.linkedin.com/pulse/ article/20130610025112-69244073-will-smart-companies-interview-your-kids.

Prencipe, L. (1997). Use the "Show-Me" Interview. *Network World* 14(49), 59. Retrieved from ProQuest.

Rosen, L. (2009, June 5). Why Interviews Are Not an Effective Means to Tell if a Job Applicant Is Lying on their Resume or Job Application. *Employment Screening Resources*. Retrieved from http://www.esrcheck.com/wordpress/2009/06/05/ how-to-tell-if-someone-is-lying-at-an-interview-hint-it-helps-to-have-a-coin-handy-2/.

Slovensky, R., & Ross, W. H. (2012). Should Human Resource Managers Use Social Media to Screen Job Applicants? Managerial and Legal Issues in the USA. *The Journal of Policy, Regulation and Strategy for Telecommunications, Information and Media* 14(1), 55–69. DOI: http:// dx.doi.org/10.1108/14636691211196941.

Traci K., & BrightMove, Inc. (2010, October 11). Us vs You. Pros and Cons of the Panel Interview. Retrieved from http://www.brightmove.com/ pros-and-cons-of-the-panel-interview/.

Wheeler, K. (2011, September 27). Why Interviews Are a Waste of Time. Ere Recruiting. Retrieved from http://www.ere.net/2011/09/27/why-interviews-are-a-waste-of-time/.

Chapter Nine

Improving Management's Ability to Identify, Develop, and Promote Internal Talent

In previous chapters, I looked at some of the methods that healthcare corporations can utilize to help them identify the best hires. Healthcare organizations that are able to land excellent candidates time and again will be a step ahead of their competitors. However, the best companies don't just excel at finding good candidates, they are also adept at developing their in-house talent.

In my experience, healthcare organizations that possess strong internal development and promotion systems have mastered two key tasks. First, executives and managers at these corporations are adept at helping workers to develop key skills, as well as learn new ones. Second, these healthcare companies do an excellent job of identifying which of their employees are best suited to fill key management and specialist roles.

In this chapter, I delineate a few techniques that readers can utilize to improve their organizations' employee development and internal promotions systems. Some of my suggestions might appear to be common sense; however, I have noticed that, time and again, executives and managers do not adhere to them.

9.1 The Two P's: How They Hinder Internal Development and Promotion Programs

At this point, I think it is worthwhile to discuss the two P's—power and politics—as they relate to healthcare corporations. Every organization needs to exercise control over these two elements if it wants to successfully develop and promote its internal talent. In the next few paragraphs, I will briefly focus on the ways in which the two P's permeate contemporary healthcare workplaces. At the same time, I will suggest methods that management can utilize to keep these forces from negatively impacting its internal talent development and promotion programs.

9.2 Power and Its Effect on the Development and Promotion of Internal Talent

Every company I have ever worked for—and likely every organization in the United States with more than a few employees—consists of men and women who possess varying degrees of power over fellow workers. In using the term "power," I refer to situations in which one individual or group "exert[s] [coercive] influence or control over others" (Hoff & Rockmann, 2012, 191). Many of these transactional relationships are legitimate. Most corporations would cease to exist if they did not contain some type of hierarchical structure that granted specific people the authority to tell others what to do and when to do it. Healthcare organizations also need to employ gatekeepers—individuals who ensure that employees follow corporate rules and regulations. Companies that lacked these personnel relationships would likely quickly devolve into a state of chaos. In my experience, even relatively flat organizations need to delineate some type of power nexus.

Hoff and Rockman, in their analysis of power relationships in the workplace, denote two key types of power-based arrangements—"structurally derived power" and "culturally derived power" (they also delineate a third type of power source, "knowledge-based . . . power," which I will not cover) (Hoff & Rockmann, 2012, 193–194). I think that their views on this issue accurately describe what I have seen in the workplace. I will briefly touch on each type of association and demonstrate how it can hinder the development of internal talent.

9.3 When Managers Use Too Many Sticks and Not Enough Carrots

As Hoff and Rockman note, power relationships naturally derive from a company's organizational structure (Hoff & Rockmann, 2012, 193–194). Although this definition can describe a number of different arrangements, I am most concerned with the relationship between an executive or manager and the employees who report directly to him or her. In my experience, many of these leaders do not know how to utilize their power over their subordinates. Sometimes, they rely on overt force and coercion to motivate workers, when some other type of technique would work better. In other instances, the executives and managers might be justified in using some level of coercion to manage the workforce; however, they take it too far.

Most readers have probably experienced these types of situations firsthand; they understand that exploitive or abusive associations can negatively impact employee morale and productivity. However, many readers might not realize that these relationships can also adversely affect a healthcare corporation's employee development and promotion programs. To wit, talented workers—the ones that a company wants to keep around—are usually the people that can most easily find jobs at other firms. As such, they are often the first ones to jump ship when their bosses act in a confrontational or oppressive manner. In these instances, the companies in question lose potential star managers, directors, and high-level specialists as well as valuable employees. Over the course of my career in healthcare and in other industries, I have worked with several star employees who jumped ship for this reason. These people loved their jobs and were satisfied with their pay; however, they felt, rightly or wrongly, that their managers were not treating them with respect and dignity.

In my experience, supervisors who dictate too much via fiat and critique can negatively impact the development of talented employees in other ways as well. Most importantly, these leaders can create tension packed environments, filled with overly anxious staff members who are always, to borrow an old cliché, "looking over their shoulders." At least some experts would agree with me; their studies have demonstrated that this type of office atmosphere hinders employee growth and learning (Schuh, Zhang, & Tian, 2013, 638). People who work in these environments often do not have the necessary autonomy to try things out and to learn from these experiments. They tend to focus on surviving and so do not spend any time acquiring new skills (Maslow, 1998, 21, 106–107, 267–269). If individuals are given the lead on a project, they focus too intently on ensuring that the X's and O's are covered to work on their leadership skills. Finally, these employees might come to believe that a strict authoritarian management style is the norm, and employ this tactic if and when they are promoted.

I do not want to lead readers to believe that I oppose the use of authoritarian management styles in all situations. There are many instances in which this type of leadership stance is warranted—and in the best interests of the company (and by extension, the employees). As an example, executives and managers who oversee call centers might find it beneficial to employ this type of management style. They might be able to utilize more authoritative methods if customer service agents adhere to a limited script and the department is mainly interested in ensuring that these employees meet predetermined efficiency and effectiveness metrics. In another example, a doctor who is working on a code blue patient might need to give commands to his or her nurses and tech support staff. He or she should expect these workers, in most situations, to follow the orders without question—as a patient's life is at stake. These are just a couple of the numerous occasions in which a leader might find it desirable to act via fiat.

However, even in these instances, healthcare leaders should respect their employees' basic rights as well as their dignity. They should utilize non-authoritarian management methods whenever feasible. This is because it is too easy for executives and managers to cross the line and unnecessarily use heavy-handed tactics or fear to motivate workers. I will posit an experience in my own life that I think will help elucidate my meaning.

9.4 A Real Life Example—How Poor Management Skills Can Have a Negative Impact on the Workplace

I got my first taste of healthcare management while working as an accounts receivable team lead for a mail order pharmacy. During the first part of my tenure, I tried to enforce all company regulations to the letter. I would reprimand subordinates for violating even the most miniscule company rules and regulations. At the same time, I held my coworkers to the highest of standards and critiqued even the smallest of mistakes. Compounding the situation, I did a poor job of listening to my fellow employees' needs and in answering their questions. I did not necessarily lack a sense of empathy; I simply did not yet have the necessary leadership experience and skills.

Needless to say, my fellow employees were less than satisfied with this arrangement. Some of them were afraid to try innovative techniques for fear that they might fail. Few of these individuals wanted to take on projects that would give them some autonomy (and provide them with the opportunity to develop key skills, including leadership skills), because they did not want to "mess up." Other people, from what I understand, found it difficult to learn in the type of environment that I had created. Some might have started looking for other jobs. In these instances, the fault was on me; my authoritarian, perfectionist style of management kept my employees from working—and learning—to their full potentials.

Eventually, the workers complained loud enough—and in this case rightly so—about my harsh dictatorial style, that the manager requested me to "tone it down." From that point onwards, I softened my approach. My missteps are repeated on a daily basis by managers and executives in healthcare departments around the country. They create an environment that stifles employee growth and initiative, which drives the best workers away.

9.5 Other Sources of Power and Their Effects on Employee Development

Hoff and Rockman also note that power relationships can derive from cultural underpinnings that are independent of—or intertwined with—a company's organizational chart (2012, 194). For those readers who are unfamiliar with the term, culture refers to a group's "shared beliefs, customs, [and] practices" (Bing Dictionary, 2014). Following this logic, a healthcare organization can empower certain people by means of its traditions or unwritten rules.

To understand the role that culture might play in abetting an employee's level of power, one only has to look at a family-run company. The family members who are employed by these organizations oftentimes exercise far more power—or at least command a level of respect—that is much greater than their job titles would suggest. These individuals are often able to exercise power over employees in other departments, including managers and directors who are, at least technically, their superiors. Family members, regardless of their official positions in the organization, usually have a say in a company's strategic direction and in other high-level decisions.

In many cases, this type of structure works well, especially for smaller companies. The individual family members can provide a series of checks and balances. And regardless, a family that owns (or at least has a majority stake) in a company has the right to run the business as it sees fit. At the same time, I think readers can identify some potential issues relating to employee development and promotion that might result from this type of structure. Most importantly, in some of these organizations, family members will not necessarily promote employees based on merit. Instead, these leaders choose to advance an individual up the ladder—or not—based on how well they like him or her. At the same time, the family members' views on employee development, even if severely shortsighted, will hold sway throughout the company, as the various department heads will be unwilling to go against the wishes of these people.

Of course, family-run healthcare corporations are not the only ones that might exhibit these shortcomings. Any organizational culture can revolve around an elite group of individuals who base their promotions on personal preference, as opposed to merit. They might also intentionally seek to hinder the growth and development of employees that they do not like. Finally, these corporate elites often insist that managers utilize certain types of training and development styles, regardless of the efficacy of these techniques.

One can further project this down to the department level, where a manager, especially one who controls a large number of employees, acts more like a lord who spreads his or her largesse on favored employees. At the same time, the leader will actively, or sometimes even unconsciously, hinder the growth and/or promotion of employees who he or she does not like. The discussion on corporate power structures and their influences on employee development and promotion leads me to the next key topic—company politics.

9.6 Corporate Politics

Most healthcare organizations—and indeed almost all companies with more than a few employees—contain some political elements. When I use the word politics, I am referring to situations in which employees form alliances with their peers, or they actively try to curry the favor of higher-ups, in an effort to achieve their aims (Hoff & Rockmann, 2012, 198). Human beings are social creatures, so one should expect them to engage in these behaviors. In fact, in many instances, office politics can serve beneficial purposes for companies. For instance, employees might work together to convince management to ameliorate a negative corporate practice or to adopt an excellent idea. However, office politics can also limit a company's ability to effectively develop and promote internal talent, and this situation can have deleterious consequences for the organization as a whole.

When readers think about office politics, the one obvious type that might come foremost to their minds is the manager–employee relationship. In this type of situation, a leader—an executive, a director, a manager, or perhaps even a high-level specialist—will utilize his or her power to help favored employees obtain training (e.g., leadership training), allow them to control key projects, or help them to advance within the corporation. At the same time, some of the employees will actively try to please this individual in order to share in his or her largesse. On the flip side, the leader will ignore or even attempt to hinder the growth, development, and promotion potential of workers that he or she does not like—regardless of their, experience, skills, or potential.

This type of relationship goes hand in hand with the structural and cultural power arrangements that I discussed earlier. However, even managers and other key leaders who strive to be evenhanded can make decisions that negatively impact their healthcare companies' abilities to create and maintain meritocratic employee promotion/development programs.

In my experience, healthcare corporations more closely resemble confederations than they do unified machines or organisms. Managers and directors of these companies often tend to put the interests of their own departments over those of their respective organizations. This phenomenon occurs for a number of reasons; however, one of the key factors relates to organizational assessment techniques. To put it simply, from what I have seen during my tenure in the healthcare field, companies tend to rate managers on how well their individual departments perform, without any vision of how one area's performance might impact other departments within these organizations. This type of assay incentivizes department heads to maximize their productivity, revenue, and other metrics—even if these actions negatively impact other areas of the company. At the same time, these individuals develop a myopic view of reality that focuses primarily on their own department's needs.

In this type of corporate environment, each manager treats his or her department as a sort of modern day fiefdom. Department heads work the rounds—by forming alliances with superiors and peers—to try to maintain or even enhance their department's position within the organizational hierarchy. In tribal cultures like this, managers and directors tend to work well with their peers, when their interests coincide; however, these individuals—or members of their respective departments—will often clash with each other when their varied needs or views do not mesh.

Sometimes directors or managers can hold grudges or otherwise express enmity towards their peers, even when their departments do not compete with each other for resources. These individuals might have developed an antagonistic relationship as a result of a situation that occurred a number of years in the past. However, their egos will not let them overcome their mutual animosities toward one another. In some cases, the relationship might be one-sided. The manager/director might hold a grudge against a fellow coworker, without any reciprocation by the other party.

In other cases, managers and directors might not hold any overt animosity towards one another at all. Yet they still—sometimes unconsciously—perceive each other in a negative light. For instance, the accounts receivable manager might not outwardly argue with the head of sales; however, he or she nonetheless believes that members of the sales team are not as capable as other employees of succeeding in leadership positions. Sometimes, these types of biases might be valid; however, more often than not, they are without merit.

One can argue that it's human nature for managers and employees alike to put the needs of their respective departments over those of the company as a whole. In many cases, it is actually advantageous for companies to foster this type of environment, as it can create a sense of intradepartmental comradery and can motivate managers and employees to work harder (as their focus is limited to maximizing their department's metrics). At the same time, this type of corporate tribalism can have a deleterious impact on the growth, development, and promotion of talented employees.

These manifestations of office-based politics can hinder the growth, development, and especially the promotion of talented employees. In fact, despite their differences, all of the various types of intradepartmental and interdepartmental issues that I discussed in the previous few paragraphs can impair the employee development and promotion systems in similar ways. Here are three of the most important ones.

- **The Patronage System ("Who You Know")**
  In these instances, managers, directors, and other leadership personnel within the organization will rely on interdepartmental relationships, patronage, and extra-regulatory negotiations (e.g., a system in which one person helps another individual, with the assumption that the "debt" will be repaid at some future time, and which contradicts or circumvents the corporation's written regulations) to help them in securing promotions—in other departments—for their favorite employees. In some cases, a key leader in the healthcare company will actively support any of his or her subordinates who demonstrate a desire to move up in the company. This becomes a problem when the officer utilizes extra-regulatory means to abet his or her staff.

  At the same time, the term can refer to situations in which managers or other key personnel give leadership roles to favored employees, without regard to that individual's skills and accomplishments relative to his or her coworkers. For instance, the marketing manager at a hospital might decide to promote one of his or her friends to the team lead position, even though that person is not the best-qualified candidate within the department. This same type of behavior can lead healthcare leaders to choose some employees over others when it comes to delegating high-profile tasks. For instance, the manager of the accounts receivable department might give a favored employee the first opportunity at taking the lead role on a key project.

At the same time, healthcare leaders can also impede certain people from getting promotions, from securing lead roles on important projects, or from obtaining other key developmental training. Politically minded leaders can set up these roadblocks within their own departments by refusing to acknowledge employee claims for more work or for a chance at a promotion. They can also hinder talented individuals in other departments from moving up the internal corporate ladder.

- **Strife and Discord**
  In this scenario, a healthcare leader tries to thwart the aims of a disliked peer in another area of the company by actively working to impede that "competitor's" staff members from advancing within the company and by attempting to keep them off of key committees and project teams. From my perspective, this behavior occurs more often in smaller companies, where individual managers and directors can exert more power. However, this type of situation can take place in any organization, given the right circumstances.

- **Not in My Department**
  This phrase refers to instances in which managers or directors refuse to consider employees from certain areas for leadership or specialist positions in their departments. The healthcare leaders will hold fast to their positions, even when these workers are the most-qualified candidates for the position. I am not referring to instances in which the department head eschews highly talented candidates due to a lack of experience in a key area. The "not in my department" motif only denotes instances in which a leader shuns all internal applicants from specific departments because of biases (or grudges) that he or she holds. This is a bigger issue than some readers might realize, because, in many healthcare corporations, the department manager has the final (and sometimes only) say with regard to internal transfers and placements related to his or her area.

9.7 The Seniority System

I have witnessed instances in which a healthcare organization's promotion system was based on seniority, instead of on merit. In these scenarios, the employee in the department with the longest tenure gets first choice at any opening. Some executives might perceive this system as beneficial because it achieves two goals. For one thing, they might argue that this type of promotion scheme will help them retain skilled workers. Ergo, these leaders believe that employees will be more likely to remain with the organization if it promotes based on seniority. This is especially true in situations where workers can only expect minimal annual increases in wages or salaries unless they move up the corporate ladder. At the same time, some executives see seniority-based promotion systems as a way of rewarding employees for their loyalty to an organization.

Healthcare companies that promote individuals or give them key assignments based primarily on seniority realize some benefits with regard to employee retention. They might procure other advantages as well. However, I believe that these organizations will usually lose more than they gain from this type of arrangement. First, they lose out because they do not place their most talented people in key specialist and leadership positions, which might impact these organizations' effectiveness and efficiency metrics. At the same time, their most talented employees will likely look for jobs at other, more proactive companies. In the end, healthcare organizations that utilize a seniority-based system might (or might not) retain a higher percentage of their workers; however, in my opinion, they often will be hard-pressed to keep their most talented people from jumping ship.

9.8 Promotion and Development Systems That Favor the Aggressive Employees

At some healthcare companies, managers and directors actively seek out what they consider to be the most talented employees and groom them for leadership and higher-level specialist positions. However, in many healthcare corporations, the individuals who secure the best promotions within the company are the ones who most aggressively pursue these positions. In some cases, these men and women are the ones who constantly scan their organizations' job openings lists. They will also likely work hard to network around the office in an effort to secure upper-level support for their ambitious goals.

In some cases, managers who actively seek promotions turn out to be great leaders. They can use their promotional skills to advantage in motivating workers, in securing excellent deals with vendors, or by achieving other company-oriented goals. However, I have also met a number of individuals who are the exact opposite of these aggressive types. Many of them are diligent, yet quiet, workers; they neither complain about their jobs, nor do they seek to draw attention to themselves when they perform above expectations.

In some cases, managers who actively seek promotions turn out to be great leaders. They can use their promotional skills to advantage in securing excellent deals with vendors, or by achieving other company-oriented goals. However, not all of these people are worthy of taking on the mantle of leadership.

At the same time, I have met a large number of individuals who are the exact opposite of these aggressive types. Many of them are (or were) diligent, yet quiet, workers; they neither complain about their jobs, nor do they seek to draw attention to themselves when they perform above expectations. Their superiors, if they did not get to know these men and women personally, might overlook them when searching for new leaders. However, that would be a mistake.

Unassuming people can sometimes make great leaders. What they lack in flair or showmanship, they more than make up for in other ways. They are often excellent listeners and are more than willing to empathize and support their employees. They are also, at least in my experience, often adept at managing through compromise and are more than willing to praise their employees when they perform well. I remember one such individual who I worked with a number of years ago. She was a quiet person who never said much and never actively (at least publicly) sought a promotion. She ended up becoming a manager in one of the company's revenue cycle management departments. From what I noticed, she did an excellent job in leading her team. She led by example by means of her hard work ethic and through her ability to understand the needs of her employees and the challenges they faced on a day-to-day basis.

I am not the only one who can attest to the value that unassuming people can bring to a corporation, especially when they are given a chance to lead. People have recognized this fact for many millennia. The Roman legend (based on a true story) of Lucius Quinctius Cincinnatus praises the ideal of the reticent leader. Cicinnatus was a Roman farmer (albeit, likely, a wealthy one), who reluctantly took up the leadership mantle in 458 B.C.—accepting the position as the de facto dictator of Rome when it was threatened by an enemy. He managed to defeat the invading armies, but that is not why he was celebrated in Roman lore. Instead, his compatriots praised him for "giving up the reins of power when the crisis was over" and heading "back to his farm" (Anonymous, 2014).

Healthcare organizations that utilize an internal promotions system that puts the onus on employees to submit applications for open positions might be poorly situated to identify these reticent leaders. This is especially true for healthcare firms in which managers, by and large, do not take an active hand in encouraging talented but unassuming employees to apply for available jobs. Ironically, smaller healthcare organizations, though lacking the HR budgets of their larger peers, might be better at identifying these types of people. At a small company—at least the ones I have been associated with—the directors, and even the c-suite personnel, often get to know each employee personally. They, therefore, have a better chance of spotting talented, non-aggressive (at least with regard to self-promotion) staff members. Nonetheless, any healthcare organization is at risk of missing out on developing and promoting the best talent if it does not have some standardized system in place for identifying reticent leaders.

9.9 Ways to Maximize Employee Development and Promotion Systems

To sum up the discussion to this point, if a healthcare organization wants to excel at developing its internal talent, it has to accomplish several objectives, which include:

- **Limiting The Influence of the Two P's**
  As I noted previously, healthcare organizations will find it extremely difficult, if not impossible, to eliminate all forms of power abuse and political maneuvering. Even if they could, it would be too costly to achieve this goal. Besides, healthcare organizations depend on power and political arrangements to help them manage employees and to achieve their overall goals. They should, therefore, eschew trying to totally ditch the two P's. Instead, healthcare companies should work to limit the two P's when they have a deleterious impact on the development and promotion of internal talent.

- **Limit the Negative Effects of Patronage**

  The patronage system draws on elements of both power and politics. More to the point, it is part of human nature. In my experience, human beings, being the social creatures that they are, will naturally gravitate to using a system of favors—I will do this task for you if you do that job for me—to achieve their personal aims.

  As I noted previously, healthcare corporations can sometimes benefit from these types of arrangements. And, anyway, it does not make sense from a cost–benefit perspective for these organizations to try to eliminate this type of employee behavior. What healthcare companies should do is to try to find ways to ensure that the patronage system does not hinder the growth, development, and advancement of talented personnel.

- **Say "No" to the Seniority System**

  In the next chapter, I will delineate some techniques that healthcare organizations can utilize to keep valued, veteran employees. However, I believe businesses should not try to retain employees by using tenure to decide who gets promoted.

- **Do Not Forget to Look for Reticent Leaders**

  As I noted in the previous section, the unassuming people can, in the right circumstances, turn out to be excellent leaders. They can certainly serve in high-level specialist positions, such as internal auditing and strategic management posts. A healthcare business needs to find a way to fully utilize these employees if it wants to maximize its potential. However, these individuals will often refrain from actively seeking these types of promotions. Companies will have to think outside the box in order to identify, develop, and promote these reticent workers.

9.10 Create the Right Culture and Use Key Information Technology (IT) Tools to Identify and Develop Workplace Talent

A healthcare leader who wants to create an effective employee development and promotion system first needs to ensure that his or her company possesses a corporate culture that contains strong meritocratic elements. The organizational environment should be one in which managers feel encouraged (and perhaps obligated) to nominate employees for key tasks and for promotions based on their perceived accomplishments. The healthcare company might not be totally able to eliminate promotions by fiat or through "backroom deals" (and perhaps there are advantages to keeping some vestiges of these systems around). However, an organization that adheres to meritocratic principles will be able to keep the politics to a minimum.

Healthcare leaders who want to create this type of culture—at least with regard to internal promotions and hiring—would have to know two things. First, these men and women would need to be cognizant of exactly what elements are necessary to develop and maintain this type of corporate environment. Second, these leaders would have to convince their employees to adopt these new methods. In almost every case, management would have to find a way to replace an existing set of norms with the ones that I discuss in this chapter. The only time this phenomenon would not exist is when the healthcare organizations are nascent. In these instances, the respective company's management team (or leader, in the case of small organizations) is free to set the ground rules.

9.10.1 How to Create the Right Culture

In this section, I will focus on the cultural elements that are most conducive to creating and maintaining optimal internal employee development and promotion programs. I will not devote much time to delineating the steps that a healthcare leader would have to follow in order to alter his or her organization's culture. Suffice it to say that it is difficult for healthcare corporations—or for any business—to make significant changes to its employees' traditions and accepted ways of doing things (Bolman & Deal, 2008, 374–378).

At the same time, healthcare organizations should make the effort to change corporate habits and behaviors when this tactic makes sense from a cost–benefit perspective. I believe that it is certainly worthwhile for healthcare companies to create systems that match employees to job types based on their skills, experience, and potential. Healthcare organizations also benefit when they are able to successfully develop and promote internal talent. In my experience, the closer that a company comes to achieving these two aims, the more efficiently it runs—all other things being equal.

Many of this book's readers work for healthcare organizations that already do a good job of developing and promoting internal talent. In these cases, their organizations will only have to make minor changes (if any) in order to accomplish the goals set forth in this chapter. However, a number of readers are probably not so lucky; their corporations' cultures might be beset by some of the issues that I discussed earlier in the chapter. Their businesses would have to make wholesale changes to office cultures in order to properly develop and promote internal talent. In my experience, it is usually relatively easy for companies to make small changes, and, as Bolman and Deal illustrate in their book, it is more difficult to alter a corporate culture in more significant ways (2008, 374–378). In either case, readers, who want to learn more about this topic—changing corporate cultures—can choose from any number of excellent books that are already on the market. Most of these volumes will provide step-by-step instructions on how to introduce and maintain new organizational initiatives that run counter to the current corporate culture.

9.10.2 Developing and Maintaining a Culture That Supports Optimal Development and Promotion Programs

Before a healthcare organization can alter its corporate behaviors and traditions to accommodate an optimal employee development and promotion process, it must have some idea as to what this type of culture looks like. In some ways, a healthcare corporation's answer to this question will be unique. It will depend upon a number of factors that are somewhat specific to that particular company. It might include elements such as that entity's history; its external and internal environments; and its mission, vision, and values. At the same time, I believe there are several cultural motifs that companies can use to help guide them in their attempts to optimize their worker development and promotion systems. These topics include:

- **Focus on Merit**
  Healthcare organizations need to foster working environments that are closer to meritocracies than to feudal fiefdoms. The cultures in these organizations will be directed toward compensating employees based primarily on their accomplishments, though other factors, such as seniority, might play a role. As an offshoot of this process, healthcare leaders in these types of organizations will naturally seek

to develop talented employees. Management will also be keen on matching each staff member with jobs that fits his or her particular skills, experiences, and temperaments.

- **Management Is Close to Its Workforce**
  In order for a healthcare corporation to optimize its employee development and promotion system, its management has to be able to identify talented workers who do not aggressively promote themselves. In my experience, this phenomenon will only occur on a consistent basis if the organization's leadership actively engages its employees. Directors, managers, and even c-suite leaders have to take an interest in their subordinates' work. This requires them to get to know these individuals as people and not just as cogs in a machine. It might be more difficult for hierarchically structured companies to espouse cultures that encourage these types of relationships; however, this task is not impossible.

- **Treat Employees with Dignity and Respect**
  Many healthcare jobs will, by their nature, be stressful and require long hours in the office. Examples of these types of positions would include nursing, employed physicians, and some call center positions. Despite that fact, in my experience, the most productive workplaces are ones in which management treats employees with respect and dignity. People will be more willing to "give a 100 percent" if they feel like they are more than just a number. More importantly, employees who work in these types of environments might be more willing to put in the extra effort to learn new skills, to take risks, and to perform other tasks that will help them to grow as individuals and as potential leaders and specialists.

- **The Cultural Message Is Holistic**
  Many healthcare organizations are very diverse. A hospital, for instance, will employ a wide range of worker types. These individuals will come from all walks of life and possess a varied array of skills, experiences, and credentials. In some cases, the company might manage facilities and offices in numerous locations throughout a state—or perhaps in many states. Regardless of its level of diversity, a healthcare corporation has to find a way to ensure that all of its employees—or at least most of them—understand and adhere to its key cultural tenets, especially as they impact its worker development

and promotion system. Both management and frontline staff have to buy-in to these cultural tenets in order for them to be successful.

Healthcare corporations that possess these key cultural traits will be in a much better position than many of their peers to create and maintain optimal employee development and promotion systems. At the same time, these organizations might be better able to leverage IT tools to further enhance their programs.

9.10.3 Leveraging IT to Enhance Employee Development and Promotion Systems

As I noted previously, healthcare corporations that want to create and maintain optimal employee development and promotion programs have to ensure that they create cultures that are conducive to fostering these types of systems. At the same time, they can utilize IT tools to help them develop and maintain these work environments, to assist management in matching employees with the correct jobs, in helping to identify potential leaders, and in other, related tasks.

I denote two schemes that healthcare corporations can use both to guide employee development and to identify the best personnel for open jobs from a list of internal candidates. They include information that will help IT personnel, working in coordination with management, to implement these systems companywide.

9.10.4 Using IT to Aid in Creating a Skills Development and Training Checklist

I believe that even relatively small healthcare organizations can derive benefits from creating a structured employee leadership skills development program. I feel that, as part of this process, management should implement a documentation process for monitoring employee advancement through the training regimen. Companies can work with outside vendors to create a checklist system, or they can utilize in-house talent and readily available office tools, such as Microsoft Project and Excel, to achieve this objective. In Figure 9.1, I have posited a how-to-guide for creating and implementing this type of checklist.

Skills Development and Training Checklist—Key Features

Each organization's checklist system will be unique but it should:

- Include a documentation system that is accessible to relevant executives, managers, and other personnel.
- Delineate a series of training programs with assigned goals. They should include predetermined skills and leadership development projects within the employee's department, as well as cross-training exercises in other departments.
- Set a series of deadlines for completion of these training assignments and/or create a checklist for denoting completion of these projects.
- Incorporate a skills checklist with a ranking system. For instance, the company might feel that empathy is important and will include it as one of the abilities on the list. Relevant managers will use a ranking system to note a particular employee's progress (or regression) with regard to mastering this talent.
- Require the manager who oversees the worker's participation in one of these pre-set training exercises to update the training checklist and skills sections.
- Allow relevant personnel to update the system at other times (when the employee is performing duties that are not related to any specific training module).
- Focus, to the greatest extent possible, on using binary or quantitative marks. This will allow managers to quickly monitor an employee's progress while at the same time ensuring that these leaders do not waste time entering or reviewing lengthy notations.
- Ensure that the system keeps track of the people who enter/modify employee information. At the very least, the system should note the author/editor and access dates and times.

Goals

Management can guide the development of key personnel within their respective organizations. More specifically, they can at least attempt to ensure that the employees learn and develop (or at least are exposed to) important leadership skills before they move up in the organization. At the same time, managers and executives can monitor these workers' development (or lack thereof). The system should also limit employer bias by obtaining input from several different leadership personnel and via ensuring that there is some level of accountability.

Figure 9.1 A how-to-guide for creating and implementing a skills development and training checklist. Each organization's documentation process will differ, as it will need to conform to that company's specific features, such as its size, culture, and so forth.

An AI-Driven Internal Candidate Selection System—Key Features

The AI system should:

- Include an employee database that contains relevant hiring information, including each worker's skills, work experiences, job approval ratings, length of tenure, salary, and so forth.
- Be secure yet accessible by relevant personnel when necessary.
- Allow employees to update relevant parts of their personnel files, including adding any work experience that they procured outside of the workplace. However, these opportunities must be limited (e.g., employees could add information twice a year as part of their review process) in order to ensure accuracy and accountability.
- Update itself whenever new information is entered.
- Contain an AI component that allows HR to enter specific skills, experience, and so forth, for a new opening. The AI system would then search through candidate files to identify the best potential applicants.
- Automatically alert internal applicants once HR has vetted and approved the list.
- Allow employees who were not selected by its automated process to apply for the position. This will allow HR to identify qualified candidates that the automated system might have missed.

Goals

Healthcare organizations can streamline their internal candidate application and selection processes, thereby making them more efficient. Healthcare companies can leverage the system to help them do a better job of finding the best candidates for specific job openings.

Figure 9.2 An example of an automated, AI-driven internal candidate selection system. Many healthcare organizations might not yet be able either to create or to purchase such a system. However, they should be able to do so within the next few years (as costs come down and technology improves).

9.10.5 Using IT to Help Create an Internal Candidate Identification System

Most healthcare organizations probably utilize one of three methods to identify internal candidates for open positions. In the first system, the organization's HR personnel will alert department managers to job openings and ask these people to let HR know if they are aware of any employees who might qualify for the position. At the same time, HR staff will post the job opening on a message board (either a real board or a virtual one) and ask employees to email them. Companies might also utilize a more formal method that requires internal applicants to fill out online applications, submit their résumés, and perform other tasks—which mirror the steps that an external applicant would take.

All three of these techniques are, to some extent, inefficient and perhaps ineffective. In all three instances, HR staff will waste time and energy duplicating key aspects of the external hiring process. At the same time, HR might overlook candidates who do not apply, or who do not receive referrals from management (in many cases because the department head wants to retain the employee). Healthcare corporations could ameliorate or even eliminate these problems by utilizing an internal hiring system that can identify potential matches based on easily accessible, real-time information.

Healthcare corporations can achieve these results in two ways. The first method would require the company to keep an employee dataset that is updated frequently and which contains important data on each worker. Whenever a position opens up, HR staff and/or hiring managers would mine this data to identify a short candidate list for job openings. Alternatively, management, working with vendors or in-house IT personnel, could create an artificial intelligence (AI) system that could perform the same functions. In Figure 9.2, I provide information that IT staff and management can use to help them create an internal candidate identification system that utilizes AI technologies.

References

Anonymous. (2014). Lucius Quinctius Cincinnatus. *Encyclopedia Brittanica*. Retrieved from http://www.britannica.com/EBchecked/topic/117993/Lucius-Quinctius-Cincinnatus.

Bing Dictionary. (2014). Definition of Culture (n). Retrieved from www.bing.com.

Bolman, L. G., & Deal, T. E. (2008). *Reframing Organizations: Artistry, Choice, and Leadership*. San Francisco, CA: Jossey-Bass.

Hoff, T., & Rockman, K. W. (2012). Power, Politics, and Conflict Management. In L. R. Burns, E. H. Bradley, & B. J. Weiner (Eds.) (2012). *Shortell and*

Kaluzney's Health Care Management: Organization Design and Behavior (pp. 188–220). 6th ed. Clifton Park, NY: Cengage Learning (Delmar).

Maslow, A. H. (1998). *Maslow on Management.* New York, NY: John Wiley & Sons.

Schuh, S. C., Zhang, X., & Tian, P. (2013). For the Good or the Bad? Interactive Effects of Transformational Leadership with Moral and Authoritarian Leadership Behaviors. *Journal of Business Ethics* 116(3), 629–640. DOI: 10551-012-1486-0.

Chapter Ten

Ideas That Managers and Executives Can Use to Increase Employee Satisfaction

In previous sections of this book, I stated that healthcare organizations can improve their chances of thriving over the long term if they hire the right people for open positions and if they possess solid employee promotion and development programs. While those things are true, I believe that most successful healthcare organizations perform well in one other key area. Namely, they cultivate supportive workplace cultures.

In this chapter, I focus on the day-to-day management of employees. Specifically, I argue that successful healthcare organizations create workplace cultures that foster employee satisfaction. I contend that this fact is important because contented employees, on average, are more efficient and effective. At the same time, I provide evidence that demonstrates a correlation between employee-satisfaction metrics and retention rates. Delving deeper into this topic, I delineate some of the key features that are found in worker-friendly corporate cultures. I finish up by positing some ideas that a healthcare leader can use to help his or her company improve its relationship with its workforce.

10.1 A Review of the Topics Discussed in Chapter 9

In Chapter 9, I talked about some of the ways in which a healthcare corporation's culture is integral to the success (or failure) of its internal worker development and promotion programs. I noted that workplace environments that encourage or allow managers and other employees to accumulate, manipulate, and sometimes outright abuse power are not the most conducive to maximizing this type of nurturing. I also suggested that healthcare organizations should keep the political elements to a minimum if they want to create and maintain robust employee-improvement programs. Finally, I pointed out that healthcare organizations that blindly reward the most aggressive employees, or the ones with the most seniority, will have difficulty ensuring that open positions are filled with the best-qualified internal candidates.

By contrast, in my experience anyway, the healthcare organizations that do an excellent job of developing internal talent are the ones that—to the greatest extent possible—accurately assess the strengths and weaknesses of each member of the workforce. These corporations promote employees based on merit and fitness for the specific job openings available. Their development and promotion systems limit the negative effects of the two P's—power and politics. Finally, these organizations are good at identifying talented employees who are not self-promoters.

In order to create this type of environment, healthcare leaders need to create protocols that carefully regulate the employee development and promotion process. They also need to continuously support their organizations' enforcement of these rules and regulations. When possible, healthcare executives and other pertinent staff should utilize information technology (IT) to help them implement and maintain effective employee development and promotion programs.

10.2 How to Retain, Manage, and Motivate Employees

In this chapter, I will discuss some methods that healthcare organizations can utilize to manage, motivate, and retain their employees. I will once again focus on corporate culture because, in my opinion, it is the most important factor influencing and mediating workers' behaviors and activities. At the same time, I will refrain from relying on academic motifs to structure this section, as I feel that one can find plenty of books that utilize this formula. Rather, I will rely primarily on my own observations, garnered over many years of working in healthcare and in other fields, to help me fill out this narrative. I will cite some academic and expert-level research, when appropriate; however, these texts will usually only serve to buttress or expand upon my observations. I feel that I will best serve my readers by providing them with "on the ground" accounts and practical information.

10.3 Culture and Its Importance in Worker Management

I touched on corporate culture, in a general sense, in the last chapter. However, I will discuss the topic in a bit more depth here. I think that readers will benefit from this conversation, as my views on workplace culture often inform and underpin my suggested employee management strategies.

As I noted in the previous chapter, one can define an organization's culture as its stakeholders' "shared beliefs, customs, [and] practices" (Bing, 2014). I think that most people would agree that it is difficult if not impossible for one to fully delineate a healthcare corporation's (or any business's) workplace culture. Although an objective viewer might be able to identify key aspects of a particular company's employee culture, he or she would be hard-pressed to isolate all of the values, beliefs, and especially the daily interactions that vivified it.

Nonetheless, a healthcare organization's culture influences its employees' official and informal interactions with each other, as well as with other key stakeholders. Management relies on their organization's norms to help them in formulating new rules and in deciding how to enforce current regulations. The company's workers utilize cultural markers to help them mediate their interactions with peers and other stakeholders, to aid them in determining what they can and cannot do while at the office (and sometimes to determine what actions are taboo even when they are performed outside of the workplace), and to guide their daily work activities (Wilhelm, 1992, 72).

In my experience, the companies that do an excellent job in both retaining and managing their respective workforces usually possess several key cultural features in common. They include:

- **A Belief That Transparency Is Important**
  Most of the employees whom I have been affiliated with have placed a high regard on corporate transparency. Workers realize that their firms have to keep some things private or even dissemble from time to time in order to protect proprietary information. However, they want management to be honest with them, whenever possible. Researchers have demonstrated that employees, by and large, prefer to work for companies that encourage both management and front-line staff to act with integrity and honesty (Asacker, 2004, 43). In fact, in one employee survey, "Nine out of 10 workers polled [said] they value[d] integrity as much as income" (Savoye, 2000, 3).

- **A Desire to Treat Employees Fairly**
  Workers perform best when they believe that management treats them with respect and dignity. As a corollary to this principle, staff members believe that their supervisors will treat them fairly during reviews and disciplinary hearings. Many employees, at least in my experience, also want their companies to have written policies that describe the disciplinary/penalty process in detail and, at least on paper, guarantee that they will have a chance to defend themselves (e.g., the system guarantees employees some level of due process).

  As a corollary to this topic, it goes without saying that people work, in part, to earn money. However, I think that a large number of Americans would agree that their wages represent only one factor in the equation. In my experience, employees, by and large, do not work solely, or even primarily, to earn as much money as possible. Instead, they view their earnings as a sort of yardstick that indicates their company's level of respect for them as workers and as human beings. In other words, when someone asks for a raise, he or she is often saying, "I feel that my employer can demonstrate its respect for my work by giving me a just raise."

- **The Acknowledgment of the Fact That Each Employee Is a Unique Individual**
  Most of the people whom I have come into contact with during my years in the healthcare field (and in other industries) want one thing above all others—to be recognized as individuals. They want their managers, and, more importantly, the higher ups—at least the director but also including the c-suite in small companies—to know them by name. These men and women would also like their superiors, as

well as their peers in the office (without being too nosy), to ask after their well-being, their families, and other personal aspects of their lives. In other words, to use an old cliché, "Employees want to be treated as human beings and not just as numbers." In fact, in my experience anyway, people will sometimes stick with companies that do not achieve some of the other key aims in this list, as long as management treats them like "family."

- **A Belief in Meritocracies**
  Few healthcare corporations can ever aspire to the lofty goal of becoming full meritocracies, in which management rewards employees solely based on their skills, their work ethics, or their accomplishments. Healthcare leaders must sometimes take into account office politics, vendor relationships, community needs, or other, non–merit-based factors when deciding who to hire, who to promote, who to reward for their efforts (and how to reward them). This is especially true when it comes to selecting members for internal committees. For instance, a director or c-suite executive might not believe that anyone in the revenue cycle management department can contribute much to a patient safety committee. However, he or she will choose an individual from that department in order to "keep the accounts receivable personnel happy."

  Nonetheless, although healthcare companies cannot hope to become true meritocracies, they should strive to create a culture that institutes, to the greatest degree possible, a merit-based system. In my experience, most employees—even some of the ones who take advantage of office politics to gain an advantage over their peers—prefer to work for companies that reward workers for their hard work and that attempt to match staff with the jobs that they are best suited for. What is more, it is not just American and European workers who feel this way. Panjak Bansal, writing in Business Today, states that Indian workers—if they have a choice—look for companies that promote a "culture of meritocracy and transparency" (2011). Most importantly, as one business expert notes, "Employees aware of merit-based promotions and responsibilities are more apt to possess a positive work ethic and opinion of your company" (Vaishnavi, 2013).

- **Make An Effort to Ensure That the Employee's Work Is Meaningful**
  Many people will spend a half century or longer working in the healthcare field. They want, of course, to earn money and secure

basic benefits. However, perhaps more importantly, they want to feel like they are contributing towards the greater good—or at least towards something larger than themselves. Almost all individuals, running the gamut from the lowest paid workers to the CEO, desire meaningful work (Fairlie, 2011, 17). A healthcare organization that cannot help its employees to realize this goal will have a larger problem in retaining and motivating these workers.

- **An Earnest Desire to Allow Employees to Maintain a Sense of Work–Life Balance**
One of the hot topics in the business circles centers around the principle of work–life balance. In this scenario, many employees prefer to work for companies that allow them to "split their time and energy between work and the other important aspects of their lives" (Heathfield, 2014). Many experts believe that people who work for companies that provide work–life balance incentives such as "flexible work schedules" and employee-friendly time-off policies are happier and more productive (when they are at the office) than they would be otherwise (Amabile & Kramer, 2012; Staff of the Corporate Executive Board, 2009).

  As a corollary to this topic, employees often suffer from burn out. The term can mean a number of different things. On the one hand, people often say they are burnt out when they are physically and mentally exhausted and this feeling persists over a longer period of time. Psychology Today notes that people in this state can also experience issues related to "cynicism, depression, and lethargy . . ." (Anonymous, 2014). In my experience, employees who are "burnt out" almost always have difficulty in mustering up the will or inner strength necessary to perform their tasks. They are usually also more prone to exhibit negative emotions, such as anger, aggression, irritation, and so forth.

  Employees who are suffering from this condition are not necessarily dissatisfied with their employers. Sometimes, these individuals get burnt out because they took it upon themselves to put in too many hours at the office or in the clinic; they might also have volunteered to perform too many tasks at once. However, too often, companies create these problems by overworking their staffs. This issue is especially problematic in some healthcare industries, including at hospitals and nursing homes, where management has significant incentives (and sometimes feels intense pressure) to do more with less or has to deal with labor shortages (e.g., in the nursing field) (Brimmer, 2013; Favaloro, 2013; Fernandez, 2011).

Although "burnt out" workers might not always be dissatisfied with their companies, I feel that the two topics—employee fatigue and worker dissatisfaction—are closely enough intertwined to include worker burn out as a corollary to the topic of work–life balance. In any case, management at any healthcare company needs to work hard to ensure that employees maintain a good work–life balance as a strategy to keep these individuals satisfied as well as to ensure that they do not burn themselves out.

10.4 Why Healthcare Companies Should Care about These Six Features

I have chosen these six cultural features because I feel that they are integral to employee well-being. In my experience, employees want to work for companies whose cultures, to some extent, possess these traits. As readers can garner from the citations in the last section, a number of research studies corroborate my observations.

Most leaders, at heart, would love nothing better than to cultivate workplace cultures that foster employee happiness. However, they might refrain from focusing on this issue because they do not see how such an initiative would improve their corporation's bottom line. In response to this meme, I hope, in the next few paragraphs, to show that there is a strong correlation between a company's employee-satisfaction rates and key metrics such as productivity, quality, and, ultimately, profits. Specifically, satisfied employees are less likely to leave a company for a new job, they tend to work harder, they produce higher quality work, and they often engage in other activities that benefit their employers.

It stands to reason that people who are content with their work life are less likely to actively search for new job opportunities (Catlette & Hadden, 2000, 32–34). In my experience, individuals who are satisfied with their current employers are also more willing to turn down unsolicited job offers, even when they can realize a significant raise or garner additional perks if they accepted the hostile offer. As a result, healthcare organizations that create supportive employee cultures should, all other things being equal, achieve higher employee-retention rates.

This fact is important because healthcare organizations generally want to keep their employee retention rates as high as possible. In my experience, companies with large numbers of veteran employees can benefit from these individuals' company-specific experiences and knowledge (a popular term for this collected wisdom is "institutional memory"). As important, healthcare firms that maintain low turnover rates can save money on training, unemployment payouts, and new employee recruitment efforts. They also realize significantly fewer lost-opportunity costs than their peers, who have difficulty keeping employees on-board. This is because managers and directors of low-turnover companies do not have to spend as much time perusing through résumés and interviewing potential new hires, thereby allowing these men and women to devote more time to performing their primary tasks.

Healthcare companies with employee-friendly cultures should, all other things being equal, possess a workforce that is more engaged than would otherwise be the case. This is because contented employees, on the whole, tend to work harder than disenchanted ones. They tend to put in longer hours at the office without complaint (or without complaining any more than would be considered normal). They also spend more time per hour working on company-related tasks—with fewer breaks—than their dissatisfied peers. I can attest to the validity of this claim from my personal observations. Researchers who have studied this issue tend to agree with my anecdotal insights (Amabile & Kramer, 2012; Maciver, 2004, 2–3; Oswald, Proto, & Sgroi, 2014, 2–13).

Just as important, contented employees frequently perform better on daily tasks and projects than their unhappy peers. In my experience, satisfied employees achieve superior results in part because they do a better job of focusing on the task at hand. They are not as often distracted by work-related worries or as easily agitated with some poorly thought-out company policy or management decision. Perhaps most importantly, at least in my experience, people who are satisfied with their workplace environments usually want to excel—to please a manager, their fellow employees, or other stakeholders (such as customers).

I feel that these are three of the main ways that healthcare organizations can benefit from creating employee-supportive cultures that reflect the six principles I listed earlier. However, these companies can realize other advantages as well. For instance, an individual's level of disenchantment with his or her company is one of the many factors (along with psychological and ethical ones) that might lead that person to steal from his or her employer (Singleton & Singleton, 2010, 51–52). At the same time, contented employees might be more likely to recommend the organization to friends and family—who then later become that organization's newest patient or its most recent hire. These are only a couple of the other instances in which a company's treatment of its employees directly or indirectly impacts its bottom line in a positive way.

10.5 Special Considerations for Clinical-Based Healthcare Companies

Up until now, my discussion of workplace environments could probably apply to firms in any field. That makes sense given that healthcare organizations share many features in common with companies in other industries. If companies in any field, including in healthcare, do not follow the six principles that I listed earlier, or for some other reason fail to satisfy their employees' needs, they will likely suffer—at least in the long term. However, healthcare firms—at least the ones that provide clinical care—do differ in significant ways from most other organizations. I delineated some of these differences in the first few chapters of this book. One variance lies in the diversity of the industry's workforce, which runs the gamut from minimum wage laborers to autonomous or semiautonomous clinical workers and physicians. I will discuss this topic in more depth in a later portion of this book. Another key dissimilarity revolves around the client–patient relationship.

Health services organizations, including hospitals, nursing homes, and home health agencies, which provide clinical care to patients, need to pay especial attention to their employees' satisfaction levels. If frontline workers, such as clinicians, techs, or nurses, become disgruntled, they could end up harming or even killing patients. In theory, it is easy to understand why this is the case, if one considers what I said earlier about the connection btween worker contentment and quality of service. Although the research on this issue is to an extent limited, at least some studies do show a direct correlation between "employee satisfaction" and patient care (Larson, 2012). More importantly, researchers have also demonstrated a connection between worker-satisfaction rates and the number of medical errors that occur (Lee, Lee, & Schniederjans, 2011, 1311–1325).

Granted, worker satisfaction is only one of many factors that can lead to patient safety issues at a health services organization. Other things, including employee training, systemic flaws in safety procedures or protocols, and understaffing (which can also lead to employee disenchantment), play a part as well. However, that does not mean that hospitals, nursing homes, and other health services providers should avoid the topic. Instead, they should consider employee satisfaction along with other issues when they look at ways of improving patient safety in their facilities.

10.6 A Case in Point—The Disgruntled Employee

I remember one situation that occurred while I was still in college that hammers home the correlation between an employee's feelings of satisfaction with his or her organization and that individual's work habits. Although this scenario took place outside of the healthcare field, I think readers will find it to be a valuable addition to the discussion in this chapter.

At the time, I was still an undergraduate and was working part-time in the summers as a bank teller. One day I decided to visit one of the local area businesses during my lunch break in order to purchase some food. I happened to get the chance to interact with a new employee—the individual had been working for the corporation for less than a week. The person handled my purchase with a high level of energy and cheerfulness. If I had the opportunity to fill out a survey, I would have given her the highest marks for customer service and attention to detail. I asked if she liked her job, and she said, "I love it."

I came back to the same spot a week later and interacted with the same person behind the counter. This individual's demeanor, within the span of one week, had radically transformed. Although she did not make any mistakes in adding up my purchases, she no longer greeted me, nor did she give off an aura of cheeriness. Instead, she brusquely tallied up my goods and handed my bag to me with machinelike, emotionless movements. I ventured to ask her if still liked the job, and this time she stated, "It is awful."

Although this individual did not work in the healthcare field, her story nonetheless provides a stark reminder of the dangers involved when a company does not place enough of the focus on its employees. Even the most energetic, capable employees will find it difficult to perform their jobs admirably if their work culture is not supportive.

10.7 The Other Side of the Argument

In previous sections, I laid out six key features that every healthcare organization wants to have in place in order to maintain acceptable employee-satisfaction rates. I then went on to discuss why it is important for healthcare companies to keep their employees contented. Finally, I provided an example that demonstrated the link between employer behaviors, worker satisfaction, and deficiencies in on-the-job performance.

In an ideal world, all healthcare leaders would make sure that their management teams created and maintained supportive corporate cultures. These individuals would work to ensure that their companies did an excellent job in promoting the six cultural features that I listed earlier in this chapter. People would be lauding these companies for their treatment of employees, their meritocratic systems, their transparency, and so forth. However, in reality, even the most determined healthcare executives might find it difficult to fully realize the goals mentioned in the first part of this chapter.

A healthcare corporation might struggle to create and maintain a truly supportive workplace environment for any number of reasons. Some of these factors are completely under its control and can be altered with only a minimal financial impact on the company's bottom line. For instance, the organization might contain a number of abusive directors or managers—or the entire corporate culture might be centered on the motto that "might makes right." Employees are likely not going to give the organization high marks in areas such as "the treatment of workers" and "creates a meritocratic environment." The healthcare entity might be able to fix these issues with only minimal outlays of cash. For instance, it could retrain the abusive managers and, only as a last resort, replace them. The company's management could spend some time analyzing the current corporate culture and looking for cost-effective ways to make it more employee friendly. Maybe the management team finds that the organization can alter its culture by making rather inexpensive changes to company policies and by tweaking the ways in which its workers interact with each other.

Although some healthcare organizations' employee-management problems might stem from non-monetary issues (e.g., bad management, poorly constructed employee policies, etc.), in many cases, these companies might be forced to sacrifice employee well-being in order to achieve financial goals. For example, nursing homes, hospitals, and other healthcare providers sometimes have to get by with less than optimal staff to patient/resident ratios in order to keep costs down. In a related move, a health services company might ask already tired employees to work mandatory overtime because it is cheaper for the entity to pay workers for the extra hours than it is for it to hire new staff. I could posit a number of other examples to backup this point; however, the bottom line is still the same in each case. Healthcare organizations sometimes make the conscious choice to anger workers and (or) to overwork them in order to meet earnings targets. In my experience, the more precarious the firm's financial situation (e.g., the closer the company is to filing for bankruptcy), the more willing it is to make these trade-offs.

Sometimes, healthcare organizations with suboptimal employee cultures might suffer from a third type of problem, which combines elements from the two types already mentioned. The corporations' issues might stem from the non-monetary factors discussed in the first set of examples; they may include things like poor management, misguided policies, and so forth. Unlike in the first set of examples, management is aware of these issues and wants to fix them; however, they do not have the available resources to act on these desires.

As a case in point, assume that a healthcare company is not understaffed, but its employees are still unhappy with it for one reason or another. The leaders of the company realize that they could improve worker morale by raising salaries or by means of some alternative method, such as by boosting everyone's annual allowed paid time off. However, they do not have the funds to execute this maneuver. Additionally, they cannot make any other significant changes—including retraining or releasing certain personnel—for similar reasons.

10.8 Solutions Should Be Creative, Cost-Effective, Authentic, Planned, and Multipronged

Obviously, it is easiest for healthcare leaders to ameliorate employee satisfaction or burnout issues when their companies have excess cash. A CEO, director, or department manager who wants to increase employee morale can more easily accomplish these things if he or she has a sizeable pot of money to draw from for activities, bonuses, retraining, or other activities. However, in my experience, healthcare leaders can often still improve employee-satisfaction metrics even if they have relatively little in the way of resources. The key to their success lies in their ability to come up with ideas that are creative, cost-effective, authentic, planned, and multipronged—what I will refer to as CCAPM.

I have included a more detailed description of each segment of the CCAPM strategy in the following sections.

- **Creative**
  As I noted previously, sometimes healthcare leaders want to improve employee-satisfaction metrics, or ameliorate issues with employee burnout; however, they do not think they have the necessary resources to accomplish this task. Occasionally, these individuals might not have any options available to them, but oftentimes even the most cash-strapped CEOs, directors, or managers can find ways to improve the morale of their employees or even to help workers overcome fatigue. They simply have to think outside the box. They might ask themselves (or others), "Can I make any changes to corporate culture or otherwise do anything to benefit my employees—without spending much money in the process?" I think readers who think through this question will be surprised at some of the ideas they might come up with.

- **Cost-Effective**
  When possible, healthcare leaders should choose the most cost-effective policies that are possible to achieve desired results. This might seem like common sense to many people. However, too often—in my experience anyway—executives and/or department managers do not follow this course of action. Of course, sometimes a healthcare leader will not have this option available to him or her; in those instances, the individual will have to utilize whatever is available.

- **Authentic**
  As a Forbes article notes, healthcare leaders gain the respect of their employees by being authentic (or seeming to be anyway) (Quast, 2012). To put it another way, executives, directors, and managers need to introduce new initiatives to employees in a way that seems genuine and heartfelt. After spending years in the healthcare workforce, around a wide diversity of people, I believe that the most

important aspect of any plan to boost employee morale is its perceived level of authenticity (from the workers' perspectives). Sometimes, staff members will celebrate a new management proposal,
even when they think it is ill-advised or that it does not improve
their work environment, as long as these people believe that management is trying—that they have the best interests of their employees
at heart.

- **Planned**
Management at both the executive and departmental levels needs
to carefully think through any employee morale improvement
schemes, even ones that seem straightforward and simple. This does
not mean that healthcare leaders should create a Plan-Do-Study-Act
(PDSA) program for each and every action they take that impacts
worker morale. However, these individuals should take enough time
to ask two questions. First, they should ask, "How will the different groups of workers in my department/organization perceive my
actions?" Healthcare leaders cannot please everyone, but especially
if they are trying to boost employee satisfaction, they should only
choose initiatives that positively impact a large majority of staff.
Second, healthcare leaders should carefully think through the process to ensure that their decisions will not have any unintended,
deleterious consequences. They should undertake these steps even
for relatively small decisions—as seemingly minor choices can have
significantly outsized (and sometimes negative) consequences.

Consider the example of the department manager who orders
pizza for his 30-member staff as a thank you for their hard work on
the latest project. He has worked with many of the employees for a
long time and knows their food tastes; however, he has recently hired
three or four new members. He does not yet know too much about
them. The manager does not take the time to ask his employees what
they would prefer on their pizzas; he just assumes, since he likes
various meats, that they will like meat pizzas as well. So, he orders
several pepperoni, sausage, and ham pizzas. When the pizza arrives,
he hands them out to his team. At that time one of his workers
steps forward and asks him if there are any vegetarian selections. He
sheepishly responds, "No, I didn't think anyone would eat them."

In this scenario, the manager attempts to do something to reward
his employees for their hard work. He is undertaking a seemingly

simple staff initiative—an action thousands of healthcare leaders probably take each week. However, he ends up potentially harming his business relationship with one of his new workers because he did not take the time to think through the potential scenarios. In this case, he did not stop to ask himself if any of his employees could potentially be averse to meat products.

- **Multipronged**
  Anyone who has worked for a small company with a tight budget—or even a large organization with a tight budget—knows that the best initiatives are the ones that accomplish several different objectives. In my experience, these types of strategies yield more bang for the buck than linear or one-dimensional ones. In regard to employee morale–boosting schemes, the best ones not only achieve this goal but also directly accomplish some other departmental or organizational objective, such as increasing worker efficiency or effectiveness.

10.9 Using IT and Data Management Tools to Aid in Improving Employee Satisfaction

In today's corporate world, healthcare leaders can utilize a number of IT and data management tools to help them create and maintain positive employee cultures, while at the same time achieving secondary goals, such as increasing worker productivity (see the bullet point on multipronged goals). In many cases, management does not have to purchase expensive IT equipment or hire additional staff to help them accomplish these tasks. Quite to the contrary, they can use basic, everyday IT tools, such as email, word processing systems, basic video capture equipment, and rudimentary HTML or XML coding to help them cultivate employee-friendly cultures.

Corporations can utilize these basic IT tools to reinforce cultural norms, to create bonds between employees at all levels and their employers, as a pedagogical tool to help workers imbibe corporate values, as a method for reifying workplace beliefs, and as a marketing tool—to convince employees to view their workplace as a second home. In the short space allotted to me in this book, I will focus on one particular area of concern, the bonds between the c-suite and frontline workers. I will demonstrate how upper management can leverage basic IT tools to develop positive relationships between themselves and their subordinates—even the ones that they never see in person.

10.9.1 Communication

The term "communication" might be the most important one in the health-care leader's vocabulary. Everyone knows that an executive or manager must be able to communicate his or her project goals, requirements, dead-lines, and so forth, to employees if he or she wants these workers to per-form well. However, in my experience, a healthcare leader's emails, spoken words, and indirect communiqués (e.g., by way of a gesture) can go a long way in helping to create and maintain an employee-friendly environment. By the same token, this individual's direct and indirect communications to employees can just as easily destroy this culture.

This is because a leader's communicative interactions with employees not only serves as an information relay channel, but it also provides them with cues to the executive's or manager's levels of trustworthiness, integrity, fairness, compassion, empathy, and so forth. Workers use these verbal and non-verbal cues to help them rank the leader on a scale from "This is someone I can lay down my life for" to "Avoid this individual at all costs."

At large companies, I have noticed that upper-level management often has significant difficulty in creating these types of positive bonds with their frontline employees and others who rarely come into contact with the directors, let alone the c-suite. In many cases, the corporate leaders have little or no place in the employee's everyday life. This situation can be problematic because, as I mentioned previously, workers' sense of job satisfaction is tied to their relationships with their supervisors—including the c-suite leaders. I believe that if these people do not feel any emotional attachment to upper management, they will be more willing to steal from the company, to get angry with the organization, and to engage in other harmful actions.

On the other hand, if employees believe that the c-suite cares about them as individuals, they are often more satisfied with their jobs—and the roles they play within their respective companies. They will often be willing to "go the extra mile" to help that organization succeed.

Upper-management personnel succeed or fail in creating these bene-ficial bonds via their communication (or lack thereof) with the workforce.

Given that many of these people cannot communicate directly with their frontline staff and middle managers on a regular basis, they have to find other methods to interact with these workers. In the next section, I demonstrate some ways in which they use basic IT tools to help them create these positive bonds—and thereby increase employee-satisfaction rates. These techniques include:

- **Get Creative with Company Emails**
  In many healthcare corporations, managers and executives use emails as their primary tool for communicating with some employees. Senior-level management—in my experience anyway—almost always chooses to communicate with lower-level employees via this medium. Their emails might convey valuable information; however, they are rarely personalized. Instead, they come across as cold, distant missives—which are just as likely to have come from Mars as from the c-suite.

  In my experience, most employees who read these missives do not feel that the leaders actually care about them. In fact, many workers do not even open the e-letters. In short, although these message might convey vital information, they do not help management to build cultural bridges. Sometimes, these messages actually do the opposite—even if they do not contain any overtly negative words or demonstrate any bad intentions. Healthcare leaders can help to ameliorate this issue by using some simple IT fixes, including:

  ○ **Replace the "Dear Employee" or "Hi All" Introduction with the Person's First Name**
    Management can score a big win with employees simply by personalizing the mass emails. Replace the "Dear Employee" with "Dear [Employee's First Name]." What is more, this is an easy process; all one needs is mail-merging skills and an updated employee database. Healthcare leaders can improve upon this one further if they can use that worker's nickname.

  ○ **Add a Photograph Signature to the Email**
    In large companies, employees usually have some type of relationship with their department managers; however, they often do not have any personal connection to their department directors. Workers know even less about the c-suite leaders; sometimes,

these employees might not even know the names of these individuals. In my opinion, healthcare leaders at the director level and above can help to bridge this gap by adding something as simple as a photograph to their general emails. It may sound simple, but I have noticed that people can more easily relate to others when they can see what the other individual looks like.

○ **Surprise Employees with Congratulatory Emails**
In large companies, c-suite leaders and directors can sometimes bridge the relationship gap between themselves and their numerous employees by occasionally sending out an unexpected congratulatory email to a frontline employee who has performed well at a task or overall. In order to be effective, the e-message should be unexpected, it must be short, and it needs to contain a personalized phrase or sentence. As most readers will acknowledge, a message of this sort gains authenticity when it contains these elements.

○ **Utilize Video**
Many employees receive a significant number of office emails per day; most—if not all of these missives—are in text. At the same time, these men and women likely receive numerous mass emails—on topics that are only of marginal interest. I do not think that any reader will be surprised to learn that workers sometimes do not read the mass messages. This is a shame, as it often represents the only connection—in many large companies anyway—that they have with upper management. As a way to break this cycle, healthcare leaders in the c-suite (and perhaps the level below that in some organizations) should consider—once or twice a year—including a video in the email. Assuming that the video message is a surprise and contains interesting information, I believe employees will watch it. More importantly, it helps the leader to overcome the "disembodied actor" syndrome. Employees see that he or she is a "real person."

○ **Create an Interactive "Get to Know Me/US" Email**
Healthcare leaders can create virtual bonds between themselves and their employees, especially frontline workers who never see them, by sending what I like to call a "Get to Know Me/US" email. The message should contain a brief bio and a few factoids

about the CEO, CFO, director, and so forth. Upper management can help to deepen these connections by making the email interactive. It takes only a little time and a bit of knowledge of HTML or XML to add a link to the message with an interactive biography webpage that employees can visit.

○ **Send a Personalized Condolence Email**
The saddest moments in most employees lives occur when someone they love passes away. From a business standpoint, leaders of small companies can use these occasions to reinforce upon the bereaved employees the notion of the company as a family. The CEO or other high-level executive will demonstrate this fact by do things such as sending flowers to the worker, going to his or her loved one's funeral, or sometimes personally offering his or her condolences to the bereaved person.

Unfortunately, healthcare leaders at large companies do not have the opportunity to take this step. They can do something similar—on a virtual level anyway—by procuring a list of employees who have recently lost loved ones and using the company's email system to send a short, personalized condolence note. Management can obtain the necessary information in a variety of ways—one easy one is to work with HR to identify any employees who apply for bereavement time off (see Figure 10.1).

• **Create an Interactive Series of Biographies on the Employee Portal**
Many healthcare corporations, especially larger ones, maintain an HR sponsored employee portal. Workers can access these sites to view information on their salaries, pay periods, available sick days, and so forth. Savvy companies will also posit other information here, such as the employee manuals. This is also a place where the c-suite executives and directors can place short biographies about themselves—as a way for worker to get to know them.

• **Utilize the Computers' Background Screens**
At most healthcare organizations, a large number of employees will have access to a computer. They are often the ones to turn these machines on in the morning and off at the end of their workday. Many other workers will access a computer at some point in the day. A healthcare corporation could and should make use of the backgrounds on the initial/sign-in screens to disseminate information,

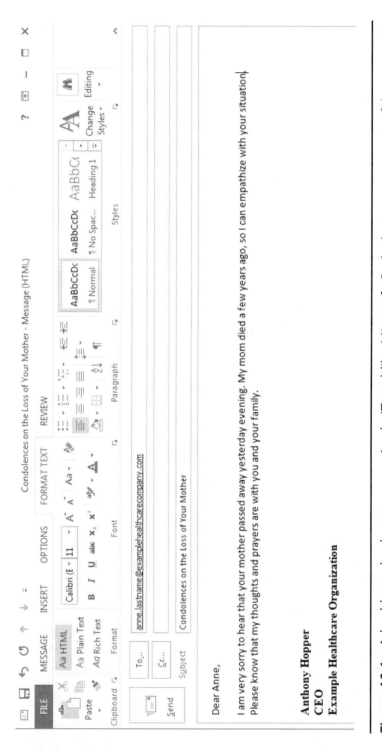

Figure 10.1 A healthcare leader can use a simple IT tool like Microsoft Outlook to convey a powerful message. In this instance, the leader has sent a condolence email to a grieving employee. The executive might never have met this individual in person; yet, in three short sentences, he has created a connection based on a shared experience—the loss of a parent.

remind employees about important events, and, on occasion, to acquaint workers with their upper management. This tactic, when used judicially, can prove effective at achieving these aims because of its level of visibility. Everyone who logs in will be exposed to the information. If the data is unique, that individual—out of curiosity—will read/view it.

These are only some of the ways that c-suite–level executives and directors at medium and large healthcare organizations can, to use an old cliché, "get to know their employees" without ever seeing these men and women in person. More importantly, they do not need to utilize high-tech IT equipment to help them achieve these results. They just need to step outside of the box and utilize the basic IT tools that they have readily available to them in creative ways.

10.10 Summing Things Up

In today's business world, healthcare leaders need to ensure, whenever possible, that their employees are at least moderately satisfied with their working environments in particular and with their companies in general. Health services organizations that achieve this goal will gain a competitive edge over their competitors. After all, as almost any healthcare leader will attest to, a corporation's labor force is its most valuable asset.

Every healthcare organization is, to some extent, unique, and health-care leaders will have to mold their employee-management schemes to fit their particular companies. With that said, I believe that all healthcare leaders should include these key areas in their stratagems.

- Ensure that the healthcare organization's employee culture possesses the six features listed toward the beginning of this chapter: maintain transparency, deal with employees fairly, treat them as individuals, reward workers based on merit, offer them meaningful work, and ensure that they balance work and social activities.
- When implementing employee-management strategies, remember CCAPM (creative, cost-effective, authentic, planned, and multi-pronged strategies)
- Use IT and data management tools to aid in creating an employee-friendly culture.

References

Amabile, T., & Kramer, S. (2012). Employee Happiness Matters More than You Think. *Bloomberg Businessweek*. Retrieved from http://www.businessweek.com/debateroom/archives/2012/02/employee_happiness_matters_more_than_you_think.html.

Anonymous. (2014). Psych Basics: Burnout. *Psychology Today*. Retrieved from http://www.psychologytoday.com/basics/burnout.

Asacker, T. (2004). Ethics in the Workplace: Start with Honesty. *T + D* 58(8), 42–44. Retrieved from ProQuest.

Bansal, P. (2011, February 6). Build HR Strategy around the Brand. *Business Today*. Retrieved from http://businesstoday.intoday.in/story/pankaj-bansal-on-hr-strategies-to-promote-brand/1/12529.html.

Bing Dictionary. (2014). Definition of Culture (n). Retrieved from www.bing.com.

Brimmer, K. (2013, April 2). Nurse Understaffing Impacts Quality of Care, Leads to Increased Infections. *Healthcare Finance*. Retrieved from http://www.healthcarefinancenews.com/news/nurse-understaffing-impacts-quality-care-leads-increased-infections.

Catlette, B., & Hadden, R. (2000). Prepared to Go, but Eager to Stay. *Workforce* 79(8), 32–34. Retrieved from ProQuest.

Fairlie, P. (2011). All Generations Want Meaningful Work. *Canadian HR Reporter* 24(11), 17. Retrieved from ProQuest.

Favaloro, M. (2013, August 14). Understaffing Cited As Major National Nursing Home Problem. *The Legal Examiner*. Retrieved from http://norfolk.legalexaminer.com/nursing-home-elder-abuse/understaffing-cited-as-major-national-nursing-home-problem/.

Fernandez, E. (2011, November 29). Low Staffing and Poor Quality of Care at Nation's For Profit Nursing Homes. University of California San Francisco. Retrieved from http://www.ucsf.edu/news/2011/11/11037/low-staffing-and-poor-quality-care-nations-profit-nursing-homes.

Healthfield, S. (2014). Work-Life Balance. *About Money*. Retrieved from http://humanresources.about.com/od/glossaryw/g/balance.htm.

Lee, D., Lee, S. M., & Schniederjans, M. J. (2011). Medical Error Reduction: The Effect of Employee Satisfaction with Organizational Support. *The Services Industry Journal* 31(8), 1311–1325.

Maciver, D. (2004). Make Your Team Happy—Make Them Work Harder! *Human Resource Management International Digest* 12(5), 2–3. Retrieved from ProQuest.

Oswald, A. J., Proto, E., & Sgroi, D. (2014). Happiness and Productivity. *JOLE*, 3rd version. Retrieved from http://www2.warwick.ac.uk/fac/soc/economics/staff/eproto/workingpapers/happinessproductivity.pdf.

Quast, L. (2012, September 17). 5 Tips for Employers To Earn Respect From Employees. *Forbes*. Retrieved from http://www.forbes.com/sites/lisaquast/2012/09/17/5-tips-for-employers-to-earn-respect-from-employees/.

Savoye, C. (2000, June 15). Workers Say Honesty Is Best Company Policy, Nine in 10 Employees Say They Value Integrity as Much as Income: Will this Lead to a New US Bottom Line. *The Christian Science Monitor*. Retrieved from ProQuest.

Singleton, T., & Singleton, A. (2010). *Fraud Auditing and Forensic Accounting* (4th ed). Hoboken, NJ: John Wiley & Sons, Inc.

The Staff of the Corporate Executive Board. (2009, March 27). The Increasing Call for Work Life Balance. *Bloomberg Businessweek*. Retrieved from http://www.businessweek.com/managing/content/mar2009/ca20090327_734197.htm.

Vaishnavi, V. (2013). Five Must-Follow Rules for a Successful Office Culture. *Forbes*. Retrieved from http://www.forbes.com/sites/vickvaishnavi/2013/03/28/five-must-follow-rules-for-a-successful-office-culture/.

Wilhelm, W. (1992). Changing Corporate Culture—or Corporate Behavior? How to Change Your Company. *The Executive* 6(4), 72. Retrieved from ProQuest.

Chapter Eleven

A Review of Some of the Unique HR and IT Challenges Facing Rural Hospitals and a Guide to Tackling These Issues

In general, rural healthcare organizations, and especially rural community hospitals, have to deal with a number of locality-specific issues. One key challenge that they face is in trying to generate sufficient revenue in areas with low-population densities and higher percentages of elderly, poor residents. Rural hospitals also have difficulties in procuring enough skilled personnel. As a result, they sometimes find it difficult to operate efficiently and effectively. As a corollary to the first two problems, rural hospitals have problems optimizing their information technology (IT) and human resources (HR) infrastructures.

These obstacles are endemic to rural hospitals and are not easy to solve. In fact, it might be impossible to come up with any remedies that completely solve these issues. Nevertheless, I think that healthcare leaders who work for rural hospitals (and for other rural health services organizations) can improve their IT and HR processes, as well as increase productivity levels at their institutions. Most importantly, these beneficial changes should positively impact their organizations' bottom lines.

11.1 Looking Backwards

In this book, I started out by providing readers with a brief history of the healthcare system. I then demonstrated why healthcare organizations—at least in today's environment—should focus their efforts not only on hiring the best workers, but also on retaining them. I have provided readers with general information on key HR and IT-related topics. More importantly, I have posited methods that HR directors, c-suite executives, IT directors, and even middle managers can utilize to attract talented employees. I have also put forth some strategies that healthcare leaders can use to motivate and retain their workers.

At the same time, as I noted in the book's first chapter, the healthcare field is extremely diverse. It comprises companies that run the gamut from "mom and pop" durable medical equipment suppliers (where I got my start), with no clinical functions, to large, multi-chain, integrated hospital systems that focus on patient care. If experts compared the healthcare universe to the scientific classification chart for animals (which most readers probably remember from their high school biology classes), the healthcare industry would be akin to the kingdom classification. It is the second highest point on the chain, representing the juncture at which animals are separated from plants and fungi, among others.

Acknowledging this fact, I have tried to present information in a way that is helpful for readers who come from a variety of different healthcare backgrounds. At the same time, I have also carved out space in this narrative to focus specifically on the needs of smaller healthcare organizations and ones that have significant resource limitations. After all, it is the smaller and more resource-challenged companies that most often need to come up with creative, cost-effective solutions in order to thrive—or sometimes just to survive—in today's marketplace.

With that said, I think it is worthwhile to focus some time on an important segment of the healthcare industry—the rural healthcare network—which faces a unique set of obstacles. Many of these corporations not only have to deal with financial issues, they also have to contend with other problems, including a shortage of trained professionals, sparsely populated service areas (contributing both to labor shortages and patient-access issues), poverty, and a graying population. For providers in rural areas, some of these issues—perhaps all of them—will only become more acute over the coming decades.

At the same time, I will touch on subjects, including provider relationships with semiautonomous and independent professionals (doctors and nurses), which are not covered in depth in other parts of this book. As a result, I think that all readers—not just ones that work for rural healthcare organizations—can use some of the information in this chapter.

11.2 Rural Health Systems—A Unique Set of Problems and HR-Related Solutions

When one mentions the rural health system, it is taken for granted that he or she is referring to the whole range of healthcare organizations—both public and private—that inhabit this sphere. Just focusing on the private operations alone, one can point to a wide diversity of companies in the healthcare ecosystem, including hospitals, nursing homes, home health agencies, an array of vendors and suppliers, as well as pharmacies and other stores that specialize in selling healthcare-related items. Most of these entities have to deal with problems such as labor shortages and demographic concerns that are endemic to—or at least more pronounced in—rural communities (Burrows, Suh, & Hamann, 2012, 1–4). At the same time, each of the health services provider types has to deal with unique variants to these issues.

I could devote an entire book to the issues facing rural healthcare providers; however, I do not have that much allotted space. As a result, I will focus my attention on rural community hospitals. These entities are usually the most complex organizations in these localities, and, as such, they have to deal with most (if not all) of the problems facing rural healthcare providers in general. As a result, I feel that readers who hold non–hospital-related health services jobs can still learn something from this section. At the same time, I will only touch on topics that deal with IT-, human resources (HR)–, and employee management–related topics.

11.3 Community Hospitals in Rural Areas

At one point in time, the majority of US citizens lived in rural areas. Although most Americans now live in urban and suburban areas, around 20 percent of them still reside in rural areas (Burrows, Suh, & Hamann, 2012, 1). In all, approximately 1980 rural hospitals "provide essential health care services to nearly 54 million people" (AHA, 2014a, 2014b). As I noted in the first chapter of this book, community hospitals did fairly well between the mid-1940s through the 1970s, due to funding from federal and state governments for things such as infrastructure and by means of generous healthcare reimbursement payments (see Chapter 1).

However, since that period, these hospitals, as a group, have struggled for a variety of reasons. I think one can—at least for the purposes of this brief analysis—divide the problems facing these institutions into two areas. On the one hand, rural hospitals have to deal with resource limitations. Their financial concerns stem, at least in part, from the demographic challenges they face, which I will discuss shortly. At the same time, these healthcare organizations often find it difficult to locate and retain key personnel.

11.4 Community Hospitals and Revenue Challenges

Community hospitals located in rural areas have to deal with several issues that limit their potential revenues. I have listed some of the more important ones below.

- **Hospitals Have Difficulty in Keeping Inpatient Numbers Up**
  Rural hospitals often have problems maintaining viable inpatient census numbers. This problem centers on a number of factors relating to general trends in reduced inpatient admissions, as well to population issues (e.g., smaller, more dispersed populations) in rural areas. (O'Donnell & Ungar, 2014; York, Kaufman, & Grube, 2014, see Chapter 1).

- **Higher Poverty Rates in Rural Areas**
  At the same time, these hospitals' patients, as a whole, are poorer than their urban counterparts. In 2012, 17.7 percent of US citizens living in rural areas were classified by the government as poor (with

incomes below the poverty threshold). By comparison, only 14.5 percent of people living in urban areas had incomes below the poverty threshold (Farrigan, 2014).

- **Other Population-Based Demographic Issues**
  Rural community hospitals not only have to deal with a group of people who are, on average, poorer than their urban counterparts. These facilities also have to cope with a population that is both older and sicker than similar populations in cities and suburbs (Ormond, Zuckerman, & Lhila, 2000, 1–5). In short, what this data means is that rural community hospitals often have to contend with a more complex and diverse case mix than their counterparts in more populated parts of the United States. These issues would not necessarily be problematic if private and public sources of funding would adequately compensate these community hospitals for the level of care they provide to rural patients. Sadly, this is not the case.

- **Lack of Private and Public Funding**
  I do not think it is any secret that private insurers, on average, tend to reimburse hospitals at higher levels than both Medicare, and, especially, Medicaid. With that fact in mind, rural community hospitals are at a disadvantage relative to their urban counterparts. That is because "the proportion of the nonelderly population covered by private health insurance—predominantly employer sponsored coverage—falls as county of residence gets more remote" (Ormond, Zuckerman, & Lhila, 2000, 2). And, as I noted in Chapter 1 of this book, government payers have gotten stingier over the past few decades, when it comes to remunerating hospitals for both inpatient and outpatient services (see Chapter 1). And the government reimbursement rates might be cut again as a result of policies in the Affordable Care Act, thereby further hampering the ability of rural hospitals to generate positive earnings (Morgan, 2014).

In short, rural community hospitals face a number of funding challenges. At the same time, they are often smaller than their urban counterparts, which means it is harder for them to maximize gains and limit expenses through economies of scale (Evashwick, 2005, 54; Roney, 2012). When combined with the labor supply issues, which I will discuss in a moment, it is no wonder that many rural hospitals struggle to survive.

In fact, according to one source, "more than half of all rural hospitals are currently experiencing negative total margins" (Morgan, 2014).

Although these financial issues probably have a number of implications for rural community hospitals, I am chiefly concerned with two of the important downstream effects. On the one hand, I would like to explore how these facilities' cash problems impact their ability to develop or purchase/lease the IT infrastructures that are necessary for identifying and retaining the best employees. I will come back to this issue later on in this chapter. At the same time, I would like to look at the relationship between the financial difficulties facing many rural hospitals and their ability to maintain adequate staffing levels and retain these employees.

It goes without saying that cash-strapped facilities—and this situation is indicative of a large number of the nation's rural hospitals—are going to have a difficult time maintaining adequate staffing levels, especially skilled workers, who command higher wage premiums. Unfortunately, rural hospitals, while they have to deal with financial constraints, also have to navigate a tough labor environment—where, in many cases, the demand for skilled workers is greater than the supply.

11.5 Rural Hospitals—Problems in Finding and Keeping Skilled Workers

Rural hospitals, on average, not only have to deal with significant resource constraints, they also have to navigate a labor market that contains a dearth of key skilled workers, such as nurses, allied health professionals, IT professionals, and doctors. In fact, many of these shortages are severe (Burrows, Suh, & Hamann, 2012, 2–3). As an example, one article estimated that "[o]nly about ten percent of physicians practice in rural America despite the fact that nearly one fourth of the population lives in these areas" (National Rural Health Association, N.D.).

There are a number of resource-based (or financial) reasons why rural hospitals have difficulties finding enough skilled workers and independent physicians to cover their operational requirements, as well as their patients' needs. For one thing, rural hospitals cannot afford to pay the same salaries that their urban peers can. For instance, a 2005 study of registered nurses showed that R.N.s "residing in rural areas" made approximately $7000 to $9000 less per year than their counterparts who were working for hospitals that were located in a city or suburb (Skillman et al., 2005, 6). Rural hospitals also cannot compete with urban ones when it comes to salaries for IT professionals (Hollander, 2014). Another issue, which is totally outside of rural hospitals' control, relates to Medicare reimbursement. In short, Medicare reimbursements do not remunerate rural physicians at the same rate as urban ones. Granted, rural doctors might have lower overall expenses, but the difference in reimbursement rates is still an issue that might discourage some doctors from setting up shop in a sparsely populated area (Barnard, 2012).

Of course, one can point to a number of potential resource advantages that rural hospitals might have when it comes to hiring new employees. For one thing, employees who live in rural areas, usually have lower cost of living expenses, especially for a key expenditure—a home payment or a rent bill. I can attest to this fact firsthand. I lived in a rural area of Virginia for a short period of time, and, on average, I paid 30 percent less per month for my apartment compared to a similar model in the nearby city. At the same time, workers usually do not have to worry about issues such as congested roadways, which will decrease their lost-opportunity costs (something that economists, at least, do quantify in financial terms). Finally, the federal government does, in this instance anyway, try to help rural areas (at least the ones that receive "underserved" designations) attract key healthcare personnel, by means of, among other things, its loan forgiveness programs (Health Resources and Services Administration, 2014).

Perhaps the biggest stumbling block that rural hospitals have in trying to hire and retain qualified, much less highly capable, workers does not involve any financial issues. In fact, even if these hospitals were flush with cash, they might still have a problem in bringing enough key employees on board. To wit, nurses, doctors, IT professionals, and other skilled workers do not want to live in rural areas because of the lack of entertainment and cultural opportunities. At the same time, employees who are single face another problem—the dearth of potential partners (for short- or long-term relationships).

People will differ with regard to the biggest hindrance facing rural hospitals when it comes to recruiting and retaining important personnel. However, I believe that the key problem can be summed up by the cliché, "There is just nothing to do in this town." In short, highly skilled employees prefer to live in cities and suburbs where they can choose from a laundry list of restaurants, and where they can partake in any of a thousand different cultural or entertainment pursuits. More importantly, they do not have to travel too far to find these opportunities. Someone who lives in a city or suburb of any size will find a shopping mall, movie theater, or other leisure-based facility that is located within a few miles of his or her residence. If that person wants to locate a group to hang out with, he or she can choose from any number of different ones, using Meetup.com or some other, similar website.

People living in cities and most suburbs also have numerous options if they decide to stay indoors. For instance, they have ready access (for a price) to high-speed Internet service, allowing them to easily surf the web or to participate in any of a number of online activities. If they are hungry, they can choose from a variety of different restaurants that will deliver food to their doors.

By contrast, men and women who choose to work in rural locations often do not have ready access to this varied array of cultural and entertainment options. They might have to travel for 30 minutes to an hour to reach the nearest shopping mall of any size or many of the other aforementioned amenities. If they prefer not to take these long trips "into town," then their options are often limited to a few restaurants, a small movie theater (if they are lucky), and so forth. They are not likely to be able to attend large concerts, go to musicals and plays, and to participate in similar events that urban and suburban dwellers take for granted.

At the same time, I can state from experience that these individuals, if they choose to stay at home, will have a limited amount of entertainment and food options available. They might be able to count on ordering in food from one restaurant, but only if they are lucky enough to live within its delivery range. Many of these people will not be able to access high-speed Internet, and some might even get cable (though most of them should have access to a dish network provider).

These issues are a significant deterrent for many people who might otherwise consider taking a job with a rural hospital. As an AP article implies, married couples might be even less inclined to accept these types of jobs, as both the employee and his or her spouse would have to concur in the move (Barnard, 2012). On the flip side, people who are single might not want to relocate to the country because they perceive that it is more difficult to find a potential spouse or life partner in this environment. This attitude makes sense, given the small, dispersed populations and lack of traditional public meeting places.

11.5.1 Rural Hospitals and the Impact from Shortages of Doctors

Rural hospitals also have a labor supply problem, which they seemingly have little control over, and that is the supply of specialist doctors and primary care physicians. I think readers are already cognizant of the importance of the former group, so I will not go into much detail with regard to the issues that might result when a locality suffers from a shortage of key specialist physicians. However, primary care doctors are also important to rural hospitals. As most people know, the latter group provides basic health services to the general population. This fact is important for rural hospitals because studies have shown a positive correlation between the number of primary care physicians in an area and emergency room (ER) visits—more doctors equates to fewer trips to the ER (Kelly, 2011). Rural hospitals can benefit from this trend if the reduction is in Medicaid patients, or other individuals whose visits typically represent a net loss for these facilities. Many rural hospitals also rely on primary care providers to staff their emergency rooms (Casey, Wholey, & Moscovice, 2007, 1). Finally, primary care physicians might perform other services, including serving on hospital boards, mentoring newcomers (MDs) to the area, and overseeing nurse practitioners. These practices can either directly or indirectly benefit rural hospitals.

These are some of the reasons why the dearth of physicians in the area, including primary care physicians, is a negative not only for rural communities but also for the hospitals in these localities. As a result of these shortages, rural hospitals might have to deal with higher rates of unnecessary emergency room visits. These entities may also have issues in procuring enough doctors (or other qualified personnel) to staff the emergency rooms, which might impact patient safety (Casey, Wholey, & Moscovice, 2007, 1–4). If the county has a dearth of key specialists, the rural hospital's inpatient census, surgery rates, and other ancillary service measures might be negatively impacted. And rural hospitals likely lose out on other benefits that accrue from having an ample supply of physicians in the area.

Of course, a community can partially compensate for the lack of primary care physicians, if it contains a sizeable number of physician assistants (PAs) and nurse practitioners (NPs). Depending on the state, these individuals can perform many of the same duties as a primary care doctor. Many rural communities have, in the past few decades, come to depend on these alternative sources of care. However, the supply of these providers might be about ready to shrink, due to the fact that the "proportion of PAs entering generalist practice has declined, and the number of NPs has fallen dramatically in recent years" (Burrows, Suh, & Hamann, 2012, 4).

11.6 Dearth of Employees Takes Its Toll on Rural Health Systems

Rural hospitals, and for that matter all rural healthcare providers, suffer when they cannot recruit and retain enough qualified staff to meet their facility's needs. Some of the problems that entail from this situation include:

- **Project-Planning Disruptions**
  Rural hospitals—or any provider that does not possess a critical mass of key employees—will have to forego certain important projects. At the same time, management might not be able to roll out new initiatives or introduce new technologies into the work environment as quickly as they would like. As a result of these problems, hospitals might lose potential revenue. They might also incur additional expenses as a result of their failure to implement cost-saving improvements or their lack of celerity in rolling out new initiatives. Rural hospitals' planning issues can be especially painful with regard to the introduction of electronic medical records (EMRs). As one article notes, these entities are having difficulties meeting federally mandated health information technology (HIT) meaningful use deadlines, which could result in these hospitals being unable to collect the sizeable sums offered by the federal government as an incentive for reaching certain HIT goals (Roney, 2012).

- **Productivity Issues**
  When rural hospitals—or any corporation for that matter—operate with less than the ideal number of staff, they will find it difficult, if not impossible, to accomplish all necessary tasks in a timely manner (Roney, 2012). For instance, an understaffed accounts receivable (or insurance coding and billing) department will fall behind in processing and submitting claims for payment. It will also have difficulty appealing claims in a timely manner. As a result, the hospital will be

slower in receiving reimbursement for the services it has provided, which has obvious impacts on both revenues and expenses. One will find these types of productivity issues in any department that is operating with less than the ideal number of employees.

- **Lack of Redundancy**
  I can state from experience that companies which are understaffed face significant hurdles when it comes to replacing workers who have to take an extended leave of absence, or who depart the organization on short notice. They simply do not have the available person power to move other staff members over to fill in for the lost personnel. Even when these entities could theoretically shift an employee to an open position, they cannot do so because they have not trained anyone to work in the needed role.

I have touched on just a few of the potential issues that can arise when rural hospitals have to do more with fewer employees. However, even rural hospitals that are fully staffed might also have to deal with project-planning disruptions and productivity issues if they cannot retain employees (e.g., they have high turnover rates) or if they find it difficult to recruit new, skilled workers to replace the ones who leave for cushier jobs in urban areas.

11.7 Rural Health Systems Need to Employ Creative, Synergistic, Labor-Related Solutions

As I noted in the previous sections, rural hospitals, as a whole, are facing a number of obstacles that—if not unique to them—are more prevalent in the localities that they service. These hospitals have to confront significant resource challenges that might limit their ability to implement some of the IT- and HR-related processes that are mentioned in other sections of this book. They also have to deal with labor shortages among key position types that are related to issues with rural areas in general.

Resource-challenged rural hospitals that are still independent and have to deal with the labor issues discussed in this chapter might try to merge with a larger hospital chain. In taking this step, they can hope to access additional resources from the parent company and achieve some economies of scale. However, there is no guarantee that they will be able to find a partner. These facilities might also not obtain the hoped-for benefits from such a merger if the parent organization decides they are not worth the investment. Finally, the chain's corporate executives might, at some point, decide to close down one or more rural hospitals under their control, if that decision makes sense from a cost–benefit perspective.

Even if a rural hospital is part of a larger corporation, its management will usually still oversee many of (or even most of) the aspects related to recruitment and employee retention. It will also likely have to confront a challenging labor environment in which many of the variables are beyond its control. I believe that rural hospitals have to adjust to this environment by thinking out of the box. This is because, as demonstrated previously in this chapter, neither rural hospitals nor any other entities, such as government organizations, have been able to remedy the labor-related issues by means of traditional methods.

When such cooperative action does not violate federal or state laws, rural hospitals might also want to partner with other agencies or groups to sponsor projects. Rural hospitals can benefit in numerous ways from entering into these types of associations. For one thing, the facilities can spread the risk burden among multiple entities. For resource-challenged rural hospitals, this might allow them to (a) take on more projects, and (b) engage in more creative ventures that pose higher risks but also offer larger potential returns. When these facilities work with local partners to accomplish labor-related objectives, they demonstrate that they are responsible community members as well. These tactics might not only benefit the hospitals in question, they may also help the specific localities as a whole.

11.8 HR and Employee Management Initiatives Should Meet Four Key Objectives

Regardless of whether rural hospitals utilize creative, synergistic methods to handle their labor issues, I believe that they should seek to accomplish several objectives, which include:

- **Achieve Optimal Staffing Levels**
  Although this goal might be impossible for some cash-strapped rural hospitals, they should seek to ensure that, to the greatest

extent possible, they possess the minimum (and perhaps more than the minimum) number of employees that are required in order to achieve adequate productivity, efficiency, efficacy, patient safety, and patient-satisfaction objectives. By adequate, I envision facilities that have enough staff to properly handle all of their key clinical and non-clinical procedures and to allow these institutions to implement important initiatives in a timely manner.

- **Maintain Relatively High Retention Rates**
  As I noted in a previous part of this chapter, rural hospitals do have some issues when it comes to recruiting and retaining certain types of workers. Rural hospitals, as a group, will probably always have more problems with employee retention, especially with regard to key personnel, than their urban peers (LaSala, 2000, 13–15; Simone, N.D.). At the same time, each hospital will have a different set of concerns with regard to these issues. Nonetheless, every rural hospital should be keen on improving employee-retention rates.

- **Achieve High Rates of Employee Satisfaction**
  Rural hospitals will likely find it easier to meet retention goals if they can keep employees satisfied. As I noted in the previous chapter, employee retention is directly correlated with job-approval measures. Management at rural hospitals, unlike their peers at urban facilities, will not only have to concern themselves with their employees on job-satisfaction rates. These leaders will also likely want to find ways to ensure that their workers are content with their lives outside of work.

- **Get More Bang for the Buck When It Comes to IT and Data Management**
  Earlier, I alluded to the fact that most rural hospitals have fewer IT staff on hand than do their urban counterparts. They also have to do more with less when it comes to purchasing (or leasing) and using hardware, software, and other IT or data management–related technologies (Hollander, 2014; Roney, 2012). At the same time, rural hospitals have just as much of a need for these IT personnel and infrastructure as their urban peers. In fact, rural hospitals might benefit more than their counterparts from using IT to offset a dearth in staffing or to help them recruit, retain, train, and develop staff. Therefore,

a rural hospital wins whenever it can find a way to boost its IT capabilities without having to impinge upon some other key area.

11.8.1 Rural Hospitals: Four Sample Solutions to HR and Employee Issues

Like any other large business, each rural hospital will possess strengths and weaknesses that are unique (at least in intensity) to that institution. Individual facilities will also have to deal with localized challenges. For instance, one rural hospital might be located in a severely economically distressed area. Another facility might be situated in a county whose population is wealthier but also older than surrounding localities. In another case, a hospital might luck out and find enough capable IT professionals, whereas its counterpart in the next county tries to operate without a sufficient number of those types of employees.

At the same time, I think that these organizations do, at the meta-level, have many of the same concerns and seek similar outcomes. With that in mind, I have posited four examples of the types of creative or synergistic solutions I have been discussing in this chapter. Each of my suggested fixes meets at least one of the four key objectives discussed in the previous section.

- **Work from Home—Wherever Home May Be**
  One of the growing trends in business management, at least in the past few years, is telecommuting. Rural hospitals can take advantage of this phenomenon to employ workers who live too far away to drive to the facility each day. By taking this step, these organizations could potentially expand their labor pools (Green, Lopez, Wysocki, & Kepner, 2009, 2–3). These facilities could also offer some employees the option of telecommuting as an incentive. Some of their workers who would otherwise leave for a job in a city or suburb (or perhaps a job with another employer in the rural area) might decide that the telecommuting option is attractive enough to offset any negatives, such as lower pay or a dearth of entertainment options. In the future, rural hospitals, working with physicians groups and other healthcare providers, might come to rely on telemedicine to allow patients to communicate with doctors and other

healthcare providers without actually having to drive to a facility (Anonymous, N.D.; Burrows, Suh, & Hamann, 2012, 7).

The idea of telecommuting, even its derivation—telemedicine— is not a new one. Many hospitals, in both urban and rural areas, allow some employees to telecommute. However, given their special set of challenges, perhaps rural hospitals should consider permitting a larger percentage of their employees to telecommute (at least some of the time). With that said, any healthcare leader who wants to take this action needs to be aware of some of the downsides related to telecommuting. For instance, he or she will need to adopt methods to ensure that telecommuters meet productivity and efficiency standards. At the same time, management at these institutions needs to make sure that their telecommuting schemes do not violate legal codes, especially the Health Insurance Portability and Accountability Act (HIPAA).

- **Train Your Own Workers**
  Some rural hospitals have been dealing with shortages in IT workers by training nurses or other employees for these specialist positions (Hollander, 2014). This is a tactic that more facilities might want to adopt with regard to IT personnel—and perhaps for a wider range of positions. It allows rural hospitals to place capable employees in key jobs, while at the same time hopefully increasing the retention of these worker types.

  Ideally, hospitals want to hire or promote credentialed people to specialist jobs, as these people can demonstrate that they went through the proper training. However, rural hospitals often do not have that luxury, especially for IT-related positions. They sometimes have difficulty finding a qualified person who is willing to accept the lower pay and distinct living conditions that come with working for hospitals, located in rural areas (Hollander, 2014). These facilities can encourage their employees to obtain credentials in needed areas by supplementing their formal education and training. However, it takes time—sometimes a significant amount of time—for employees to procure an associates, undergraduate, or master's degree. In many cases, rural hospitals cannot wait that long.

  With that in mind, I believe that rural hospitals might be able to accomplish three key objectives when they train their own staff to take over specialized jobs in IT or in other areas. First, management can train individuals, who they know and trust, for these positions. The leadership staff will likely already be familiar with these employees' intelligence levels, people skills, work ethics, and so forth. If managers or directors train and promote the right people for these jobs, they will often excel in their new positions (given time), regardless of any lack of formal education. Second, these individuals most likely already have deep ties—both to the community and to the hospital. If treated well, they are less likely to leave for other jobs—especially positions in urban areas. Third, a person who receives his or her training primarily in-house might not have the necessary credentials to secure the same type of job at another facility; hence, that individual will have a significant incentive to stay put.

- **Work with Other Local Hospitals to Get Things Done**
  As I noted previously, resource-challenged rural hospitals, which also have to deal with labor shortages, can seek to merge with hospital chains. They can also outsource some key tasks, such as IT and billing-related services, to third-party vendors. I have already noted some of the potential problems with mergers, and the latter strategy is also not without risks. For one thing, rural hospitals that outsource often give up significant control over operational decisions. At the same time, a hospital that outsources a department runs the risk of harming its relationship with employees, as well as with the community (Brooks, 2014; Bucki, N.D.; Mehring, 2005).

  As an alternative, rural hospitals might be able to share resources, expenses, and personnel related to IT and perhaps to other facility activities as well. For instance, several rural hospitals in a region can group together—or work with a larger, urban hospital—to apportion EMR services, staff, and other technologies. This type of arrangement is potentially a win–win for all parties, as the co-op can attain efficiency and productivity gains due to economies of scale and increased purchasing power, which each individual facility could not hope to achieve on its own (Hollander, 2014; Reddy, Purao, & Kelly, 2008). At the same time, these hospitals can rightly claim that they are doing the best that they can to employ local people (even if those individuals live in the next county).

  Of course, healthcare leaders at a hospital that wants to create these types of associations will first have to ensure that their proposed schemes do not violate anti-trust laws (or any other state or federal legal codes). However, if they pass legal muster, these types of co-ops might prove to be a useful addition to a rural hospital's list of potential strategic initiatives.

- **Create Cultural and Entertainment Opportunities for Employees and Doctors**
  As I have already noted, rural hospitals often have to operate with less than the ideal number of staff—at least in certain areas. At the same time, some of these institutions might have difficulty in retaining key employees, as well as in finding replacements for these departed workers. These workforce issues can have a deleterious effect on a hospital's efficiency, its effectiveness, its productivity, its customer satisfaction ratings, and, ultimately, on its bottom line. As I have also demonstrated, these facilities can face some of the same issues when the communities that they serve have difficulties in attracting enough specialists and primary care doctors.

  Due to resource-related issues, rural hospitals might have to ask more of the employees that they do have on staff. These people might have to put in longer hours on the job than their urban counterparts. Among other things, they also might have to shoulder more responsibilities and to handle more tasks (per person) than their peers at city and suburban hospitals. Physicians, especially general practitioners, will most likely have to see more patients and deal with a more complex array of issues (especially financial issues) than will their peers in the cities and suburbs.

  Given these workforce-related challenges, it is imperative that rural hospitals find ways to keep employee satisfaction at high levels (see the previous chapter for some suggestions). Ideally, these institutions want to go beyond this step and create a culture in which employees see the hospital as more than just a job landing site; they come to love it as they would a favorite sports team or a nation-state. I have found that people who possess a sense of loyalty to the institution itself—and not just to their fellow workers—are more likely to eschew other job offers. They also tend to be more accepting of potentially adverse working and living conditions (e.g., longer hours, fewer entertainment and cultural options, etc.).

  Just as important, rural hospitals—to a much larger degree than their urban counterparts—should focus on providing their employees access to cultural, social, and entertainment outlets. As a first step, rural hospitals could work with departmental champions and dedicated IT personnel (either volunteer or paid) to create central message boards or other sites that allow employees to identify and communicate with coworkers who share similar interests. These institutions should also try to schedule a number of employee-centered extramural or intramural events, as a way to help offset the lack of entertainment options available in the larger community. The hospitals might also be able to invite area physicians to these events, without violating Stark laws. Finally, rural hospitals should seek to work with other key public and private stakeholders to create a series of community-based events in an effort to provide further cultural and entertainment options for employees and their families, as well as for local physicians.

Rural hospitals need to go the extra mile when it comes to helping their employees find social, cultural, and entertainment options to fill their leisure hours because this strategy provides these facilities with a good chance of boosting retention. Namely, hospital workers who feel like they are a part of the community, and who have ample opportunities both to meet others with similar interests and to engage in activities they enjoy, will likely be more inclined to stay put.

11.9 Summing Things Up

In conclusion, rural hospitals, as a whole, are facing a number of headwinds. On the one hand, they are having trouble generating enough revenues to survive. These institutions' financial problems are often the result of demographic factors that are beyond their control. On the flip side of things, rural hospitals are finding it difficult to recruit and retain key personnel. These institutions' labor issues are only exacerbated by their lack of income.

Given these challenges, rural hospitals, more so than their urban and suburban peers, need to adopt strategies that maximize employee-satisfaction rates—with regard to work and leisure time. They should also seek to implement other initiatives that will allow them to operate at optimal levels, retain workers, and make the best use of their IT budgets. Management at these facilities should not hesitate to introduce creative (yet proven) strategies when traditional initiatives fail to produce the needed results.

References

American Hospital Association. (2014a). Fast Facts on US Hospitals. Retrieved from http://www. aha. org/research/rc/stat-studies/fast-facts.shtml.

American Hospital Association. (2014b). Rural Health Care. Retrieved from http://www. aha. org/advocacy-issues/rural/index.shtml.

Anonymous. (N.D.). Telemedicine Technology—Here, Now & Emerging. Emory University. Retrieved from http://www. emory.edu/BUSINESS/et/telemed/.

Barnard, J. (2012, September 1). Boomers Retiring to Rural Areas Won't Find Doctors. *Associated Press*. Retrieved from http://www.bigstory.ap. org/article/boomers-retiring-rural-areas-wont-find-doctors.

Brooks, C. (2014, May 16). The Pros and Cons of Outsourcing Your HR Department. *Business News Daily*. Retrieved from http://www.businessnews daily.com/6428-pros-cons-of-professional-employer-organizations.html.

Bucki, J. (N.D.). Top 6 Outsourcing Disadvantages. Retrieved from http://operationstech.about.com/od/outsourcing/tp/OutSrcDisadv.htm.

Burrows, E., Suh, R., & Hamann, D. (2012, January). Health Care Workforce Distribution and Shortage Issues in Rural America. National Rural Health Association. Retrieved from file:///C:/Users/eland_000/Downloads/HealthCareWorkforceDistributionandShortageJanuary2012.pdf.

Casey, M., Wholey, D., & Moscovice, I. (2007, August). Rural Emergency Department Staffing:

Potential Implications for the Quality of Emergency Care Provided in Rural Areas [Policy Brief].

Upper Midwest Rural Health Research Center. Retrieved from http://rhrc.umn. edu/wp-content/files_mf/caseyedstaffing.pdf.

Evashwick, C. J. (2005). *The Continuum of Long-Term Care* (3rd ed.). Clifton Park, NY.: Delmar Cengage Learning.

Farrigan, T. (2014, February). Poverty Overview. United States Department of Agriculture. Retrieved from http://www. ers.usda.gov/topics/rural-economy-population/rural-poverty-well-being/poverty-overview.aspx.

Green, K. A., Lopez, M., Wysocki, A., & Kepner, K. (2009, August – Revised). Telecommuting as a True Workplace Alternative [Document HR021]. Institute of Food and Agricultural Sciences, University of Florida. Retrieved from http://edis.ifas.ufl.edu/pdffiles/HR/HR02100.pdf.

Health Resources and Services Administration. (2014). Nurse Corps Loan Repayment Program. Retrieved from http://www.hrsa.gov/loanscholarships/repayment/nursing/.

Hollander, C. (2014, May 17). Rural Hospitals Get Creative in Staffing for IT Needs. *Modern Healthcare*. Retrieved from http://www.modernhealthcare. com/article/20140517/MAGAZINE/305179979.

Kelly, E. (2011, June 2). More Primary Care Doctors, Fewer ER Visits. Families USA. Retrieved from http://familiesusa. org/blog/more-primary-doctors-fewer-er-visits.

LaSala, K. B. (2000). Nursing Workforce Issues in Rural and Urban Settings: Looking at the Difference in Recruitment, Retention and Distribution. *Online Journal of Rural Nursing and Health Care* 1(1), 8–17.

Mehring, J. (2005, June 19). The Downside of Outsourcing. *Bloomberg Business Week*. Retrieved from http://www.businessweek.com/stories/2005-06-19/the-downside-of-outsourcing.

Morgan, A. (2014, May 1). Rural Hospitals Closing at Alarming Rate. *Rural Health Voices*. Retrieved from http://blog.ruralhealthweb.org/2014/05/rural-hospitals-closing-at-alarming-rate/.

O'Donnell, J., & Ungar, L. (2014). Rural Hospitals in Critical Condition. *USA Today*. Retrieved from http://www.usatoday.com/story/news/nation/2014/11/12/rural-hospital-closings-federal-reimbursement-medicaid-aca/18532471/.

Ormond, B. A., Zuckerman, S., & Lhila, A. (2000). Rural/Urban Differences in Health Care Are Not Uniform Across States. Urban Institute. Retrieved from http://www.urban. org/publications/309533.html.

Reddy, M. C., Purao, S., & Kelly, M. (2008). Developing IT Infrastructure for Rural Hospitals: A Case Study of Benefits and Challenges of Hospital-to-Hospital Partnerships. *Journal of the American Medical Informatics Association* 15(4), 554–558.

Roney, K. (2012, May 24). 6 Biggest Meaningful Use Challenges for Rural Hospitals. *Becker's Health & CIO Review*. Retrieved from http://www.beckershospitalreview.com/healthcare-information-technology/6-biggest-meaningful-use-challenges-for-rural-hospitals. html.

Simone, K. G. (N.D.). Recruiting Physicians Today. NEJM Career Center. Retrieved from http://www.nejmcareercenter.org/minisites/rpt/rural-hospitalist-recruitment-challenges/.

Skillman, S. M., Palazzo, L., Keepnews, D., & Hart, L. G. (2005, January). Characteristics of Registered Nurses in Rural vs. Urban Areas: Implications for Strategies to Alleviate Nursing Shortages in the United States. Center for Health Workforce Studies. Retrieved from http://depts.washington.edu/uwrhrc/uploads/CHWSWP91.pdf.

York, R., Kaufman, K., & Grube, M. (2014, January). Where Have All the Inpatients Gone? A Regional Study with National Implications [blog]. *Health Affairs*. Retrieved from http://healthaffairs.org/blog/2014/01/06/where-have-all-the-inpatients-gone-a-regional-study-with-national-implications/.

Chapter Twelve

A Review of Key Topics and a Look at Future Trends

I have touched on a number of key themes in this book that relate to human resources (HR), information technology (IT), and data management. In a traditional conclusion, I would simply review the topics that I have covered in this book. However, in this instance, I do not think that the narrative would be complete without a discussion of the key technology-based trends that will help to shape not only healthcare HR and IT strategies but, indeed, the entire health services universe in the years and even decades to come.

I have discussed most of these trends at different points in the book. I will expand on some of them here, while at the same time I will try to project these trends into the future. More importantly, I will demonstrate how healthcare leaders can use this knowledge to help them to prepare their managers and staff for the coming changes and, at the same time, to take advantage of any advances in healthcare technologies and data management systems.

I will integrate some of the key topics from previous chapters into this discussion. Specifically, I will argue that technology will become more ubiquitous in Americans' everyday lives. Many of these systems will also continue to show improvements—on a routine basis—in terms of their processing abilities, memory capacities, intelligence, adaptability, and endurance (e.g., longer battery lives).

Assuming that this techno-environment comes to fruition in the next few decades, I will delineate why healthcare leaders will want to place a heavier reliance on artificial intelligence (AI) and IT methods and systems in the coming years. I will posit, in general terms, some of the potential advances in AI and indicate ways in which healthcare executives and managers can leverage these new technologies and ways of thinking. At the same time, I will ponder what type of employee might be best able to succeed in these technology-heavy work environments.

12.1 Technology Is Becoming More Ubiquitous

In previous sections of this book, I noted that technology is becoming more integrated into Americans' everyday lives. Readers of this text, like the US population in general, probably would not agree on the extent of these interrelationships. They would also differ with regard to what the future holds in terms of human–technology interactions. Some experts have even gone so far as to predict that humans and machines will "merge" in the not too distant future. In this scenario, men and women will utilize bionic parts, highly advanced AI technologies, and other technologies to augment their skills, extend their lifespans, and to enhance other aspects of life (Farrar, 2008). A number of these technology mavens believe, as a corollary, that human-level AI systems will take over many of the complex, highly skilled jobs that are currently performed by human beings (Ghose, 2013).

Although most people might consider this scenario to be farfetched, almost everyone would agree that advances in technology have significantly altered the way that many Americans—and indeed people around the world—conduct their personal and work lives. In just a few short decades, computers and other technological wonders have, among other things, helped to transform the way that people communicate with each other, learn, travel, store information and photos, and analyze data. I discussed these changes at some length in Chapter 2 of this book; I do not feel it would be worthwhile to review that material here. More important to this discussion is the fact that these trends are likely to continue into the future.

12.2 Future Advances in Technology Will Impact Almost All Areas of Healthcare

I think most Americans, if asked, would probably agree that the technology revolution will continue into the indefinite future. Companies and entrepreneurs will create better, faster, and smarter computers. Society will continue to develop new technologies, which will potentially allow both people and corporations to become more efficient and effective—at least in certain tasks. It does not take an auger to predict that individuals in the future will develop even more intimate relationships with technological devices and software. These interconnections might eventually put an end to some low-tech products and processes that are even now being marginalized by their IT brethren.

These trends will likely have a significant effect on many areas of healthcare. In fact, the continued advances in IT might, at some point in the future, impact almost every aspect of the healthcare corporation. For instance, as I noted in Chapter 1, hospitals (and doctors) can utilize advancements in medical technology to help them improve patients' lives. However, these facilities' interest in these technologies helps to drive up their expenses and to increase hospital-to-hospital competition. For their part, patients are using the Internet to access medical information that they would have had difficulty obtaining in previous generations, thereby changing how they view their relationships with their physicians (who are no longer the sole arbiters of this knowledge) (Weiner & Biondich, 2006, 35–36). These trends are not likely to slow down or stop anytime soon. What is more, they represent only two of the myriad number of ways that changes in technology have and will continue to impact healthcare organizations.

Just as important, many of these technological advancements are highly disruptive for both society in general and for the healthcare industry in particular. These changes do not necessarily take place at a measured, orderly pace—with one device or item slowly replacing its predecessor. Instead, the environment more closely resembles a frothy sea. New devices and software programs often appear and are dethroned within a matter of years. The ones that are not totally overhauled often get significantly modified (updated) every so often. The disruptive nature of these trends should continue well into the future (Manyika et al., 2013, 1–5).

At the same time, individuals and businesses frequently do not keep pace with the advancements in technology, especially in IT. Their homes and facilities contain a menagerie of new tech and antiquated systems. From a healthcare worker's standpoint, this means that he or she, ideally, needs to be aware of the new tech applications as well as the older models. Additionally, this employee often needs to be able to comfortably shift back and forth between 21st-century technologies and 20th-century tools. This is the case now, and, as I will note later in the chapter, it will become even more important over the next few decades.

12.3 Five Specific Trends Related to the Technology Revolution

In the previous section, I discussed general trends related to advancements in technology that are currently impacting—and will continue to affect—both society at large and the healthcare industry in particular. Here, I want to focus on five key, specific aspects of the technology revolution that are especially relevant to the healthcare human resources (HR) topics that are the subject of this book.

- **Third-Party Knowledge Creation**
  One of the key trends that will impact healthcare in the coming years and decades is the fact that researchers, experts, and others are constantly performing tests and obtaining new information on a variety of health services–related issues. This trend does not move straight up, as the results of inquiries/studies often contradict each other; however, over time, the line does move up. That fact is probably obvious to every reader. What might be surprising is just how fast new information is being accumulated or learned. According to one source, "[O]n average human knowledge is doubling every 13 months" (Schilling, 2013). This time rate will likely constrict (e.g., knowledge will be accumulated over a shorter period of time) in the coming years (Schilling, 2013).

- **Paperless Workplaces**
  As the technology revolution has progressed, healthcare workplaces have slowly transitioned from paper-based environments to virtual ones. I discuss this phenomenon in Chapter 2. However, I think it is important to note one key aspect of this issue here. Namely, this trend has recently picked up steam, at least in some segments of

the healthcare industry, as ever larger numbers of doctors and hospitals have started to purchase (or lease) and use electronic medical records (EMR) systems (Hsiao & Hing, 2014, 1–4; King & Adler-Milstein, 2013). The federal government, via the passage in 2009 of the American Recovery and Reinvestment Act, has played a large part in the industry's push to go paperless—at least at the clinical level (Hsiao & Hing, 2014, 1–4; King & Adler-Milstein, 2013). This fact is important because it almost certainly guarantees that the proportion of clinical-based health services providers, such as doctors and hospitals, which are adequately utilizing EMRs, will continue to increase over the next few years.

- **Data Collection Increases**
Over the past couple of decades, healthcare organizations have automated many tasks that were previously performed by human beings. At the same time, these IT systems have rapidly progressed with regard to memory storage, processing speed, analytical abilities, and (reduced) cost (see Chapter 2). The combination of these factors, along with other non-technological variables, such as government regulations and an increasing focus on personalized care, have allowed (and sometimes even forced) healthcare organizations to collect and store ever-increasing amounts of data (Horowitz, 2012). In fact, a 2012 article pointed to a research report stating that "[h]ealth care organizations are accumulating 85 percent more data than two years ago [in 2010]" (Horowitz, 2012). This trend is likely to continue well into the future (Horowitz, 2012).

Although healthcare organizations have been successful at collecting and storing larger amounts of data, they have not been as proficient in translating this data into meaningful, usable information. Many large corporations, in a number of different industries, suffer from this problem. An Oracle study, which surveyed over 300 c-suite leaders in "11 industries [including healthcare]," noted that "60% of executives rate their companies unprepared to leverage the data and cite significant gaps in people, process, and tools" (Oracle, 2012, 3, 5). Like their brethren in other industries, healthcare organizations are experiencing some of the same issues in optimizing the use of the data that they collect (Kayyali, Knott, & Van Kuiken, 2013). The challenge for healthcare leaders in the upcoming years will be in finding ways to ameliorate this issue.

- **Machines Replacing Human Beings**

  Most adults, if they stop to think about it, will readily be able to cite instances in which computers, robots, or other machines now perform jobs that were once the sole domain of human beings. One does not need to go too far back in time to find numerous want ads for mail runners and file clerks; email and electronic filing systems, such as EMRs, have (or are in the process of) eliminated these positions. These are just two of the many instances in which machines have replaced men and women. In other cases, automation is reducing the need for human minds and muscle.

  This trend will not die down anytime in the near future. In fact, it might pick up steam. Some researchers believe that automated systems will make inroads into a wide number of jobs that are currently the domain of human beings. They run the gamut from low-wage positions, such as "retail sales," to higher-salaried jobs, such as "budget analysts" (Shinal, 2014). With regard to clinical positions, robots might supplement or even replace men and women in some clinical areas related to diagnosis, caregiving, and pharmacy management (Aquino, 2012; Klein, 2011; McNickle, 2012).

  The jobs that are most likely to be taken over by high-technology systems are ones "mainly consisting of tasks following well-defined procedures that can easily be performed by sophisticated algorithms" (Frey & Osborne, 2013). In other words, healthcare workers whose jobs follow a certain limited set of procedures or that rely on predictable, linear processes might eventually find themselves competing with AI or IT systems. From experience, I can attest to the fact that the machines eventually win out in these contests.

- **A Little of the Old—A Little of the New**

  I think that one of the most important tenets of the technology revolution is also the one that will be the most obvious to readers of this book. That is the fact that the aforementioned trends are not progressing in smooth, predictable patterns. Instead, both individuals and companies often make do with a hodgepodge of new IT devices and more antiquated systems. I think most people can sympathize with the workplace scene in which a team or individual utilizes a sophisticated data analysis program to complete one task and, a little while later, falls back on the "pen and paper method" to complete a different assignment. At the same time, many healthcare workers will utilize a number of different software and hardware tools (of varying degrees of sophistication), as opposed to being able to rely on an integrated system, to complete their daily array of tasks. I think both of these trends will continue to persist for the foreseeable future because healthcare companies—for a number of reasons, including financial and cultural ones—are often slow to transition from older generation systems to newer ones.

12.4 Healthcare Organizations' Revenue Streams Will Remain Unpredictable

In Chapter 1, I focused on several trends over the last few decades that have had a deleterious impact on hospitals. In Chapter 11, I followed up on this discussion by delineating some of the unique financial problems that rural hospitals face. As I noted in those sections, one can impute many of these issues to other types of health services organizations. Therefore, it is important for readers to note that a significant number of the issues that I touched on in Chapters 1 and 11 will continue to negatively impact healthcare organizations' bottom lines for the foreseeable future. They include:

- **Medicare and Medicaid Reimbursements Might Shrink Further**
  Over the course of the last three decades, the federal government has passed legislation that has served—more often than not—to reduce Medicare and Medicaid reimbursements (see Chapter 1). At the same time, the Centers for Medicare and Medicaid Services (often as a result of federal legislation) has initiated programs, such as pay-for-performance measures and increased reporting requirements, that have hurt the bottom lines of hospitals and other healthcare providers. What is more, private insurance companies have often followed the federal government's lead and have reduced payments, limited inpatient stays, or taken other actions that negatively impacted the health services industry's revenue streams (see Chapter 1).
  No one can predict the future with certainty when it comes to Medicare payments to hospitals and other health service providers. However, I believe that the federal government is unlikely to pass

Medicare legislation that will provide a net benefit to hospitals and other health services organizations. Quite to the contrary, it is more likely to impose further cuts in Medicare spending. Why is this the case? Namely, Medicare is facing potential future funding shortfalls (Roy, 2012). Assuming that Congress' anti-tax mindset does not change (and assuming that Medicare will eventually need a cash infusion to survive), lawmakers will have few methods to remedy Medicare's financial issues, except to cut spending. Although Medicaid is different from Medicare, as most readers can attest to, many legislators in state governments as well as the federal government make it a routine habit to push for cuts to Medicaid reimbursements. As a result, healthcare organizations have to be wary of further Medicaid-related cuts.

- **Potential for Congress to Pass Other Legislation**
  As I noted in Chapter 1, Congress has passed a number of laws over the years that, at least in the short term, have negatively impacted the bottom lines of large numbers of healthcare organizations. Of course, the federal government has also enacted laws that have helped healthcare companies. From a management standpoint, I would suggest that one prepare for the worst and hope for the best. With that in mind, it makes sense for healthcare leaders to assume that Congress, at some point in the next decade or two, will pass at least one law that will negatively impact their companies.

- **The Impact of New Technologies**
  As I noted in several sections of this book, healthcare organizations can often use IT and other technological tools to help them to become more efficient, to boost productivity levels, and to reduce expenses. At the same time, healthcare organizations can impinge upon their bottom lines when they engage in costly technology wars with rivals, which causes them to spend significant amounts of money on new clinical-based systems that they then underutilize (see Chapter 1). Given the current pace of advances in clinical technologies and the continued competition between hospitals and other health services providers, I would argue that this latter issue will remain a problem for many healthcare organizations—perhaps even outweighing the benefits that could accrue from adopting money-saving IT and AI tools.

- **The Increasing Elderly Population**
  According to the US Census Bureau, "[I]n 2050, the number of Americans aged 65 and older is projected to be 88.5 million, more than double its projected population of 40.2 million in 2010" (Vincent & Velkoff, 2010, 1). On the surface, this would seem to be a boon to almost all sectors of healthcare. After all, the over-65 set are the ones who typically use the most healthcare services (see Chapter 1). However, there are plenty of unknowns here—especially looking several decades out. For one thing, the ability of many healthcare organizations to generate a profit from servicing the elderly is directly tied to the reimbursements they receive from Medicare and, to a lesser extent, Medicaid. If Medicare cuts its reimbursement rates, it will have an impact on hospitals, nursing homes, and other health services providers. At the same time, the elderly in 2030, 2040, or 2050 might be healthier than their peers today, and that fact will also change the payment dynamic. Finally, it is impossible to determine which organizations benefit to what extent from the graying of the US population without knowing who the key players are. In the future, new competitors will likely spring up to challenge the dominance of hospitals, nursing homes, and other traditional health services providers.

I have only performed a rudimentary examination of four of the more important variables that will drive revenues for hospitals and other healthcare providers in the coming decades. This is not an exhaustive list, by any means. However, from my vantage point in the present, one thing becomes clear to me. I believe that, in the future, many heathcare organizations will have to find a way to do more—to provide more care, more services, and more goods—with less money. In this environment, only the most efficient and effective companies thrive. At the very least, healthcare leaders should be cognizant of the fact that their respective companies' might suffer from external shocks.

12.5 Look for Diamonds in the Data and Knowledge "Rough"

As I noted in a previous section of this chapter, older IT and AI systems are routinely replaced by newer models. At the same time, the technology revolution is continuously allowing organizations to automate processes that were once the domain of human minds and hands. On the intellectual side of things, healthcare leaders have access to an ever-growing stream of third-party knowledge-based information on topics related to almost every aspect of their workplaces. At the same time, their organizations' computer systems are collecting and storing more data than ever before. Looking at this matter from an HR perspective, savvy healthcare executives, managers, and staff can utilize these facts to aid them in hiring the best workers, in better managing employees, and in improving workplace efficiency and productivity. These tactics will not go out of fashion in the near future. They include:

- **Occasionally Scan the Literature for New Ideas**
  In my experience, healthcare leaders currently utilize two key avenues to help them locate new, beneficial, cost-effective IT tools or to enable them to identify innovative methodologies or strategies developed by researchers or by other organizations. One way involves networking with other professionals via social media, professional organizations, or business relationships. Many healthcare leaders will also attend conferences and trade shows (or send one of their associates to these events) in an effort to acquire information that can help them in the workplace.

  In addition to these techniques, I would suggest that healthcare leaders also mine the literature for ideas on HR-related topics, such as hiring, better managing employees, and so forth. They can do this to some extent by perusing through trade journals relevant to their respective fields. However, on occasion, they should review other relevant peer-reviewed journals for helpful ideas or guides to new IT tools. Given the sheer amount of knowledge that is created on HR topics alone, one can perhaps gain an edge on the competition by mining these documents for innovative strategies and technologies. Granted, healthcare leaders will incur lost-opportunity costs for performing these searches; however, I think the benefits will often outweigh these expenses—and sometimes by a wide margin. At the same time, healthcare leaders can delegate these tasks to trusted associates, thereby decreasing lost-opportunity costs further (assuming that the subordinates make less money than their supervisors). This tactic will become even more important as the amount of knowledge generated per year increases.

- **Look for Innovative Ideas in Other Industries**
  Almost every healthcare organization checks up on its competitors. Many healthcare leaders will adopt ideas that their peers at other firms have already tried with some success. However, in my experience, some of these individuals could become more adept at noticing successful trends in other industries that can be translated into winning healthcare HR-related strategies. They can sometimes accomplish this feat by simply scanning the world around them with an eye to observing how other types of businesses accomplish key hiring and employee-management tasks.

- **Always Seek to Develop More and Better Techniques for Analyzing Data**
  As I noted previously, healthcare organizations are doing a better job of accumulating and storing data. Over the next few years, they will likely accumulate even more data on an ever larger number of topics that are both patient and organization centered (Horowitz, 2012). At the same time, healthcare organizations, like their peers in other fields, often are not adept at finding ways to use these datasets (Kayyali, Knott, & Van Kuiken, 2013; Oracle, 2012, 3, 5). I have made some suggestions in this book for ways in which these companies can use employee data to their advantage in the hiring process and/or in managing employee expectations. Savvy healthcare leaders will go further and will devote some of their respective organizations' energies to developing and testing new and better techniques, including new metrics, for using the HR-related data (as well as other datasets) that their organizations collect. They will also scan the literature and survey other companies to identify techniques that researchers or peers have successfully implemented and used.

- **Embrace Automation—When It Makes Sense**
  Healthcare leaders should purchase or lease new IT and AI tools whenever these actions make sense from a cost–benefit–culture standpoint. Although I have focused attention on using IT tools to help with HR-related tasks, when possible, I realize that sometimes organizations can actually make money if they do not invest in a new computer software program or piece of hardware (e.g., the older systems fully meet these companies' needs). At the same time, executives and managers have to weigh the impacts of any changes on their workplaces (more on that one in a moment). Nonetheless, in my life,

I have too often seen healthcare leaders leave significant amounts of money "on the table" by hesitating to purchase IT tools or to fully train staff on how to use the available software and hardware.

As the century rolls on, I think that healthcare leaders will be presented with an ever more diverse array of IT and AI tools that they could potentially integrate into their workplaces. As a result, it will likely become more paramount for executives and managers in these organizations to become adept at identifying and adopting beneficial technologies.

12.6 The 21st-Century Employee

As I noted in previous sections, the technology revolution will continue for the foreseeable future. Future devices and software systems will likely develop even closer, more intimate relationships with humanity over the next few decades. More importantly for this discussion, AI and IT tools will eventually penetrate almost every aspect of the corporate workspace.

Although that may be the case, many of the corporate environments of the future might be more complex and confusing than the ones in existence today. During the course of the day, many workers will have to move back and forth between antiquated or earlier generation technologies and newer ones. In order to complete their assigned tasks, they will have to be comfortable switching between multiple systems, ways of doing things, and even subcultures. What type of employee is best suited to succeed in this work environment?

In previous sections of this book, I talked about high-potential individuals. I suggested that they should possess high I.Q.'s and be willing to adapt to a variety of situations. I also noted that, in many cases, it did not matter—and in fact might help—if these people did not possess a specialist's background in the chosen position. I will review and expand on that discussion here.

In my opinion, the 21st-century employee should possess several key skills, including:

- **Polymaths**
  The best employees, at least the ones who work in mid-level jobs or higher, should be comfortable operating in different environments and with various cultures and subcultures. They should be able to

utilize a wide variety of IT and AI tools. Most importantly, these workers should be adept at taking what they learn in one area and applying this information to other parts of the workplace or to help solve unrelated problems. In other words, high-potential employees should aspire to be polymaths. Employees with diverse training, experience, and proclivities are less likely to be replaced by machines.

- **Willing to Change**
  In the coming decades, healthcare organizations might need to change out technologies at a more rapid pace. At the very least, they will need to add disruptive technologies (here defined as systems which alter employees' standard workflow processes) on occasion. It makes sense that employees who are more willing to adapt to changes in the environment or in their daily work lives will more easily adjust to these alterations.

- **Enjoys Learning**
  As the speed of technological change and knowledge procurement picks up, it makes sense to assume that employees will need to work harder to ensure that their skills stay relevant. In that scenario, healthcare leaders should prefer men and women who like to learn. These individuals will put in the effort to remain current with regard to their skills, to the external environment, and in their knowledge of the company's methodologies and IT tools.

- **Good People Skills**
  The value of this skill to the employee (and thus to his or her employer) will depend in part on his or her position within the corporate nexus. Someone who primarily works alone and who does not have to interact with customers might not need to develop these skills to the same extent as an employee who constantly works in teams or who routinely interacts with customers/patients.

- **High Intelligence Quotient (I.Q.)**
  As I noted in previous sections, people who possess high I.Q.'s are often better at solving complex problems, at analyzing data, and at performing a number of other tasks in the office. Assuming that the individuals possess the other skills on this list, they should—more often than not—thrive in the 21st-century office environments, as I have described them here.

Of course, healthcare organizations will not need all employees to possess these skills. Even in the coming decades, these companies will still need low-skilled workers, as well as employees who perform highly specialized or rote tasks. These individuals might not need to be polymaths or possess overly high I.Q.'s. However, I think that, in the future workforce, all employees should be willing to change their routines, when necessary, to accommodate the incorporation of new technologies into the workplace. Although these men and women do not have to enjoy learning, per se, they should be ready and willing to undertake extra training and/or to develop new skills, when required.

12.7 Building the Right Culture: Employee Satisfaction Is Key

In Chapter 10, I noted that healthcare organizations can benefit financially by achieving high employee-satisfaction rates. I delineated some of the specific ways that companies can benefit when their employees are content. At the same time, I provided readers with a guide to creating supportive workplace cultures. I feel that 21st-century healthcare organizations may eventually find it almost necessary to maintain high worker-contentment rates. They might find it difficult to replace some of the employees who leave.

Think about it for a second. In a world where machines perform many (or at some point in the future—most) of the basic, specialist, or rote tasks, the human workers will become even more valuable. Some healthcare departments might totally phase out the jobs that require little in the way of training or experience. The human employees will perform higher-level tasks that require a significant amount of knowledge, training, and experience. These people are the ones who are often hard to replace.

12.8 The Negative Impact of Bad Hires

Regardless of what the future brings, healthcare organizations will always need to utilize a large number of human workers—at least for the foreseeable future. People simply do some things better than machines. At the same time, healthcare companies will always have to be careful when hiring people to fill open positions. As I noted in Chapter 3, organizations will suffer if they hire people who subsequently do not perform well on the job, who do not get along with their peers, or who do something that opens up the company to a lawsuit. In some cases, an employer can lose a significant amount of money as the result of a bad hire (see Chapter 3).

With that in mind, I devoted several chapters of this book to the hiring process. I delineated some of the key methods that employers use to fill open positions. I focused special attention on the direct hiring process.

12.9 The Direct Hiring Process—A Model That Is Applicable to any Era

In Chapter 4 of this book, I discussed some of the different types of employment approaches that healthcare corporations utilize to fill open positions. They include:

- Contracting with employment agencies or staffing firms to identify qualified workers or to deal with short-term needs
- Outsourcing specific tasks, departments, or service lines to third-party firms
- Using interns to complete basic or specialized job tasks
- Utilizing a referral method to fill open positions
- Attending job fairs or actively hiring at colleges and universities
- Directly managing the hiring process

In Chapter 4, I focused on the first five employment methods. I provided a brief description of each technique and noted some of the benefits, as well as the disadvantages, of using each of them. Beginning with Chapter 5, I've spent a significant amount of time on the final hiring method—when healthcare companies actively manage the hiring process. Although most organizations utilize a number of the six hiring methods to fill open positions, many of them rely heavily on the sixth one. Almost all of the firms that I am familiar with use an in-house (direct) process to land some of their hires. At the same time, a large number of these hiring systems do not operate with the highest degree of efficiency or effectiveness. If they did, then the rate of bad hires would be much lower than it is currently (see the statistics in Chapter 3).

In reality, an organization's hiring practices will incorporate elements from several different methods. Acknowledging that fact, it would be impossible to write this book without instituting some artificial separation between the direct hiring process and the other methods. With that in mind, I divided the direct hiring process into three stages—first contact between the potential hire and the corporation, the initial candidate vetting process, and the interview/secondary vetting process. I focused only on certain aspects of these three steps.

I do not want to reproduce the information in the chapters on hiring here. Instead, I would like to demonstrate how HR staff, hiring managers, and other key personnel can incorporate some of the key takeaways from those sections into a corporate checklist. They can use this document to help guide them in improving their respective companies' direct hiring systems.

12.10 Setting Up a Direct Hiring System—A Checklist

In Chapters 5 through 8, I focus on the direct hiring process. A healthcare leader, HR staff member, or other pertinent company employee could use this information to create a checklist to oversee the direct hiring process at the meta-level. The checklist could form the very basic outline for a strategic plan (see Figure 12.1).

Figure 12.1 is a sample. In reality, a particular healthcare company might organize the information in a different way. The corporation would certainly include some additional questions or notations that would pertain to its unique workplace, its job market, its stakeholders' needs, the external environment, and so forth. However, I think the graphic encapsulates many of the meta-level topics that almost any healthcare organization would need to address.

Whether readers rely on my checklist or create their own documents, they do want to keep in mind some of the goals that they should strive for when creating or reorganizing their direct hiring systems. They include:

- **Eliminate the Need for Paper**
  Ideally the system should be paperless, except for paper files that are required from applicants and any other documents that need to be in paper format to meet applicable local, state, or federal laws.

Sample Healthcare Organization
Direct Hiring Process — Checklist
Created on: (Place date here)/Last Update: (Place date here)

Global Questions	Responses	Further Information	Update
How many different positions in the company?	Number here	Place notes detailing where further information on this topic can be found, including pagination if relevant.	Date
Have we discussed/created a list of universal questions?	Yes/No	Place notes detailing where further information on this topic can be found, including pagination if relevant.	Date
* Have we tied these questions to preferred employee behaviors, skills, etc.	Yes/No/ Somewhat	Place notes detailing where further information on this topic can be found, including pagination if relevant.	Date
* Do we have data to support the effectiveness/goals of the questions that do not involve basic personal information (e.g., home address, phone, etc.).	Yes/No/ Somewhat	Place notes detailing where further information on this topic can be found, including pagination if relevant.	Date
* Percentage complete?	Percentage	Place notes detailing where further information on this topic can be found, including pagination if relevant.	Date
* If Less than 100%, which areas still need work?	N/A	List the areas still needing work in this section. Place notes detailing where further information on this topic can be found, including pagination if relevant.	Date
Have we discussed/created a list of job-specific questions?	Yes/No	Place notes detailing where further information on this topic can be found, including pagination if relevant.	Date
* Percentage complete?	Percentage	Place notes detailing where further information on this topic can be found, including pagination if relevant.	Date
* If less than 100%, which jobs still need work?	N/A	List the jobs/positions that need questions added or altered. Place notes detailing where further information on this topic can be found, including pagination if relevant.	Date
Additional questions that focus on hiring issues, which are global in nature.	N/A	Place notes detailing where further information on this topic can be found, including pagination if relevant.	Date

(Continued on following page)

Sample Healthcare Organization (Continued)
Direct Hiring Process — Checklist
Created on: (Place date here)/Last Update: (Place date here)

Steps in the Process	Responses	Further Information	Update
Do we have a document that lists/describes each step in the hiring process by department/job?	Yes/No/Somewhat	Place notes detailing where this document can be found. If one does not exist, then create a plan or other process for creating a steps' chart.	Date
Do we have a process in place for evaluating/reevaluating the hiring process at the company level?	Yes/No/Somewhat	Place notes detailing where further information on this topic can be found, including pagination if relevant.	Date
* Have we completed an organization-wide evaluation within the last year?	Yes/No	Place notes detailing where further information on this topic can be found, including pagination if relevant.	Date
* If the answer is yes, did the report identify areas of improvement?	Yes/No	The organization might want to list the key areas that need improvement. It would also place notes detailing where further information on this topic can be found, including pagination if relevant.	Date
* If the answer is yes, do we have a plan in place to fix each area?	Yes/No/Somewhat	Place notes detailing where further information on this topic can be found, including pagination if relevant.	Date
Do we have a process in place for evaluating/reevaluating the hiring process at the department level?	Yes/No	Place notes detailing where further information on this topic can be found, including pagination if relevant.	Date
The organization could posit additional topics or questions that focus on each of the steps in the process. Importantly, the company might want to break the "Steps in the Process" section into subsections based on the steps in the process (e.g., candidate submission, applicant review, etc.).	N/A	N/A	Date

Interface/Web Portal	Responses	Further Information	Update
Do all buttons/submission interfaces function correctly?	Yes/No	Place notes detailing where further information on this topic can be found, including pagination if relevant.	Date
Any discernable bugs in the program/portal?	Yes/No	Place notes detailing where further information on this topic can be found, including pagination if relevant.	Date
Does the interface work smoothly on all browsers?	Yes/No	Place notes detailing where further information on this topic can be found, including pagination if relevant.	Date
What portions of the candidates' information/profiles port to our database? This section will contain a breakdown of information and items that do/do not port, along with reasons for these decisions.	N/A	Place notes detailing where further information on this topic can be found, including pagination if relevant.	Date
Additional questions that relate to the Interface/Portal	N/A	Place notes detailing where further information on this topic can be found, including pagination if relevant.	Date

Security Issues	Responses	Further Information	Update
Any issues related to privacy, network security, etc. would go here. The document would break these down by process (e.g., interface/web portal, emails/ communications, document collection/storage, etc.).	N/A	N/A	Date

(Continued on following page)

Sample Healthcare Organization (Continued)
Direct Hiring Process — Checklist
Created on: (Place date here)/Last Update: (Place date here)

HR Staff/Hiring Managers/Other Personnel	Responses	Further Information	Update
The company would list pertinent information that pertains to the number of staff, full-time equivalent (FTE) information, costs, etc. In the case of hiring managers, the organization might want to try to calculate lost-opportunity costs.	N/A	N/A	Date

Costs to Operate and Maintain Direct Hiring Process	Responses	Further Information	Update
The company might choose to include this category. If so, it would list topics that pertain to the specific costs related to operating the system. The organization might choose to break down costs by department, by process-related steps, etc. It would likely relegate most of this information to other documents (budgets, plans, etc.).	N/A	N/A	Date

Data Management	Responses	Further Information	Update
List of the generic data categories/metrics on candidates.	N/A	Note place(s) where one can find this information.	Date
* Within the last six months, have we assessed/reassessed the validity, relevancy, and reliability of each data point?	Yes/No	This section should let reviewers know where to find information on each data point.	Date
* If the answer to the above question is "No," have we scheduled an assessment for the ones not previously reviewed?	Yes/No/Somewhat	Place notes detailing where further information on this topic can be found, including pagination if relevant.	Date

Data Management (Continued)	Responses	Further Information	Update
List of the department-level categories/metrics on candidates.	N/A	Note place(s) where one can find this information	Date
* Additional questions related to these data points.	N/A	N/A	Date
The company can add questions focusing on the management and analysis of candidate data.	N/A	N/A	Date

For Future Reference: IT/AI Technologies to Review	Responses	Further Information	Update
The organization would posit topics and/or questions that center on the in-house development or purchase/lease of new IT/AI tools. The company should focus only on software and hardware that will be utilized in the hiring process.	N/A	N/A	Date

Other Topics	Responses	Further Information	Update
As needed, the organization can add additional topics to this checklist.	N/A	N/A	Date

Figure 12.1 The checklist contains some key hiring-related topics and queries. Healthcare organizations can use the checklist to help them develop, organize, and maintain their direct hiring systems.

- **The Healthcare Organization Controls the Process**
  HR, working with other pertinent personnel in the company, should set the system up in a way that allows the organization to exert the greatest control possible over the information provided by the applicants.

- **Ameliorate Applicant Bias, Fraud, and Embellishments**
  One of the organization's main goals in setting up its hiring system should be to reduce, to the greatest extent possible, candidate fraud (e.g., providing intentionally incorrect information), candidate bias, and any other information that detracts from HR's ability to gain an accurate picture of an applicant's skills, experiences, and so forth.

- **Reduce Bias on the Part of Interviewers and Other Employees**
  On the flip side, the organization wants to create a hiring process that reduces interviewer bias—and any other corporate-side biases.

- **Eliminate Extraneous Material**
  A healthcare organization's hiring process should be designed in such a way that it eliminates a good bit of the candidate information that does not apply either to the particular job specifications or to other company-based needs.

- **Tailor the Information to Fit the Job/Company**
  One key goal—perhaps the main goal of setting up the hiring process as I laid it out in Chapters 5 through 8—is to ensure that the healthcare organization's HR staff and hiring managers obtain the information that they need in order to accurately assess each candidate's fitness for (a) the open position to which he or she applied; and (b) in a more general way, whether the person is a good fit for the company as a whole.

- **Try to Ensure that the Candidate Information Is Objective— Tied to Empirical Formulas/Research**
  As I noted several times in this book, I believe that a healthcare organization can use empirically based metrics and formulas to help it choose the right person for each job (and for the company as a whole in the case of high-potential applicants).

- **Use Objective Measures When Possible**
  As a corollary to the previous bullet point, a healthcare organization should use tests and other objective methods (or at least more objective than the alternatives) to analyze a candidate's fitness for a job.

- **Reevaluate the Process**
  The healthcare organization should routinely reevaluate its hiring process. It should also measure the level of success or failure of each of its hires. The healthcare company should store this information in a database. It should create a series of measures or statistical tests to analyze the data obtained in an effort to learn which candidate elements best predict success in the workplace.

- **Use IT Tools as Effective Aids**
  In Chapters 5 through 8, I discuss a number of potential IT tools that an organization can use to help it organize the hiring process, collect and store information, analyze data, and serve as a platform for communication and transfer of information between the applicant and the pertinent hiring staff, as well as among the staff themselves.

12.11 A Guide to Developing and Promoting Internal Talent

A healthcare organization will find it difficult to succeed in the long run if it does not possess competent staff and capable managers, officers, and analysts. One way in which the corporation can procure these staff members is to hire them. However, in order to remain viable, it must also be able to match its workers to the right jobs. In Chapter 9, I attempted to demonstrate the connection between an organization's employee culture and the success or failure of its system for developing and promoting internal talent. I focused on cultural elements, centering on issues such as power and patronage, which could hamper a firm's ability to properly manage employee development and to promote the best people to management and specialist positions.

I suggested that an organization that wants to do a good job at developing the talents of its personnel and promoting the right people should attempt to create a system that, among other things, is fair, meritorious, empathetic, objective (based on empirical norms), and data driven.

- **The System Is Fair**
  To the greatest extent possible, management should try to remove the politics out of its training and promotion programs. In order to achieve this result, the organization has to find a way to ameliorate

employee cliques, manager favoritism, unjust power arrangements, and similar cultural and structural impediments.

- **The Process Is Meritorious**
  Granted, an organization could conceivably implement a worker development promotion system that is fair but not meritorious. In fact, it could theoretically utilize any method of employee development and advancement, as long as it meets certain fairness standards. However, to be successful, management must find a way to ensure that the process is meritorious. After all, what company does not want to promote the most capable people to management and mid-/high-level specialist positions?

- **Management Needs to Be Empathetic**
  An organization's executives, directors, and managers have to get to know their employees in order to be able to accurately assess each worker's skills, experiences, and potential. At the same time, management has to cultivate a work environment that is based on respect and trust if it wants staff to work hard to develop key skills.

- **The System Needs to Be Empirical/Objective**
  In order to optimize its effectiveness, any employee development and promotion system needs, when possible, to be based on empirical standards. Management should also use statistics and objective measures to analyze its workers, as well as to periodically review the effectiveness of (and search for flaws in) its employee development and promotion system.

12.12 The Data-Driven Office

Throughout the book, I emphasize the need for healthcare leaders to use empirical methods and quantifiable data, along with IT tools, to structure, manage, and analyze key aspects of their respective organizations' HR processes. Taking this a step further, they should use these methods to help them manage all aspects of their organizations—both on the clinical and non-clinical sides. At the same time, they should ensure the highest degree of interoperability, as security and finances allow.

With regard to HR tasks, healthcare organizations want to eventually reach a point at which they use IT tools to monitor numerous data points related to their employees' skills, experiences, and behaviors. They would also collect and analyze key non–employee-related workplace statistics. The goal for management should be to use this information to predict which candidates will succeed in what positions, to accurately assess the skills and potential of current employees, to identify problem workers, to tailor the work environment to maximize the staff's satisfaction, and to ascertain which corporate and department strategies are most effective in achieving HR-related goals, such as optimizing employee retention, motivating workers, and so forth.

I believe that almost all healthcare organizations can currently implement at least some aspects of this integrated IT process. However, few, if any, corporations will be able to bring the entire system—as I have described it in this book—to fruition at this time. Regardless, I feel that all healthcare leaders should spend a little time asking themselves how they would achieve this goal. That is because I believe that advances in technology will, within the next few years or decades, allow most healthcare corporations to create these holistic IT systems.

References

Aquino, J. (2012). Nine Jobs that Humans May Lose to Robots. *NBC News.* Retrieved from http://www.nbcnews.com/id/42183592/ns/business-careers/t/nine-jobs-humans-may-lose-robots/#.VQEVofnF9Mg.

Farrar, L. (2008, July 15). Scientists: Humans and Machines Will Merge in Future. *CNN.* Retrieved from http://www.cnn.com/2008/TECH/07/15/bio.tech/index.html.

Frey, C. B., & Osborne, M. A. (2013, September 17). The Future of Employment: How Susceptible Are Jobs to Computerisation? Retrieved from http://www.futuretech.ox.ac.uk/sites/futuretech.ox.ac.uk/files/The_Future_of_Employment_OMS_Working_Paper_1.pdf.

Ghose, T. (2013, May 7). Intelligent Robots Will Overtake Humans by 2100, Experts Say. *Live Science.* Retrieved from http://www.livescience.com/29379-intelligent-robots-will-overtake-humans.html.

Horowitz, B. (2012, July 18). Health Care Organizations Unprepared for Big Data Challenges: Oracle Report. *eWeek.* Retrieved from http://www.eweek.com/c/a/Health-Care-IT/Health-Care-Organizations-Unprepared-for-Big-Data-Challenges-Oracle-Report-151653.

Hsiao, C., & Hing, E. (2014, January). Use and Characteristics of Electronic Health Record Systems Among Office-Based Physician Practices: United

States, 2001–2013. National Center for Health Statistics (Centers for Disease Control and Prevention). Data Brief #143. Retrieved from http://www.cdc.gov/nchs/data/databriefs/db143.pdf.

Kayyali, B., Knott, D., & Van Kuiken, S. (2013, April). The Big-Data Revolution in US Health Care: Accelerating Value and Innovation. McKinsey & Company. Retrieved from http://www.mckinsey.com/insights/health_systems_and_services/the_big-data_revolution_in_us_health_care.

King, J., & Adler-Milstein, J. (2013, October 15). Hospital Progress to Meaningful Use: Status Update. *Health Affairs Blog*. Retrieved from http://healthaffairs.org/blog/2013/10/15/hospital-progress-to-meaningful-use-status-update/.

Klein, E. (2011, October 1). How Robots Will Replace Doctors. *The Washington Post*. Retrieved from http://www.washingtonpost.com/blogs/wonkblog/post/how-robots-will-replace-doctors/2011/08/25/gIQASA17AL_blog.html.

Manyika, J., Chui, M., Bughin, J., Dobbs, R., Bisson, P., & Marrs, A. (2013, May). Disruptive Technologies: Advances that Will Transform Life, Business, and the Global Economy. McKinsey Global Institute. Retrieved from file:///C:/Users/ahopper/Downloads/MGI_Disruptive_technologies_Full_report_May2013.pdf.

McNickle, M. (2012, January 6). 10 Medical Robots that Could Change Healthcare. *Information Week*. Retrieved from http://www.informationweek.com/mobile/10-medical-robots-that-could-change-healthcare/d/d-id/1107696.

Oracle (2012, July 17). From Overload to Impact: An Industry Scorecard on Big Data Business Challenge. Retrieved from http://www.oracle.com/webapps/dialogue/dlgpage.jsp?p_ext=Y&p_dlg_id=12350238&src=7546261&Act=4.

Roy, A. (2012, April 23). Trustees: Medicare Will Go Broke in 2016, If You Exclude Obamacare's Double-Counting. *Forbes*. Retrieved from http://www.forbes.com/sites/aroy/2012/04/23/trustees-medicare-will-go-broke-in-2016-if-you-exclude-obamacares-double-counting/.

Schilling, D. R. (2013, April 19). Knowledge Doubling Every 12 Months, Soon to be Every 12 Hours. *Industry Tap into News*. Retrieved from http://www.industrytap.com/knowledge-doubling-every-12-months-soon-to-be-every-12-hours/3950.

Shinal, J. (2014, March 21). Future Economy: Many Will Lose Jobs to Computers. *USA Today*. Retrieved from http://www.usatoday.com/story/money/columnist/2014/03/21/software-tech-economy-work/6707457/.

Vincent, G. K., & Velkoff, V. A. (2010, May). The Next Four Decades—The Older Population in the United States: 2010 to 2050. US Census Bureau. Retrieved from http://www.census.gov/prod/2010pubs/p25-1138.pdf.

Weiner, M., & Biondich, P. (2006). The Influence of Information Technology on Patient-Physician Relationships. *Journal of General Internal Medicine* 21(Suppl. 1), 35–39. DOI: 10.1111/j.1525-1497.2006.00307.x.

Appendix: Guidelines for Use on the Go

This Appendix contains important guides and checklists from the text, which have been rendered in a form that makes them easy to print/scan. This allows the readers to create portable, paper versions of each figure, which they can reference while at work. They can use these handy pocket guides to, among other things, help them set up relevant HR-focused strategic plans similar to the ones discussed in the book, to assist them in designing hiring-based pre-employment tests, or to aid them in creating templates to collect and analyze applicant and/or employee data.

Figure 4.1
Readers can print/scan this table and use it as a handy pocket-reference guide to help them decide which employment method is right for a particular task. Those readers who want to review this material in more depth can refer to Chapter 4.

Figure 5.1
Readers can use this one-page sample candidate dataset to aid them and their staffs as they work to create their own applicant-based information databases. Those readers who want to review this material in more depth can refer to Chapter 5, Sections 5.7.2–5.8, as well as to other relevant sections throughout the book.

Figure 6.1

Readers can refer back to this sample question when creating their own tests. Those readers who want to review this material in more detail can look at Chapter 6, Section 6.4.

Figure 6.2

Readers can print/scan this guide and use it to help them during the brainstorming stage—to remove the statistical and mathematical clutter in order to visualize what their particular corporation's data-processing system could accomplish. Those readers who want to review this material in more depth can refer to Chapter 6, Sections 6.3 and 6.6, as well as to other relevant sections throughout the book.

Figure 8.1

Readers of this book can print/scan this table and use it to help them and their information technology (IT) teams create the frameworks for similar systems at their respective corporations. Those readers who want to review this material in more depth can refer to Chapter 8, Section 8.8.

Figure 9.1

Readers of this book can print/scan this guide for use by their employee training and development teams. Those readers who want to review this material in more depth can refer to Chapter 9, Section 9.10.4.

Figure 9.2

Readers of this book can refer to this guide to help them envision how an artificial intelligence (AI) system might help their particular company improve its candidate-selection system. Those readers who want to review this material in more detail can refer to Chapter 9, Section 9.10.5.

Figure 12.1

Readers can print/scan these pages for use by project development teams that are tasked with creating and implementing a direct-hiring system. Those readers who want to review this material in more depth can refer to Chapter 12, Section 12.10, as well as to other relevant parts of the text.

The Pros and Cons of Five Hiring Methods (Does Not Include Direct Hires)		
Type of Hiring Method	Pros	Cons
Using Employment Agencies or Staffing Firms	* Allows the corporation to utilize additional tools and resources * Provides the company with access to needed personnel * Offers the organization the opportunity to supplement HR functions * Enables the firm to fill temporary and/or permanent positions * Allows the corporation to distribute some of the risks involved in hiring and managing employees	* Temps/Fills might struggle to understand the host company's culture * Temps/Fills may have issues adjusting to the host corporation's protocols (including customs, rules, and regulations) * Problems that derive from the employee-agency-company matrix relationships * The company gives up some control to the staffing or employment agency * The temps/fills might not satisfactorily perform their duties * Liability issues relating to the fact that the temps/fills represent the host company
Outsourcing Work	* Allows the corporation to utilize additional tools and resources * Provides the company with access to needed personnel * Offers the organization the opportunity to supplement HR functions * Enables the firm to fill permanent positions * Allows the corporation to distribute some of the risks involved in hiring and managing employees * Enables the company to focus on what it does best	* The outsourcing agency/ workers might struggle to understand and relate to the employer's culture * The outsourcing agency/ workers might have difficulty obeying or understanding the host company's protocols (including customs, rules, and regulations) * Problems that derive from the employee-agency-company matrix relationships * The company gives up some control to the staffing agency or outsourcing vendor * The outsourcing firm's employees might not satisfactorily fulfill their duties * Potential liability issues when the outsourced workers represent the host company

(Continued on following page)

The Pros and Cons of Five Hiring Methods (Does Not Include Direct Hires) *(Cont'd)*		
Type of Hiring Method	Pros	Cons
Utilizing Interns	* The host company procures a source of relatively cheap labor * The host corporation garners some additional labor resources, thereby providing it with increased flexibility *The hosting firm can leverage the internship to help it develop key relationships with universities and other institutions	* Potential liability issues due to the fact that the interns represent the host company * Interns might struggle to succeed because they do not understand the host corporation's culture * Management suffers lost-opportunity costs related to mentoring and training the interns The interns might not perform as expected, or they might engage in improper behaviors, which negatively impact the host company's bottom line
Tapping into Referrals (Direct and Indirect)	* Provides companies with another method for identifying and hiring capable employees (direct and indirect referrals) * Referrals might work harder and perform better than other types of hires (direct and indirect referrals) * Managers can trust referred employees with sensitive information right away (direct referrals) * Companies might not have to spend as much money or time in training referrals vis-à-vis other types of hires (direct and indirect referrals)	* Managers might have more difficulty in firing a bad hire (direct referrals) * Other employees might distrust or dislike the referred employee (direct referrals) * HR might not properly vet these employees (direct and indirect referrals)
Participating in Job Fairs	* Provides companies with another method for identifying and hiring capable employees * Corporations can use these events to help them identify potential hires for positions opening up in the future	* The quality and quantity of potential candidates will vary * Expenses related to attending these fairs and following up with candidates

Figure 4.1 This chart provides the reader with an overview of five of the six hiring methods discussed in this chapter, along with their pros and cons. I do not include the direct hiring method in the chart because I discuss it in detail in the next chapter.

Sample Healthcare Organization—Candidate Applications/Dataset for Open Position #31 Applications Received from February 1, 2015–March 2, 2015 (Note: Information Comes from the Online Application Form)

Candidates	Specific Attributes for Task #1 (1 = One Attribute, 5 = Five or More Attributes)	Specific Attributes for Task #2 (1 = One Attribute, 5 = Five or More Attributes)	Cultural Fit (Based on Answers to Company Specific Questions, 10–35 and Ranked 1–5)	Job Specific Quantitative Test Results (0%–19.49% = 1, 19.5%–39.49% = 2, 39.5%–59.49% = 3, 59.5%–79.49% = 4, 79.5%–100% = 5)	Job-Related Skills (1 = One Skill, 5 = Five Skills)	Average Overall Score (3.4+ Moves on to Next Round)
1	5	3	2	3	2	3
2	2	2	3	3	3	2.6
3	2	2	4	4	5	3.4
4	1	4	1	2	1	1.8
5	3	1	5	3	3	3
6	4	5	3	4	4	4
7	4	5	2	2	3	3.2
8	1	2	1	1	2	1.4
9	5	3	5	4	5	4.4
10	2	5	5	5	4	4.2
11	3	1	4	4	3	3
12	2	3	2	4	3	2.8
13	5	5	3	3	4	4
14	4	2	4	3	2	3
15	3	1	3	3	4	2.8
16	1	4	2	2	3	2.4
17	3	2	4	3	4	3.2
18	2	3	3	2	1	2.2
19	1	2	3	3	1	2
20	4	3	4	4	3	3.6
Average	2.85	2.9	3.15	3.1	3	3

Figure 5.1 A sample version of an Excel document containing candidate information that has been downloaded from the online application form. Although a real dataset would likely contain many more columns, this figure contains all of the key sections. As important, it demonstrates how an organization can create tailor-made questions and then quantify this data.

Sample Healthcare Organization
Open Position #31
Company/Job-Specific Exam
Quantitative Section

Instructions: You have 25 minutes to complete 30 multiple choice questions. Please choose the best answer to each question. Do not spend too much time on any one answer. These queries pertain to actual work-related tasks that you will be required to perform if you are chosen for this job.

Question #1: Your department has, on behalf of a client, billed Insurance A for 300 test strips. The insurance company has allowed 3/5 of your total charges. It has paid 100% of its allowed amount. Assuming your price (billed to Insurance A), per 100 strips, is $37.95, how much do you receive from Insurance A?

A. $68.31
B. $56.93
C. $70.00
D. None of the above

Question #2: . . . .

Figure 6.1 An example of a type of test that can be created in-house by even the smallest healthcare organizations.

Sample Healthcare Organization
Specific Position in the Accounts Receivable Department
Data Derived from Hires — October 10, 2001–January 18, 2013
Note: Information Comes from Candidate/Employee Tracking Information

New Hires 10/10/2001–01/18/2013	Quantitative Score on the Entrance Exam (0%–19.49% = 1, 19.5%–39.49% = 2, 39.5%–59.49% = 3, 59.5%–79.49% = 4, 79.5%–100% = 5)	Medicare Billing Experience Noted on the Employment Application Section (No = 0, Yes = 1)	Used the Term "Organized" to Describe Himself/Herself on the Employment Application (No = 0, Yes = 1)	Performance Reviews (1 = Poor, 5 = Excellent) Averaged over Number of Years with Company and Rounded	Promoted During Tenure with Company (5 = Three Promotions, 3 = Two Promotions, 2 = One Promotion, 0 = No Promotions)	Fired or Laid Off? (5 = No, 0 = Yes)
1	5	0	1	4	5	5
2	3	1	1	3	2	5
3	1	1	0	1	0	0
4	4	0	1	3	2	5
5	2	0	0	1	0	0
6	3	1	1	3	0	5
7	4	1	1	4	3	5
8	4	0	1	3	0	5
9	3	1	1	2	0	0
10	2	0	0	2	0	0
11	3	1	1	3	0	5
12	3	1	1	3	0	5
13	5	0	1	4	3	5
14	4	1	1	4	3	5

Figure 6.2   This dataset is simplistic. A real data sheet would likely contain many more columns and lines. Nonetheless, it does a good job of denoting some of the ways in which healthcare companies can utilize candidate hiring data, in combination with employee statistics, to identify key traits that denote successful workers in certain job positions. Note how a healthcare analyst can, with the help of statistics, identify interrelationships between categories or determine the cohort's medians and means in certain key areas.

Sample Healthcare Organization Open Position #31 Panel Interview Results: Candidate 12 (14 potential hires interviewed) Ranking System: 5 = Excellent/Highly Qualified and 1 = Poor/Not Qualified Note: Does Not Include (open-ended) Questions 4, 7, 9, and 15; "I" = Interviewer								
Questions	I #1	I #2	I #3	I #4	Total	Avg.	Weight	Category Score	Avg. of All Candidates
1	4	3	3	4	14	3.5	0.05	0.175	0.1759
2	2	1	4	2	9	2.25	0.1	0.225	0.3679
3	5	4	3	4	16	4	0.1	0.4	0.3893
5	4	3	4	3	14	3.5	0.1	0.35	0.4196
6	2	2	1	2	7	1.75	0.05	0.0875	0.158
8	3	3	3	3	12	3	0.1	0.3	0.3929
10	4	5	4	4	17	4.25	0.1	0.425	0.4036
11	4	5	5	4	18	4.5	0.1	0.45	0.3107
12	1	2	5	2	10	2.5	0.1	0.25	0.3429
13	3	2	3	3	11	2.75	0.1	0.275	0.3196
14	5	4	4	5	18	4.5	0.1	0.45	0.425
Total Score								3.3875	3.7054

Figure 8.1 Healthcare corporations can use a system similar to the one above to quantify company-specific interview questions. In this graphic, the interviewers ranked the candidate's responses to certain queries on a scale from 1 to 5. The HR staff transferred this data to Excel and came up with a composite score for the applicant. The hiring manager and/or HR staff can use this sheet to compare this individual's interview responses to those of his or her peers. Note that some open-ended questions could not be quantified.

Skills Development and Training Checklist—Key Features

Each organization's checklist system will be unique but it should:

- Include a documentation system that is accessible to relevant executives, managers, and other personnel.
- Delineate a series of training programs with assigned goals. They should include predetermined skills and leadership development projects within the employee's department, as well as cross-training exercises in other departments.
- Set a series of deadlines for completion of these training assignments and/or create a checklist for denoting completion of these projects.
- Incorporate a skills checklist with a ranking system. For instance, the company might feel that empathy is important and will include it as one of the abilities on the list. Relevant managers will use a ranking system to note a particular employee's progress (or regression) with regard to mastering this talent.
- Require the manager who oversees the worker's participation in one of these pre-set training exercises to update the training checklist and skills sections.
- Allow relevant personnel to update the system at other times (when the employee is performing duties that are not related to any specific training module).
- Focus, to the greatest extent possible, on using binary or quantitative marks. This will allow managers to quickly monitor an employee's progress while at the same time ensuring that these leaders do not waste time entering or reviewing lengthy notations.
- Ensure that the system keeps track of the people who enter/modify employee information. At the very least, the system should note the author/editor and access dates and times.

Goals

Management can guide the development of key personnel within their respective organizations. More specifically, they can at least attempt to ensure that the employees learn and develop (or at least are exposed to) important leadership skills before they move up in the organization. At the same time, managers and executives can monitor these workers' development (or lack thereof). The system should also limit employer bias by obtaining input from several different leadership personnel and via ensuring that there is some level of accountability.

Figure 9.1 A how-to-guide for creating and implementing a skills development and training checklist. Each organization's documentation process will differ, as it will need to conform to that company's specific features, such as its size, culture, and so forth.

An AI-Driven Internal Candidate Selection System—Key Features

The AI system should:

- Include an employee database that contains relevant hiring information, including each worker's skills, work experiences, job approval ratings, length of tenure, salary, and so forth.
- Be secure yet accessible by relevant personnel when necessary.
- Allow employees to update relevant parts of their personnel files, including adding any work experience that they procured outside of the workplace. However, these opportunities must be limited (e.g., employees could add information twice a year as part of their review process) in order to ensure accuracy and accountability.
- Update itself whenever new information is entered.
- Contain an AI component that allows HR to enter specific skills, experience, and so forth, for a new opening. The AI system would then search through candidate files to identify the best potential applicants.
- Automatically alert internal applicants once HR has vetted and approved the list.
- Allow employees who were not selected by its automated process to apply for the position. This will allow HR to identify qualified candidates that the automated system might have missed.

Goals

Healthcare organizations can streamline their internal candidate application and selection processes, thereby making them more efficient. Healthcare companies can leverage the system to help them do a better job of finding the best candidates for specific job openings.

Figure 9.2 An example of an automated, AI-driven internal candidate selection system. Many healthcare organizations might not yet be able either to create or to purchase such a system. However, they should be able to do so within the next few years (as costs come down and technology improves).

Sample Healthcare Organization
Direct Hiring Process — Checklist
Created on: (Place date here)/Last Update: (Place date here)

Global Questions	Responses	Further Information	Update
How many different positions in the company?	Number here	Place notes detailing where further information on this topic can be found, including pagination if relevant.	Date
Have we discussed/created a list of universal questions?	Yes/No	Place notes detailing where further information on this topic can be found, including pagination if relevant.	Date
* Have we tied these questions to preferred employee behaviors, skills, etc.	Yes/No/ Somewhat	Place notes detailing where further information on this topic can be found, including pagination if relevant.	Date
* Do we have data to support the effectiveness/goals of the questions that do not involve basic personal information (e.g., home address, phone, etc.).	Yes/No/ Somewhat	Place notes detailing where further information on this topic can be found, including pagination if relevant.	Date
* Percentage complete?	Percentage	Place notes detailing where further information on this topic can be found, including pagination if relevant.	Date
* If Less than 100%, which areas still need work?	N/A	List the areas still needing work in this section. Place notes detailing where further information on this topic can be found, including pagination if relevant.	Date
Have we discussed/created a list of job-specific questions?	Yes/No	Place notes detailing where further information on this topic can be found, including pagination if relevant.	Date
* Percentage complete?	Percentage	Place notes detailing where further information on this topic can be found, including pagination if relevant.	Date
* If less than 100%, which jobs still need work?	N/A	List the jobs/positions that need questions added or altered. Place notes detailing where further information on this topic can be found, including pagination if relevant.	Date
Additional questions that focus on hiring issues, which are global in nature.	N/A	Place notes detailing where further information on this topic can be found, including pagination if relevant.	Date

(Continued on following page)

Sample Healthcare Organization (Continued)
Direct Hiring Process — Checklist
Created on: (Place date here)/Last Update: (Place date here)

Steps in the Process	Responses	Further Information	Update
Do we have a document that lists/describes each step in the hiring process by department/job?	Yes/No/Somewhat	Place notes detailing where this document can be found. If one does not exist, then create a plan or other process for creating a steps' chart.	Date
Do we have a process in place for evaluating/reevaluating the hiring process at the company level?	Yes/No/Somewhat	Place notes detailing where further information on this topic can be found, including pagination if relevant.	Date
* Have we completed an organization-wide evaluation within the last year?	Yes/No	Place notes detailing where further information on this topic can be found, including pagination if relevant.	Date
* If the answer is yes, did the report identify areas of improvement?	Yes/No	The organization might want to list the key areas that need improvement. It would also place notes detailing where further information on this topic can be found, including pagination if relevant.	Date
* If the answer is yes, do we have a plan in place to fix each area?	Yes/No/Somewhat	Place notes detailing where further information on this topic can be found, including pagination if relevant.	Date
Do we have a process in place for evaluating/reevaluating the hiring process at the department level?	Yes/No	Place notes detailing where further information on this topic can be found, including pagination if relevant.	Date
The organization could posit additional topics or questions that focus on each of the steps in the process. Importantly, the company might want to break the "Steps in the Process" section into subsections based on the steps in the process (e.g., candidate submission, applicant review, etc.).	N/A	N/A	Date

Interface/Web Portal	Responses	Further Information	Update
Do all buttons/submission interfaces function correctly?	Yes/No	Place notes detailing where further information on this topic can be found, including pagination if relevant.	Date
Any discernable bugs in the program/portal?	Yes/No	Place notes detailing where further information on this topic can be found, including pagination if relevant.	Date
Does the interface work smoothly on all browsers?	Yes/No	Place notes detailing where further information on this topic can be found, including pagination if relevant.	Date
What portions of the candidates' information/profiles port to our database? This section will contain a breakdown of information and items that do/do not port, along with reasons for these decisions.	N/A	Place notes detailing where further information on this topic can be found, including pagination if relevant.	Date
Additional questions that relate to the *Interface/Portal*	N/A	Place notes detailing where further information on this topic can be found, including pagination if relevant.	Date

Security Issues	Responses	Further Information	Update
Any issues related to privacy, network security, etc. would go here. The document would break these down by process (e.g., interface/web portal, emails/ communications, document collection/storage, etc.).	N/A	N/A	Date

(Continued on following page)

Sample Healthcare Organization (Continued)
Direct Hiring Process — Checklist
Created on: (Place date here)/Last Update: (Place date here)

HR Staff/Hiring Managers/Other Personnel	Responses	Further Information	Update
The company would list pertinent information that pertains to the number of staff, full-time equivalent (FTE) information, costs, etc. In the case of hiring managers, the organization might want to try to calculate lost-opportunity costs.	N/A	N/A	Date

Costs to Operate and Maintain Direct Hiring Process	Responses	Further Information	Update
The company might choose to include this category. If so, it would list topics that pertain to the specific costs related to operating the system. The organization might choose to break down costs by department, by process-related steps, etc. It would likely relegate most of this information to other documents (budgets, plans, etc.).	N/A	N/A	Date

Data Management	Responses	Further Information	Update
List of the generic data categories/metrics on candidates.	N/A	Note place(s) where one can find this information.	Date
* Within the last six months, have we assessed/reassessed the validity, relevancy, and reliability of each data point?	Yes/No	This section should let reviewers know where to find information on each data point.	Date
* If the answer to the above question is "No," have we scheduled an assessment for the ones not previously reviewed?	Yes/No/Somewhat	Place notes detailing where further information on this topic can be found, including pagination if relevant.	Date

		Note place(s) where one can find this information	Date
List of the department-level categories/metrics on candidates.	N/A		
* Additional questions related to these data points.	N/A	N/A	Date
The company can add questions focusing on the management and analysis of candidate data.	N/A	N/A	Date
For Future Reference: IT/AI Technologies to Review	**Responses**	**Further Information**	**Update**
The organization would posit topics and/or questions that center on the in-house development or purchase/lease of new IT/AI tools. The company should focus only on software and hardware that will be utilized in the hiring process.	N/A	N/A	Date
Other Topics	**Responses**	**Further Information**	**Update**
As needed, the organization can add additional topics to this checklist.	N/A	N/A	Date

Figure 12.1 The checklist contains some key hiring-related topics and queries. Healthcare organizations can use the checklist to help them develop, organize, and maintain their direct hiring systems.

Index